1995

Evening Standard
LONDON
RESTAURANT
GUIDE

DAN
07957 773 093

1995

Evening Standard

LONDON RESTAURANT GUIDE

Fay Maschler

To Reg Gadney

First published in Great Britain in 1994 by
PAVILION BOOKS LIMITED
26 Upper Ground, London SE1 9PD
Text copyright © FAY MASCHLER 1994
Maps and design copyright © Pavilion Books 1994

The moral right of the Proprietor has been asserted.

Designed by Alyson Kyles

Cover designed by Amy Swanson and Nick Cave

Additional reporting and wine reviews by Andrew Jefford

Commissioning Editor for the Evening Standard: Joanne Bowlby

A CIP catalogue record for this book
is available from the British Library.

ISBN 1 85793 3214

Printed and bound in Great Britain by
Butler & Tanner Ltd, Frome and London

2 4 6 8 10 9 7 5 3 1

This book may be ordered by post
direct from the publisher. Please contact
the Marketing Department.
But try your bookshop first.

Maps designed by Footprint Designs,
5 Dryden Street, London WC2E 9NB

Corporate editions and personal subscriptions of the
Evening Standard London Restaurant Guide are available.
Call us for details. Tel: 071-620 1666

CONTENTS

INTRODUCTION

W RITING A RESTAURANT guide to London is a tantalizing
affair. No sooner is final copy sent to the printers than a new
place opens which by rights should be included. This, the second
edition of the *Evening Standard London Restaurant Guide*, is as
topical as it is possible to be in an annual publication. At the same
time it reflects and gives access to the extraordinarily varied and
intricate background of the established and recently opened
restaurants that have put London at the centre of the gastronomic
map. Such a phrase would have been laughable a decade ago but I
maintain that you can nowadays eat out in London and find greater
variety, a more beguiling sense of formality, deeper authenticity in
Oriental food, bolder creativity and sensitivity in cooking and as
good a sense of style as anywhere in the world. Indeed, it is revealing
when some chefs come directly from France – the country to which
in catering we have for so long genuflected – to take up positions in
luxury hotels here, just how predictable and *vieux chapeau* their
food can seem.

One of the ways in which London has opened up is through new
brooms and pricing policies sweeping through some of the grand old
institutions making them once again enticing and affordable for
Londoners. The set price menus at the Connaught, the Café Royal
Grill Room and the Ritz all compare favourably with the cost of
eating out at certain fashionable venues where grilling meat or fish
and pouring oil on rocket salads seems the apex of the chefs' abilities.
For more or less the same money, you can luxuriate in romantic,
historical rooms, be on the receiving end of professional, structured
service and, most importantly, eat the food of classically trained
chefs who are conversant gastronomically with what is new.

In the thirty restaurants included in this edition which have
opened since last year's guide went to press there is, significantly,
only one Indian place and no Chinese or Thai. Ethnic restaurants,
of course, abound and provide a valuable service, but there has been
little recent development or experimentation. One reason for this
might be the burgeoning of what you could call ethnic-British
establishments, opened by young chefs who take their inspiration
and ingredients from the world over and offer their dishes in usually
quite straightforward surroundings at reasonable cost. At the other
end of the scale there have been this year notable additions to the
roster of where you can find the finest food: from Marco Pierre
White at The Restaurant at the Hyde Park Hotel, Gordon Ramsay

at Aubergine, and Richard Corrigan at Fulham Road.

The opinions in this guide are mine. That may sound arrogant but they are based on reviewing London restaurants for the *Evening Standard* for over 22 years. But because it is impossible for one person to revisit so many places in a matter of months, I have used monitors to check the progress of some of the established restaurants reviewed. Where their reports to me differed considerably from my own opinion, I went back myself. The entries for all the restaurants are new. Andrew Jefford who has brilliantly assessed the better wine lists has also helped with restaurant inspections. There follow a few things you should know about this book which I trust will lead you – with the help of this year's much clearer maps – to some new discoveries and happy times in that best of settings: a good restaurant.

Price: The price quoted beside each restaurant is a guide to the cost of a three-course meal for one person with half a bottle of house wine (or appropriate drink) and tax.

Service: If there is a fixed charge this is stated. Optional service leaves it up to you; 10% is adequate, 15% is generous. Watch out for credit card slips left open when service charge has already been added and protest vociferously. There is no requirement to pay a fixed charge if truly indifferent service can be proved. If you want to reward out-of-the-ordinary attention, cash is much more appreciated.

Newcomers: This is a list of restaurants that opened after the end of July 1993.

Eros Awards: This distinction is not the conventional award comparable to, say, Michelin stars. The list, compiled annually, reflects not just the best cooking in London – although in most cases that coincides – but something more; a recognition of restaurants that joyfully succeed in what they set out to do, be that supply classic or modern *haute cuisine*; provide a neighbourhood restaurant that makes you want to move house; offer consistently high standards in a volatile area such as Chinatown; express one person's culinary vision; carry on a tradition with love and vigour; highlight the authenticity or regionality of a cuisine or recognize that glamour is an element in eating out and provide for it the right food, service and surroundings.

FAY MASCHLER

MAP 1

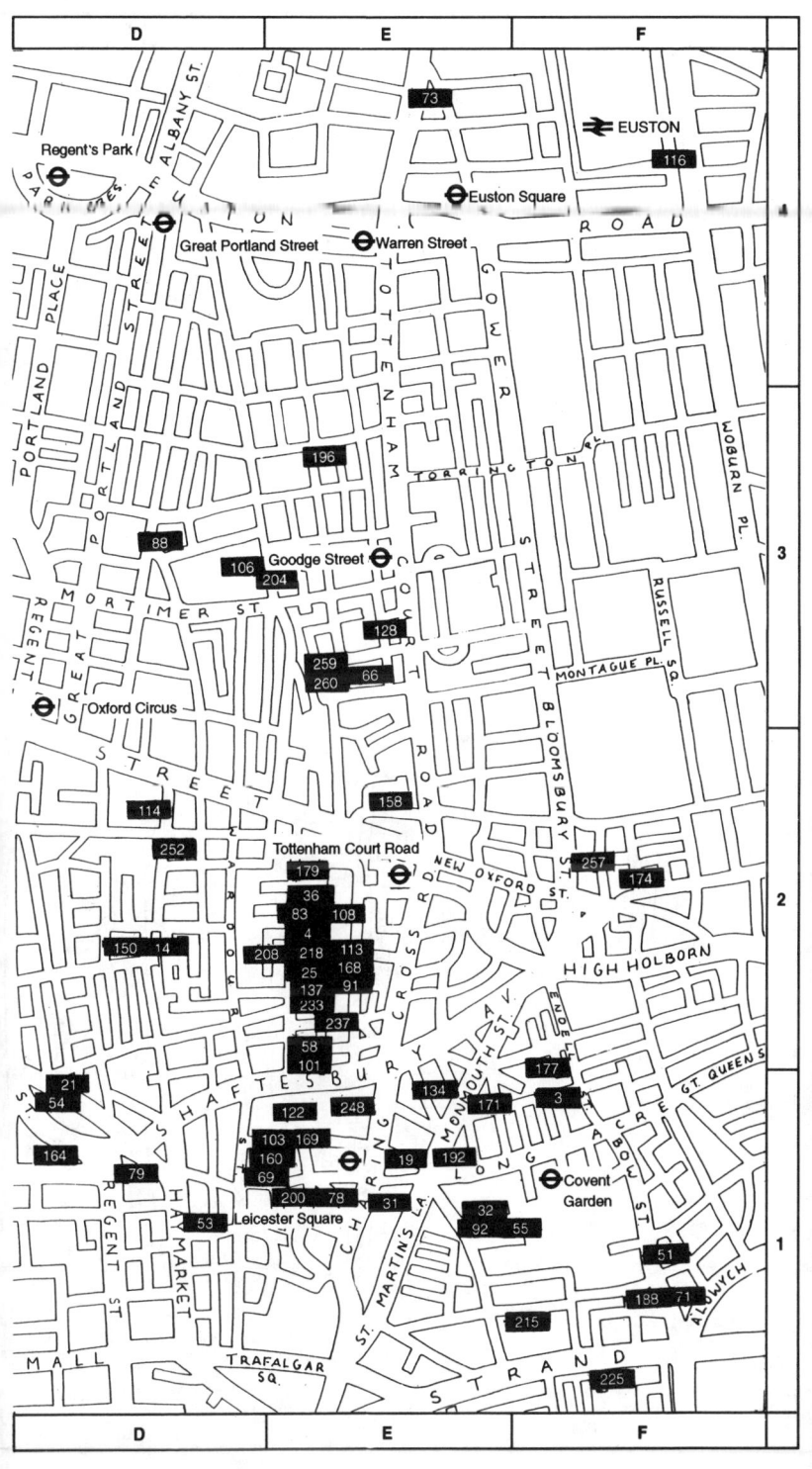

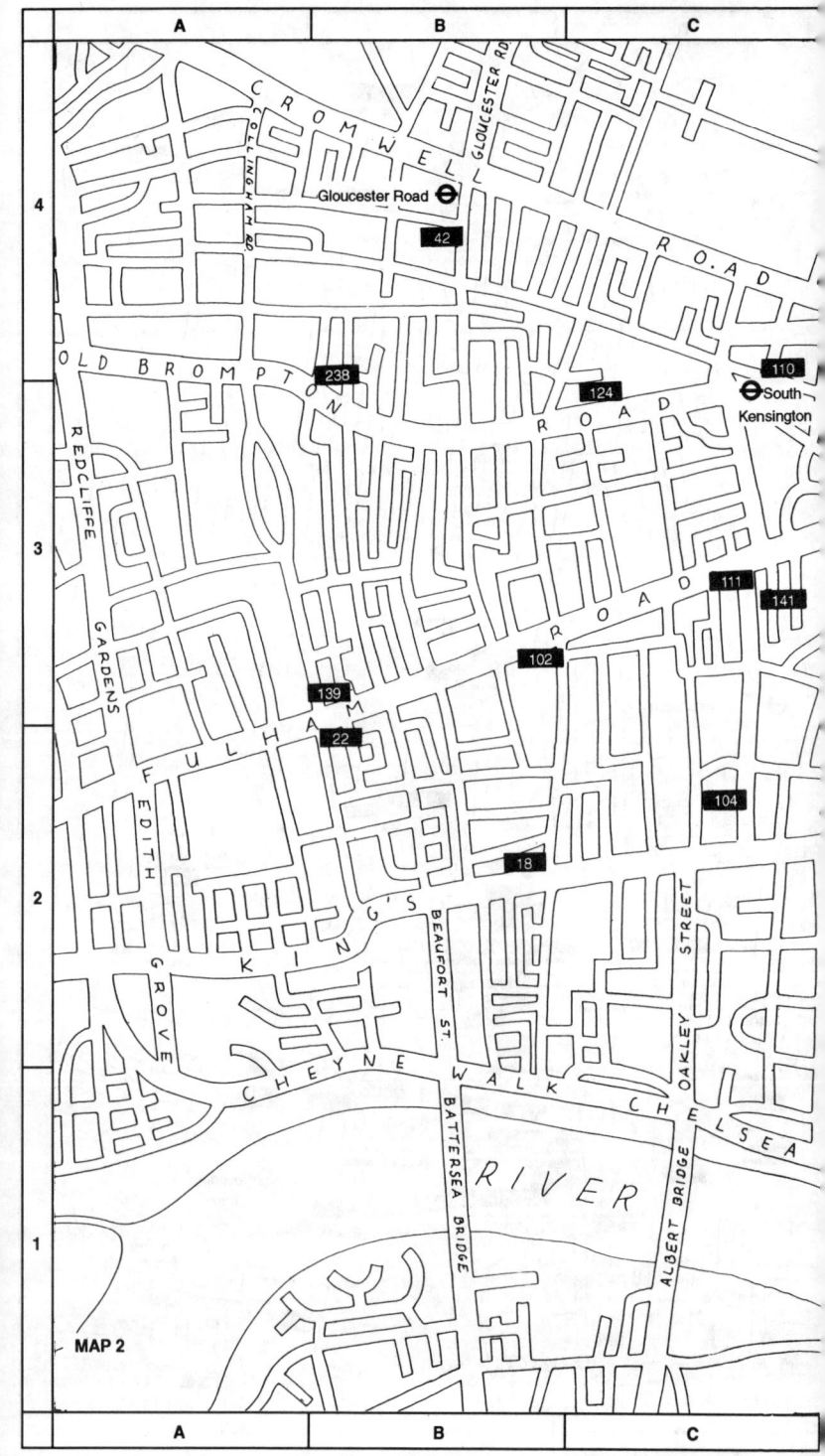

MAP 2

10

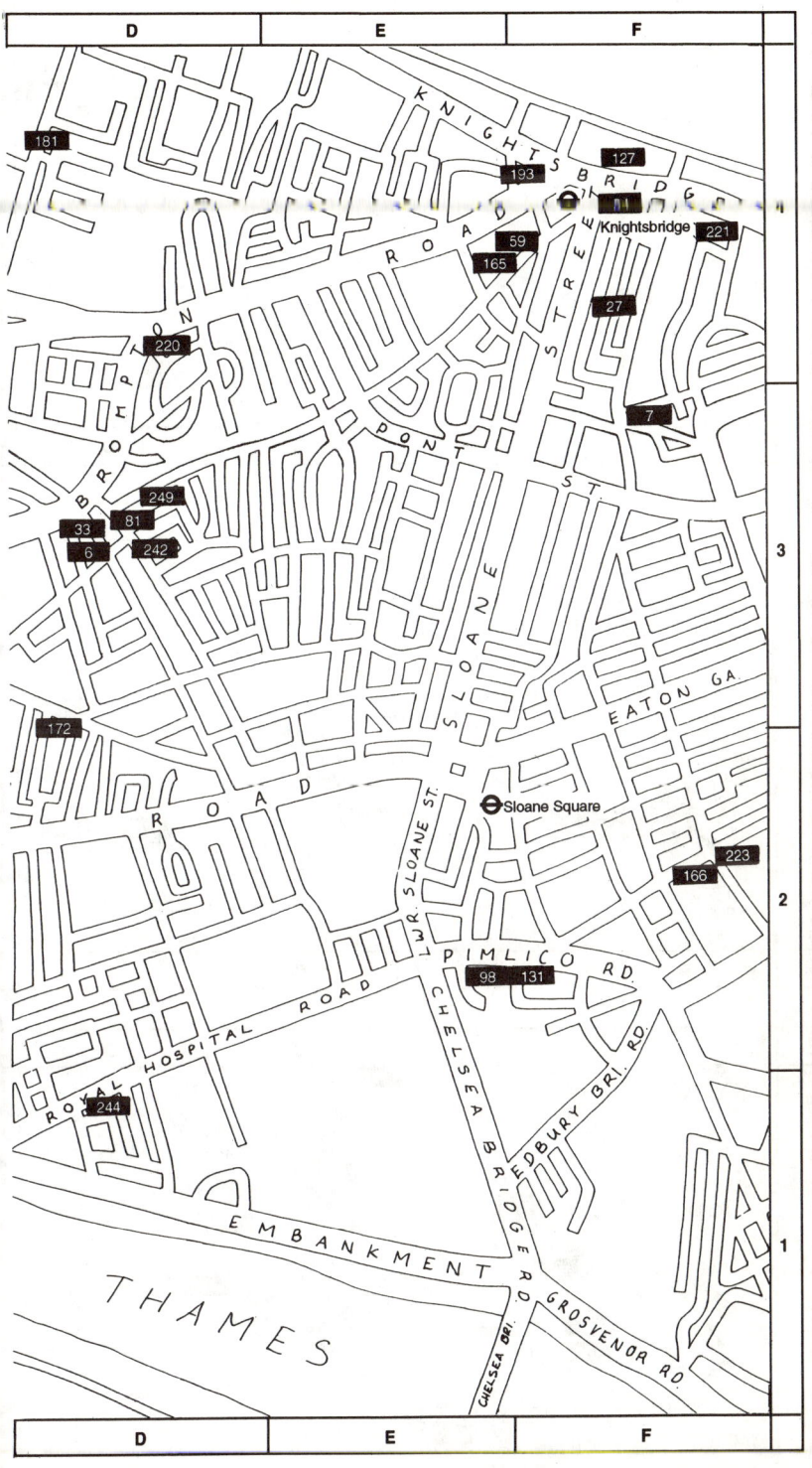

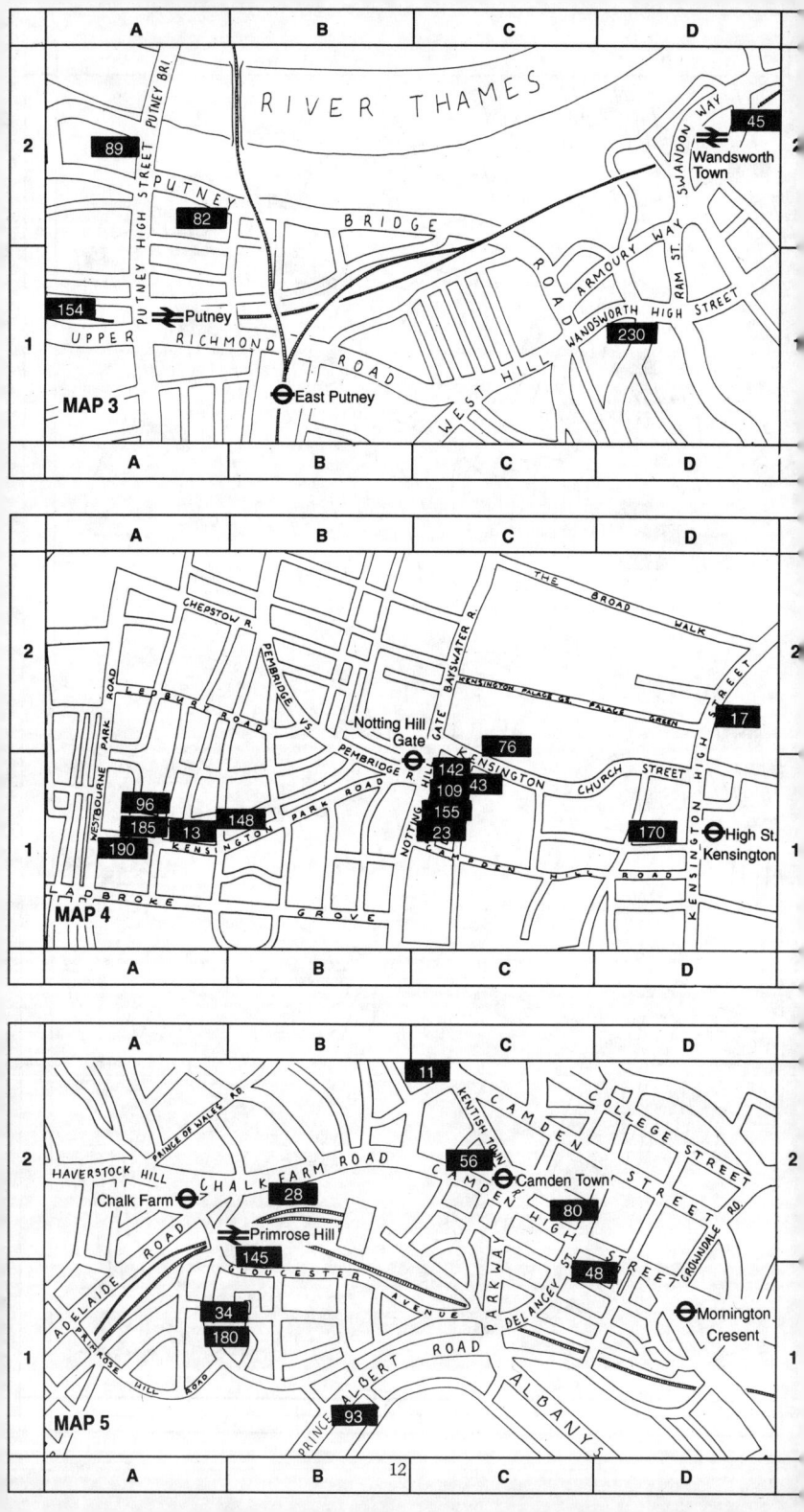

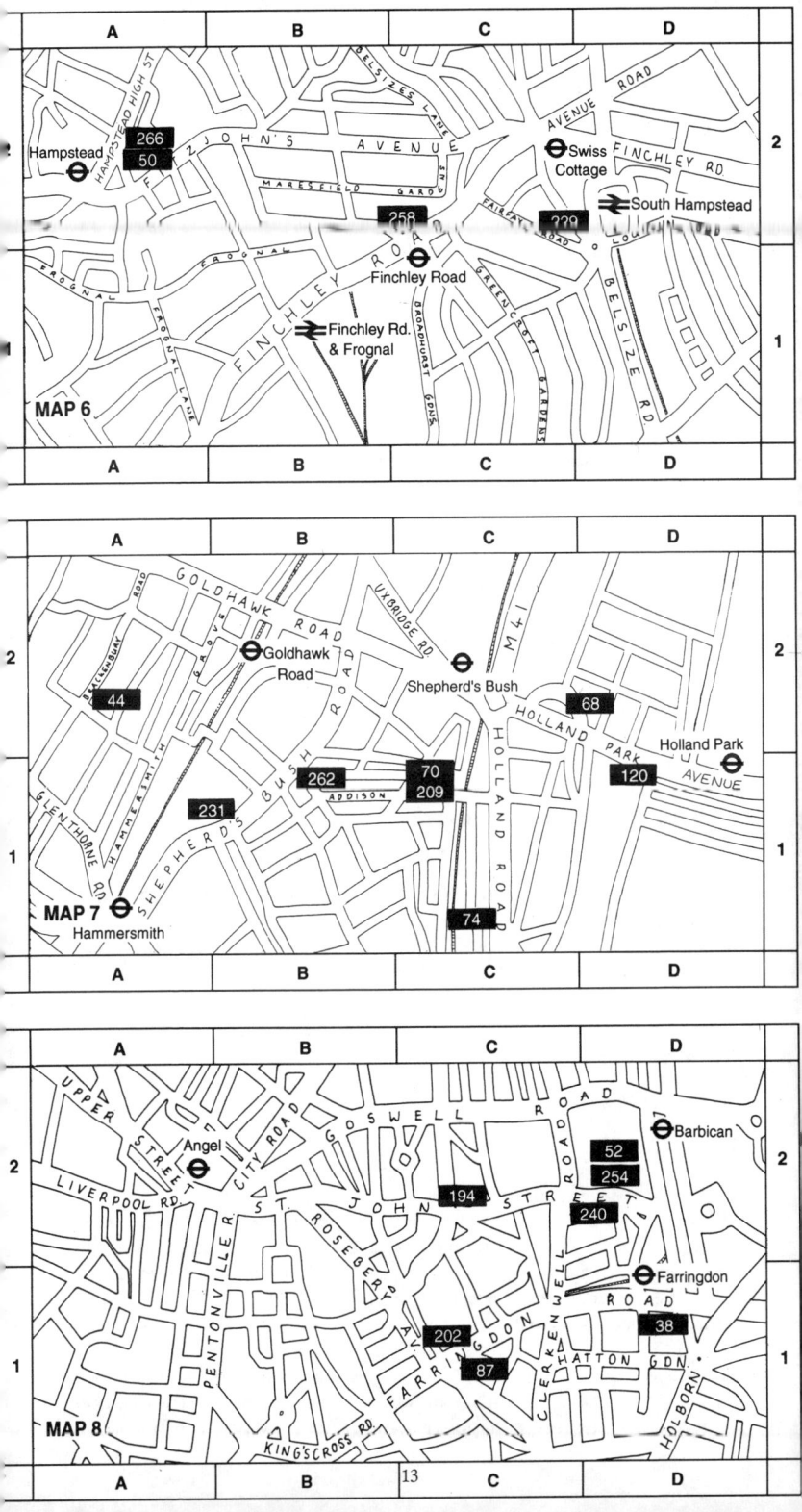

MAP 6

Hampstead

266
50

JOHN'S AVENUE
BELSIZE LANE
MARESFIELD GARDENS
HAMPSTEAD HIGH ST
FROGNAL
FROGNAL LANE
FINCHLEY ROAD

258

Swiss Cottage

AVENUE ROAD
FINCHLEY RD

South Hampstead

229

FAIRFAX ROAD
GREENCROFT
LOUDOUN RD
BELSIZE RD

Finchley Road

BROADHURST GDNS
BELSIZE GARDENS

Finchley Rd. & Frognal

MAP 7

GOLDHAWK ROAD
UXBRIDGE RD
M 41

44

Goldhawk Road

Shepherd's Bush

68

Holland Park

GROVE
BUSH ROAD
HOLLAND PARK
 HOLLAND AVENUE

262   70
       209

120

231

ADDISON

BRACKENBURY ROAD
GLENTHORNE RD
HAMMERSMITH
SHEPHERDS

HOLLAND ROAD

74

Hammersmith

MAP 8

UPPER STREET
LIVERPOOL ROAD
Angel

GOSWELL ROAD

Barbican

52
254

194

ST JOHN ST

240

STREET

PENTONVILLE RD
CITY ROAD
ROSEBERY AV
FARRINGDON ROAD

Farringdon

202   38

87

CLERKENWELL ROAD

HATTON GDN

KING'S CROSS RD

HOLBORN

13

L'Accento

16 Garway Road,
Notting Hill Gate, W2

071-243 2201 £23

'The accent is on value and hubbub'

A concentration of the loudly chattering classes fetches up at this popular, fairly priced Italian restaurant near Westbourne Grove. Noise is amplified by bare, spare decor in earthy shades and should there be a lull there is often a customer with a baby in tow whose yelps will fill it. The room at the back is slightly quieter but, perversely, not necessarily preferred. The set price menu at £10.50 for two courses with three options in each course (no price increase since last year) is a clear bargain given that main courses à la carte start at that price. However, a note on the menu advises that for an extra £1.50 starters can be ordered as a main course. Choosing the set deal, you will not be short-changed gastronomically. Pumpkin ravioli with sage, butter and Parmesan followed by guinea fowl with mushrooms and grilled polenta was one menu enjoyed this year. The fresh vegetables that accompany the main course are stipulated for you and may or may not suit the dish. Chef Andrea Beltrani is a master of pasta and risottos. Basil tagliolini with lobster, tomato and herbs and black cuttlefish risotto have both been praised. Robust dishes for hearty appetites or chilly days include rabbit stuffed with Italian sausage braised in mushroom sauce. So keen are the waiters to turn tables around efficiently that it takes some persistence to get the dessert menu. If you despair, just ask for vin santo and cantucci or maybe simply the long list of grappi.

OPEN: Mon-Sun. **HOURS:** 12.30-2.30pm and 6.30-11.30pm. **CLOSED:** Bank Holidays. **CREDIT CARDS ACCEPTED:** Visa, Access, Mastercard. **NUMBER OF SEATS:** 65. **SERVICE:** 12.5%. **SET PRICE LUNCH AND DINNER:** £10.50. Wheelchair access (but not lavatory). Tables outside seat 30. Private room seats 30. **NEAREST TUBE STATION:** Queensway/Bayswater/Royal Oak.

Adam's Cafe

77 Askew Road, W12

081-743 0572 £14

'Caff by day, couscous by night'

Friends of the Greasy Spoon might be a society worth forming for those who regret seeing the passing of caffs with their cholesterol-laden specialities or their transformation into fancy restaurants or Thai-by-night. A basically British breakfast menu is still served here during the day but the evening identity of a Tunisian restaurant is now firmly stamped on the surroundings. More space, a revamped kitchen and a longer menu make Adam's Caf almost qualify for the description restaurant but the prices, happily, do not. The only first course costing more than £2.50 is crêpe aux fruits de mer. And it costs £2.75. Popular are the deep-fried filo pastry envelopes known as briks containing either egg, tuna or mixed vegetables. Should you choose to go for a grill of meat or fish, then chorba, a lamb- based Tunisian soup, would be the ideal first course. Cous-courses are made with good-quality lamb, chicken and merguez sausages. Couscous Imperiale for two with a mixture of lamb, brochettes, merguez and meatballs is particularly recommended. Explore the North African wines. The really adventurous can finish with a fig eau de vie called boukha. The owners of Adam's Caf also own Jigsaw opposite (74 Askew Road W12, 081-734 8002) where serviceable French food is offered at £8.50 for three courses with choice in each course.

OPEN: Mon-Sat. **HOURS:** 7.00pm-12.00am. **CLOSED:** Bank Holidays. **CREDIT CARDS ACCEPTED:** None. **NUMBER OF SEATS:** 60. **SERVICE:** Optional. Wheelchair access (but not lavatory). Private room seats 24. **NEAREST TUBE STATION:** Ravenscourt Park.

Ajimura Japanese Restaurant

51/53 Shelton Street, W1 ❸

071-240 0178 LUNCH: £10; DINNER: £25

'Japanese food made accessible'

Ajimura, claims to be the longest-established Japanese restaurant in Britain which, if so, only takes us back to 1972. An increase in competition at all price levels and perhaps a realization that the gaijin can bear more reality has seen an increase in Japanese staff (replacing Scandinavians if my memory serves me well; it might be skewed by the varnished pine interior) and a monthly list of specials to augment and embroider what has become a sort of sameyness about Japanese food. There is a sushi bar where 'Tora-san' Tanizawa has been assembling the little bundles of garnished sticky rice since 1974. They are presented in various compilations, some with them with rather daft names like Nessy's Delight or Mother Ocean, or separately. There are many set lunches and dinners to turn to if the composition of a Japanese meal seems too taxing. A local clientele of Covent Gardeners can be inferred from the supply of filofax-perforated recipe postcards, the symbol denoting vegetarian dishes and the message on the chopstick wrappers; 'To help protect the environment, we only use re-usable chopsticks wrapped in re-cycled paper'. To anyone worrying about endangered bamboo groves, let me assure you that bamboo grows continually – impossible to stop. Since a Japanese meal seems ideal pre-theatre, it is worth noting that pre-theatre set price dinners from £13.00 per person are served from Monday to Friday between 6 and 7.30pm. As always with Japanese restaurants, lunch is much cheaper than dinner.

OPEN: LUNCH: Mon-Fri. DINNER: Mon-Sat. **HOURS:** 12.00-3.00pm and 6.00-11.00pm. **CLOSED:** Bank Holidays. **CREDIT CARDS ACCEPTED:** Access, AmEx, Diner's Club, Visa. **NUMBER OF SEATS:** 58. **SERVICE:** Optional. **SET PRICE LUNCH:** £8.50. **SET PRICE DINNER:** £19.50-£35. No-smoking area. Private room seats 20. **NEAREST TUBE STATION:** Covent Garden. MAP REF: 1,F/1

Alastair Little

49 Frith Street, W1

071-734 5183

(4)

BAR £25; RESTAURANT £50

'When the cat's away . . .'

Prices here have hit the roof – that's the one with little neon strip lights illuminating below bare, battered black tables laid with flimsy white paper napkins and on the walls framed illustrations that have done service as menu decoration. With Juliet Peston – once co-chef – gone and the eponymous chap away a good deal of the summer of '94 teaching in Italy, test meals have been disappointing, of a sort that invoke the morality tale of the Emperor's new clothes. Mr Little has published his recipes in *Keep It Simple* (Conran Octopus £18.99) . As well-fed and -read readers you will have recognized the dictum of Auguste Escoffier, an instruction that deserves to be ingested with a pinch of salt. Simplicity is a process of distillation rather than a plonking down of ingenuously large portions of (dreadful phrase) good, plain cooking. Alastair is capable of the former. Dishes cooked by his sous-chef such as rosti potato (presented as a fat potato cake), smoked eel, leeks and mustard; duo of terrines (one soft and yielding, one firm and marbled), various pickles and relishes exemplify the latter. Another meal delivered main courses of pigeon with a mass of lentils in a weak juice and cod awash with a vaguely Chinese dressing of soy sauce and herbs. Keep it simple, yes, but not slap-dash. Restaurant customers who say they feel short-changed if the famed chef is not present are usually told by know-it-alls like me that the real skill lies in the famed chef ensuring that his kitchen works as well in his absence. Well, it doesn't here, making the spare, noisy surroundings, the demanding prices and the take-it-or-leave-it service all the harder to take. But by the time you read this Mr Little should be back at the stove full of Italian inspiration and let us not forget, he is, on form, one of Britain's most reckonable cooks.

OPEN: LUNCH: Mon-Fri. DINNER: Mon-Sat. **HOURS:** 12.00-3.00pm and 6.00-11.30pm. **CLOSED:** Bank Holidays. **CREDIT CARDS ACCEPTED:** Access, AmEx, Visa. **NUMBER OF SEATS:** 36 in Restaurant, 18 in Bar. **SERVICE:** Optional. **SET PRICE LUNCH:** £10 in Bar, £25 in Restaurant. Bar can be booked privately and seats 16. Wheelchair access (but not lavatory). **NEAREST TUBE STATION:** Tottenham Court Road/Piccadilly Circus/Leicester Square. **MAP REF:** 1,E/2

Al Basha Restaurant

222 High Street Kensington, W8

(5)

071-938 1794

£20

'A restaurant that almost counts as a restaurant in the park'

Last year we were somewhat cynical about the views of Holland Park from this restaurant which would have required a telescopic neck like that of Alice in Wonderland after she ate the 'Eat Me' cake to get more than a glimpse. However, new floor-to- ceiling curved windows have been installed, lending an agreeable conservatory air. Other parts of the restaurant, decorated with Orientalist pictures suited to more lugubrious moods, are shrouded in gloom. There is almost no such thing as a bad Lebanese restaurant – the core clientele would not tolerate it – but even so the quality of the food at Al Basha tends to be above that honourable average. From the lists of hot and cold hors d'oeuvres here are some tried and approved choices; baba ghannouj (also known as moutabal), a purée of grilled aubergines; muhammara, a mixture of ground nuts and spices; l'sanaat salatah, lamb's tongue in lemon sauce; sawda dajaj, fried chicken livers with lemon and spices; jawaneh, grilled chicken wings; batata harra, spicy fried potatoes. Of course appetite and inclination governs an order and there is diced raw liver and lamb's testicles for those who want them. Grazing on the crudités that justify the £1.50 cover charge and a spread of small dishes usually dulls the appetite for main course grills but shish taouk, chicken fillets in garlic, should be managed. For the same reason desserts seem offered in a half-hearted manner. Coffee is good. Service is polite and regulars seem not even to have to ask for a menu; what they want is known and efficiently produced. For those who live or work in the area it is worth noting the take-away option that includes interesting sandwiches with the fillings tucked into puffy Arab bread.

OPEN: Mon-Sun. **HOURS:** 12.00pm-12.00am. **CREDIT CARDS ACCEPTED:** All major credit cards. **NUMBER OF SEATS:** 140. **SERVICE:** 15%, £1.50 cover charge. **SET PRICE LUNCH AND DINNER:** £12.50. Wheelchair access (but not lavatory). Private room seats 65. **NEAREST TUBE STATION:** High Street Kensington.

Albero & Grana

Chelsea Cloisters,
89 Sloane Avenue, SW3   ●

071-225 1048/9   **£30**

'The most exciting Spanish food in London'

Sylvia Ligonie, a native of Madrid, was not the first person to notice the sad quality of Spanish food in London but unlike other grousers she did something about it; she opened Albero & Grana with the help of Jose Antonio Garcia, who masterminded the striking decor based on the crimson and ochre colours of the bullring, and chef Angel Garcia (no relation), who directs the kitchen. Angel Garcia's previous post was at the restaurant Luculo in Madrid where he was awarded a Michelin star. His training and work experience in France tells in his gastronomic style – the result is not diluted and primped like much Spanish 'new' cooking but dramatic, vibrant and uncompromising. It is occasionally almost original, a description to be used with circumspection where food is concerned. I would advise in the first course something rustic such as olla gitana, a stew of cured ham, chicken, chick-peas and vegetables, or something more astonishing such as the lasagne of black pudding with a green pepper sauce or the stuffed griddled squid with a black ink sauce. Cold escabeche of duck liver is like no foie gras you have ever tasted before. In the main course simplicity can be satisfying as in gilthead bream baked in sea salt but this is also a moment to try regional specialities such as the Catalan guinea fowl with candied garlic and orange. Turn down the waiter's proposal of a selection of vegetables – the only English moment of the meal – but do not omit one of the pastry-based desserts such as caramelized pastry horn filled with honey ice cream and fruits or the apple and cinnamon millefeuille.

The front part of Albero & Grana is given over to a long tapas bar which is invariably packed out with a quite glamorous crowd and concomitantly noisy (the din spilling into the restaurant area). The tapas are better than the sorry offerings found elsewhere but more expensive. Recommended are scallops a la plancha, squid Abuela style, chorizo with chick-peas, eggs scrambled with asparagus and prawns and tortilla. There is also a tapas of the day. Read my lips.

THE IMPROVED WINE list at this restaurant begins to do justice to Spain's increasingly diverse wine culture. Not only is the selection better, but the list itself is more informative, if occasionally pretentious (amontillado and oloroso sherries, we are told, 'should be tasted in silence . . . like all works of art, they require an empty space in which to be enjoyed'. Er, clear the restaurant, please, we have a customer who wants a glass of oloroso.) Prices are highish and best value is to be had from the as yet nascent selections from Navarra and Valdepeñas, together with the less expensive Riojas. Ribera del Duero deserves expansion, and there's more to Penedès than Torres. Hurrah, though, for the half-bottles of fino sherry, even if £12 is a bit stiff for something whose wholesale price is a quarter that.

OPEN: LUNCH: Mon-Sat. DINNER: Mon-Sun. **HOURS:** 12.30-3.30pm and 6.00pm-1.00am. **CLOSED:** Some Bank Holidays. **CREDIT CARDS ACCEPTED:** All major cards. **NUMBER OF SEATS:** 120. **SERVICE:** 12.5% for parties of over 7. **SET PRICE DINNER:** £24. Private room seats 20. **NEAREST TUBE STATION:** South Kensington/Sloane Square. MAP REF: 2,F3

Al Bustan

27 Motcomb Street, SW1 ●7

071-235 8277 £30

'A Lebanese menu by a woman chef'

Assuming that people who go to Lebanese restaurants do so because they like Lebanese food it seems hardly worth listing dishes from among the familiar hot and cold hors d'oeuvres and main-course grills since the standard of preparation here, as in most Lebanese places, is high and fairly unwavering. For a suggestion of some items offered you could read the entry for Al Basha. However, Al Bustan's individuality lies in its Belgravia location, its female chef who, with her husband, is co-proprietor, its fancy decor expressed in perforated painted screens, intricately patterned fabrics and plenty of houseplants posing as dining room decoration and its helpful service. Last year we advised that a show of interest in the menu might bring forth some specials. Reports are that this is true but that the price of the specials can come as something of a shock. Cabbage stuffed with minced lamb in a lemon sauce priced at £21 was a case in point. Kinder to your pocket is the printed menu where you can find Al Bustan specialities such as nkhaat, exotically spiced lamb's brains fried in batter, at £5.50 or farrouj mousakhan, oven-cooked baby chicken with onions and sumac served on specially prepared bread, at £10.50. A separate section lists raw meat. Fish – prawns, Dover sole or sea bass – is sold at market price so, bearing in mind that stuffed cabbage, it is worth checking first what that will be. The dessert pastries here are notably delectable. Wine prices have come down since last year so what you might lose on stuffed cabbage, you might gain on the house St-Emilion at £12.

OPEN: Mon-Sun. **HOURS:** 12.00-11.00pm. **CLOSED:** Christmas Day and Boxing Day. **CREDIT CARDS ACCEPTED:** All major cards. **NUMBER OF SEATS:** 65. **SERVICE:** £2.50 cover charge. Wheelchair access (but not lavatory).Tables outside seat 15. Private room seats 18. **NEAREST TUBE STATION:** Knightsbridge.

MAP REF: 2,F/3

Alexandra

507 Kingston Road, SW20   **8**

081-542 4838   **£15-£25**

'The Normandy landing in Raynes Park '

It is not so easy these days to find what you might consider that typically French meal of moules Normandes, filet de boeuf Grand Veneur, tarte Tatin. In fact you might have to go – and should go – to Raynes Park. Here in homey, homely premises chef/proprietor Eric Lecras delivers the sort of dishes you cross the channel to Dieppe to locate. Creme argenteuil à l estragon; crêpe Dieppoise; magret de canard fumé; filet de rouget au safran; rognons de veau au cognac; poulet Vallée d Auge; confit de canard aux cêpes plus the above-mentioned menu are all regulars on the menu which is supplemented by daily dishes presented on the blackboard. Lecras cooks traditionally and competently. My one complaint is that the set price menus offer two or three courses plus one glass of wine and coffee. The French paradox – that the French can eat butter, cream, Calvados and duck liver and not have heart attacks – was never achieved on one glass of wine. Luckily there is a list of about twenty French wines that are priced without excessive mark-up.

OPEN: LUNCH: Sun. DINNER: Mon-Sat. **HOURS:** 12.00-2.00pm and 7.00-10.00pm. **CREDIT CARDS ACCEPTED:** Access, Mastercard, Visa. **NUMBER OF SEATS:** 55. **SERVICE:** 12.5% (optional). **SET PRICE LUNCH:** £12.80. **SET PRICE DINNER:** £12.80 (£16.95 Fri and Sat). Tables outside seat 12. Private room seats 30. **NEAREST BR STATION:** Raynes Park.

Alfred

245 Shaftesbury Avenue, W1

071-240 2566 ⑨

£22

'At ease with English food. And wine (and eau de vie)'

Alfred is the venture of Fred Taylor, a chap previously to be found behind bars – at the Groucho, then at the eponymous Fred's (now under different ownership) – rather than front of house. The premises are next to the little green at the junction of Shaftesbury Avenue and Oxford Street. Many restaurants have occupied this site but none as stylishly as Alfred with its retro-bleak interior reminiscent of an Edward Hopper painting. The lemon yellow tables made in some descendant of formica contrast with duck-egg blue gloss walls sporting Plexiglas light fittings. Tongue and groove painted a drab purple reaches up to dado level. As a design scheme it works well and its uncluttered quality – save for pretty fresh flowers – is taken up in the short, British menu. Chef at Alfred is Robert Gutteridge whose previous post was at Belgo (q.v.) a fact reflected more in the wide and deep choice of British beers offered, plus Somerset eau de vie and English cider brandy, than in the food. Dishes manage to seem indigenous without seeming themed. They can be as straight-forward as chilled cucumber and mint soup; steak with Stilton butter, chips and greens; calves' liver with bacon and onion gravy; stewed fruit with clotted cream and roasted almonds and Burchester cheese, but are cooked with the sort of care and flair you might omit at home. Where they get a little wilder – braised knuckle of bacon with pickled cabbage and split pea rissoles – they also succeed. The short wine list is an Anglo-French hybrid that makes you realize to what extent New World wines have filled the shelves of our wine consciousness. Downstairs at Alfred is a spacious bar. Alfred has achieved that rare feat of managing not to be pretentious about being unpretentious.

OPEN: Mon-Sat. **HOURS:** 12.00-4.00pm and 6.00-11.45pm. **CLOSED:** Christmas Day, Boxing Day and New Year's Day. **CREDIT CARDS ACCEPTED:** Access, AmEx, Visa. **NUMBER OF SEATS:** 60. **SERVICE:** 12%. Wheelchair access (but not lavatory). Tables Outside: seat 36. **NEAREST TUBE STATION:** Tottenham Court Road.

Al Hamra Restaurant

31-33 Shepherd Market, W1

071-493 1954/6934 ⑩

£25

'Go in a group and roam wide and free among the meze'

In an area known for its lively company and exotic appetites, Al Hamra has earned a reputation for both, albeit of a different nature. The restaurant offers an abundance of Middle Eastern promise. Indeed there is a choice of 43 cold and hot Lebanese hors d'oeuvres, culminating with dafadeh, frogs legs served breaded or Provençal, and 16 main courses of charcoal-grilled fish, chicken and meat plus daily specialities. As seems traditional, Saturday is the day for molukhieh, that viscous leaf cooked in this instance with lamb, coriander and garlic and served with rice. Particularly recommended in the first course are haliwat, tender sweetbreads enlivened with lemon juice and jawaneh, chicken wings with garlic sauce. Meals start with a heaped platter of crudités, accompanied by hot unleavened bread, olives and pickles justifying the substantial cover charge. As with other Oriental styles, the idea is to order a number of dishes to share, so the bigger the group the better.

OPEN: Mon-Sun. **HOURS:** 12.00pm-12.00am. **CLOSED:** Christmas Day and New Year's Day. **CREDIT CARDS ACCEPTED:** Access, AmEx, Diner's Club, Visa. **NUMBER OF SEATS:** 75. **SERVICE:** Optional, £2.50 cover charge. **SET PRICE LUNCH AND DINNER:** £20 plus drink. Wheelchair access (but not lavatory). 4 tables outside. **NEAREST TUBE STATION:** Green Park. MAP REF: 1,B/2

Ali's Indian Cuisine
81 Kentish Town Road, NW1   ⓫

071-284 2061   **£23**

'For once you can believe the blurbs'

Testimonials plaster the window of this small Kentish Town Indian restaurant Conscientious preparation and lively spicing continue to be factors that lift this local above many others. Service that is genial and houseproud is another plus. Two appetizers that pair well are prawn purée and the fresh-tasting sheek kebab. A tandoori dish can offset one of Ali's specialities such as the lamb-based gosht kata masala where crisp fried onions and garlic tossed with spices are the garnish that makes all the difference, lending a smoky flavour to the meat. Breads, including poppadums, are light and dry. Ali's claims to be the first Indian restaurant in the West End to have an open-air garden. Speaking Hobson-Jobson, they invite you to the 'varandah'.

OPEN: Mon-Sun. **HOURS:** 12.00-3.00pm and 6.00pm-12.00am. **CLOSED:** Christmas Day and Boxing Day. **CREDIT CARDS ACCEPTED:** All major cards. **NUMBER OF SEATS:** 35. **SERVICE:** Optional. Wheelchair access (but not lavatory). Tables outside seat 18. Private room seats 16. **NEAREST TUBE STATION:** Camden Town/Kentish Town. MAP REF: 5,C/2

Al San Vincenzo
30 Connaught Street, W2   ⓬

071-262 9623   **£35**

'One man's belief in Italian food'

Leafing through the plethora of Italian recipe books on offer – the growth area in cookery publishing – you might get the feeling that they are talking about a different country to the one portrayed on the plate in London's Italian restaurants. The joy of Vincenzo Borgonzola's cooking at his eponymous restaurant (beatified) is its singularity; the way it too veers away from a familiar formula. His is a short menu that changes regularly, reflecting growing and hunting seasons however brief those might be. You could not say that chef Vincenzo is an original since his dishes are rooted in tradition but you might say he is a loner in both the sense that his small, warmly decorated restaurant is unlike any other and also in his apparent inability to find temperamentally suited help in the kitchen. Often having to work more or less by himself, he can stretch customers' patience but the wait is usually well worth it and fortunately the restaurant, ably run by his wife Elaine, seats only 35. In choosing a meal, complexity of dishes must be balanced. Some first courses seem almost small main courses e.g. large quail cooked with orange and fennel but these could be weighed against main courses of mussels and clams sautéed in olive oil, lemon and garlic or hand-made spaghetti Pugliese style with baby octopus in a spicy sauce. To proceed another way, you could start with something as light as carpaccio of monkfish dressed with a warm vinaigrette and move on to veal chop with Parma ham and morels. Fish dishes change daily according to marketing. The dessert course also usually features an unpredictable confection. An example I tried is the Neapolitan pastry tart filled with ricotta, mixed peel, barley and orange water that in appearance resembled crumbling masonry in an old Italian hill town. The wine list complements the menu in being also quite short and also carefully considered. There is probably some Italian superstition about seeming pleased with the way things are going – the Borgonzolas like to have a good moan – but you sometimes must book a day or so ahead to secure a table in the evening.

OPEN: LUNCH: Mon-Fri. DINNER: Mon-Sat. **HOURS:** 12.30-3.00pm and 7.00-10.15pm. **CLOSED:** Christmas and Bank Holidays. **CREDIT CARDS ACCEPTED:** Access, Visa, Mastercard. **NUMBER OF SEATS:** 35. **SERVICE:** Optional. Wheelchair access (but not lavatory). **NEAREST TUBE STATION:** Marble Arch/Paddington.

L'Altro

210 Kensington Park Road, W11

071-792 1066/1077 LUNCH £9; DINNER £25-£30

If she lives in Notting Hill, take Auntie Patsy for antipasti'

The 'otherness' of L'Altro is in relation to Cibo (q.v.) the first Italian restaurant opened by Gino Taddei. The impact of the original intention – that the restaurant should specialize in fish cooking – has faded somewhat and the interesting thing about L'Altro now is not its piscine leanings but the comprehensive list of interesting, carefully prepared antipasti offered at lunchtime. Better than the components of any tapas bar, these dishes presented at prices that in the main range between £2 and £4 encapsulate ingredients and ideas you would be thrilled to find at the most ambitious and expensive of London's Italian restaurants. A selection to prove the point: oysters sautéed with spinach and shallots; grilled ciabatta with cardoons, wild mushrooms and quails; grilled Trevisana radicchio with melted goat's cheese; beetroot-stuffed ravioli with butter and sage; gnocchi with rabbit ragu; black sheets of pasta with fillets of sea bass. Perhaps a greater achievement of this kitchen is rendering the sort of items that overkill has made banal, e.g. roasted and marinated vegetables, the sort of delicacy they can and should be. Those who are affronted by chillis (such people do exist) might construe as criticism a reliance on this short, sharp shock in quite a few of the assemblies. The lunch crowd is local and sometimes literary. The wine list is usefully annotated.

OPEN: Lunch: Mon-Sun. **DINNER:** Mon-Sat. **HOURS:** 12.00-3.00pm and 7.00-11.00pm (7.00-10.30pm Mon and 7.00-11.30pm Fri-Sat). **CLOSED:** Bank holidays. **CREDIT CARDS ACCEPTED:** AmEx, Diner's Club, Mastercard, Visa. **NUMBER OF SEATS:** 43. **SERVICE:** 12.5% on parties of 5 and over. Wheelchair access (but not lavatory).Tables outside seat 8. **NEAREST TUBE STATION:** Ladbroke Grove.

MAP REF: 4,A/1

Andrew Edmunds

46 Lexington Street, W1   ⑭

071-437 5708   LUNCH: £15; DINNER: £20

'An English wine bar fulfilling fantasies about French bistros'

This self-servingly scruffy small wine bar and restaurant attracts a loyal clientele who like to think of the place as a sort of raffish club where people like them like to gather. There was a time when their indifference towards indifferent food seemed a badge of honour but now the food and more so the wines make a visit worthwhile even for 'non members'. As shopping for ingredients becomes more alluring, so cooking, or indeed assembling, gets easier and in Lexington Street the kitchen need not roam far to cull the best from the street market and the few remaining food shops of Soho. The point is proved by the daily-changing menu viz. items like coppa with fruit bread and gruyère; artichoke heart with feta and sun-dried tomato salad; roasted vegetables with goat's cheese and ciabatta, but the cramped kitchen can also run to more elaboration, for example shellfish saffron soup; best end of lamb with rosemary mash. Cheeses are well chosen. Chocolate mousse cake is something of a speciality. Some bottles on the wine list seem almost too good for the restless atmosphere in which they must be drunk but this has never stopped anyone – including me. Service understands the concept of being cruel to be kind but is invariably attractive to behold. The ground floor is considered a preferable place to sit but the low-ceilinged dark green basement of the 18th-century house has its charms too.

THE WINE LIST is short, predominantly classic and chaotically organised – yet the selections are intelligent (sherries from Valdespino, burgundy from Pousse d'Or and Jayer-Gilles, Vouvray from Huet, Chablis from Durup, Hermitage from Chave) and prices are reasonable.

OPEN: Mon-Sun. **HOURS:** 12.30-3.00pm and 5.30-11.00pm. **CLOSED:** Bank Holidays. **CREDIT CARDS ACCEPTED:** Access, Switch, Visa. **NUMBER OF SEATS:** 60. **SERVICE:** Optional. Tables outside seat 4. **NEAREST TUBE STATIONS:** Piccadilly Circus/Tottenham Court Road/Oxford Circus.   MAP REF:1,D/2

The Angel

101 Bermondsey Wall East, SE16

071-237 3608   **£30**

'One of the great views of London'

Forte Restaurants in its mission to revamp has turned the attention of the
relevant department to the three Port of London Inns it owns; the
Dickens Inn at St Katharine's Dock, the Anchor at Bankside and the
Angel at Rotherhithe. What they describe as a contemporary menu
which 'combines the comfort of traditional dishes with the elegance of
what has become termed Modern British' has been introduced into each
of these historic pubs and the result is not bad. Actually the result is to
my mind almost immaterial when you are sitting at the window of the
first-floor dining room at the Angel watching the water shiver and shrug
as it does when the tide is turning and clocking the effect of the fading
light on the dome of St Paul's; it is a moment when, if you love London,
the feeling is requited. Caesar salad, mixed crostini, halibut and salmon
carpaccio, tomato and herb salsa and capuccino mousse might strike you
as more modern than British but you could compose a meal of cream of
onion soup with Cumberland sausage followed by deep-fried skate in a
lemon and coriander batter with pease pudding and chips and spotted
dick and fresh egg custard or sherry trifle. You might be wiser to choose
steak or tuna fish from the chargrill but an undeniable effort with the food
is being made and the service I have encountered is charming,
quintessentially English. Doubtless if the Angel – established they say at
least as early as the 15th century – did not have a ghost, Forte Restaurants
Marketing Department would rustle one up, but the 'hanging' Judge
Jeffreys is reported to walk the balcony where once he enjoyed a pint of
ale whilst watching the public executions on the North bank opposite.

OPEN: LUNCH: Sun-Fri. DINNER: Mon-Sat. **HOURS:** 12.00-3.30pm and 7.00pm-
12.00am. **CLOSED:** Bank Holidays. **CREDIT CARDS ACCEPTED:** All major cards.
NUMBER OF SEATS: 50. **SERVICE:** Optional. **SET PRICE DINNER:** £15.50 (Mon-Fri
only). **NEAREST TUBE STATION:** Rotherhithe.

Anna's Place

90 Mildmay Park, N1

071-249 9379   **£20-£25**

'Warm-hearted Swedish cooking '

Swedish restaurants in London are about as plentiful as ice creams in
Hell; Anna's Place leaves you wishing that there were a whole lot more.
From its doll's-house entrance to the simple comfort of painted wood and
a host of Scandinavian artefacts, the atmosphere is one of cosy
domesticity. Gratifyingly, the food and service sustain this homey feel.
The menu which is fashioned by the eponymous, cheery Anna is short,
reasonable and suitably Scandinavian with much reliance on fish:

gravadlax; pan-fried bream; a superb warm turbot salad with a creamy mustard dressing. There is also a hearty side to Swedish food, and this is exemplified by meatballs in a thick sauce, a rich beef stew and a number of thick soups which feature in the winter menu. For dessert you could practise your Swedish by saying choklad tarta – pretty self-evident – or the more impenetrable Svenska våfflor med blåbärssylt och vispgrädde which those on their second Linguaphone tape will know to waffles with blueberry compote and cream. Wine prices are fair but drinking vodka or Swedish beer would be another way of raising your spirits.

OPEN: Tues-Sat. **HOURS:** 12.15-2.15pm and 7.15-10.45pm. **CLOSED:** 2 weeks at Christmas and Easter; 4 weeks in August. **CREDIT CARDS ACCEPTED:** None. **NUMBER OF SEATS:** 40. **SERVICE:** 10%. Wheelchair access (but not lavatory), please advise when booking. Tables outside in summer seat 15. **NEAREST TUBE STATION:** Highbury & Islington.

Arcadia

35 Kensington High Street, W8   **17**

071-937 4294   **DINNER: £28**

'More bucolic and with better food than the Ark that went before'

What was the Ark off Kensington High Street conjoined to the original Ark – more home from home to Noah – sited at the top of Kensington Church Street has become, under new ownership, Arcadia. The chef/proprietor of Arcadia is Nikki Barraclough whose roll-call of previous postings inspires confidence; Sonny's, the Carved Angel, Clarke's, Stephen Bull and Le Manoir aux Quat'Saisons. Important changes have been made both to the food offered and to the look of the place which over the years had grown shabby and dispiriting. Barraclough's food is relatively simple but has the important virtue of ingredients tasting intensely of themselves. She is a canny buyer and a canny borrower of recipes as evidenced by Joel Robuchon's chocolate tart and Alice Waters' chocolate cake. That is borrowing from the best. Dishes that typify what is available and that have been enjoyed are white bean, sage and tomato soup; crab ravioli with a shellfish sauce; ragoût of sweetbreads and kidneys with a red wine sauce (a first course despite its strapping size); roast quails with plum sauce and waffle crisps (masterly quails); salad of Appledore Farm lettuce; a selection of Perroche, Cashel Blue and Spenwood cheeses served with oatmeal biscuits and green tomato chutney. At lunchtime (including Sunday) the menu is a set price. An à la carte brunch is also served on Sundays. A problem which the fresh cream and apple-green decor has not overcome is the second-choice atmosphere to the basement when compared with the bustling ground floor, the volume of clientele that Arcadia now deserves should help the discrepancy.

OPEN: LUNCH: Mon-Fri. DINNER: Mon-Sun. **HOURS:** 12.00-2.30pm and 7.00-11.00pm. **CLOSED:** Public holidays. **CREDIT CARDS ACCEPTED:** AmEx, Mastercard, Visa. **NUMBER OF SEATS:** 78. **SERVICE:** Optional. **SET PRICE LUNCH:** £13.50 or £16. No-smoking area. Wheelchair access (but not lavatory). Tables outside seat 14. Private room seats 14. **NEAREST TUBE STATION:** High Street Kensington.

MAP REF: 4,D/2

The Argyll

316 King's Road, SW3

18

071-352 0025   **£28**

'You can imitate a menu but not necessarily its success'

Chef Anand Sastry and the Argyll have parted company; he to set up on his own and the Argyll to offer a more relaxed menu, one that strikes me as closely modelled on that of the perennially successful Le Caprice, an observation vindicated by the discovery that Le Caprice was the previous place of work of chef Tony Carey. A few more pictures on the white walls of the pleasantly plain, bare-boarded large room with doors to the street that are folded back on clement days and nights also seem a signal that this is a place where you might eat out with your pocket money rather than your life's savings. Unfortunately at a test meal, the dishes had more a sense of style than of content. Some – a Gloy-like chilled pumpkin soup and a dish of duck with an overwhelming flavour of sesame oil – were simply horrid. The change of pace in the culinary sense also happens to have coincided with the arrival of challenging restaurant alternatives nearby such as Aubergine, Fulham Road and Chez Max which is, I suppose, hard cheese on the Argyll. It is possible to eat very simply; endive with mustard dressing, rocket salad with Pecorino, rigatoni with pesto, calves' liver with bacon and parsley mash, fresh cherries on ice and it is probably sensible to do so. Sastry's hand is missed generally and in the vegetable cooking in particular. There are no steals on the wine list which to some extent is divided up by grape variety, but some interesting bottles. Service is brisk in manner rather than mph.

OPEN: LUNCH: Tues-Sun. **DINNER:** Mon-Sun. **HOURS:** 12.30-2.30pm and 7.30-11.15pm. **CLOSED:** Bank Holidays. **CREDIT CARDS ACCEPTED:** AmEx, Diner's Club, Mastercard, Visa. **NUMBER OF SEATS:** 60. **SERVICE:** Optional. **SET PRICE LUNCH:** £10 (two courses), £12 (3 courses).Wheelchair access (but not lavatory). **NEAREST TUBE STATION:** Sloane Square.   MAP REF: 2,B/2

Arts Theatre Café

6-7 Great Newport Street, WC2

19

071-497 8014   **£19**

'Bruschetta in theatre land'

Beside the small, modern auditorium of the Arts Theatre is a basement café which has established a trade that seems for the most part to be independent of the night's audience. Theatre-goers dash in and out, desperate for a drink or the loo (access to which is through the café), or sit down for a short meal, but other customers are in no hurry to be summoned by bells. A reasonably priced short menu of daily-changing modern Italian dishes is the attraction. Choices include soups – often inspired vegetable combinations – salads, garnished breads, pasta and risotti, usually a grilled chicken dish, a casserole – braised pigeon say, or braised leg of lamb with garlic – fish dishes and something to satisfy vegetarians. Reports this year have talked of wavering cooking standards and these can seem all the more serious in a spare space into which crowds of people lighting up cigarettes may suddenly pour. However, candles and flowers create warmth in the room and one waiter presides with the efficiency of six. Orecchiette with broccoli, olive oil, garlic and chilli had too much browned garlic, not enough broccoli. Chicken on thick, grilled country bread with a thin gravy and sliced braised artichokes and tomatoes (plus garlic) was satisfying but a mayonnaise-dressed potato salad was a clumsy partner to very rare cold roast beef. Desserts feature some interesting tarts and creamy-eggy confections.

OPEN: Mon-Sat. **HOURS:** 12.00-11pm (6.00pm-11.00pm Sat). **CLOSED:** Bank Holidays. **CREDIT CARDS ACCEPTED:** None. **NUMBER OF SEATS:** 28. **SERVICE:** 10%. **SET PRICE LUNCH AND DINNER:** £11.50. **NEAREST TUBE STATION:** Leicester Square.

MAP REF: 1,E/1

Les Associés

172 Park Road, N8   **20**

081-348 8944   **£27**

'The Three Burgundian Musketeers of Crouch End'

There must be something in the air in Crouch End which wafts over the rest of North London but only settles in the kitchens of this seemingly most innocuous of suburbs. Whatever it is, the result is that its residents have the pick of several creditable establishments – Le Cadre, Florians, Jashan (see entries) – whereas those who live in, say, Hampstead, Highgate or Highbury have to make do with a less inspiring selection. Les Associés vindicates this claim by offering a surprisingly versatile and sophisticated menu, one which has an authentic taste and feel of the kind you might find in any small French town. The same cannot be said of the decor which has the distinct air of a small English boardroom circa 1975, but the food overcomes this reservation. The chef's provenance is Dijon in the heart of Burgundy and despite occasional forays further afield – a bouillabaisse Marseillaise is offered with two days' notice – the food remains rooted in Franche-Comté where such dishes as la chartreuse d'escargots et sa crème d'ail; la lotte au cumin sauce safrane are both familiar and, in this case, pleasingly prepared; especially appealing is the salmis de pintadeau aux pruneaux, exhibiting just the right combination of richness and delicacy. Noteworthy is the plateau de nos fromages affinés, if only because it is rare these days, even in the haughtiest of restaurants, to find cheese taken seriously. The wine list is wholly French, burgundies the obvious choice. When you book for the evening, the assumption is that you will be there for the duration.

OPEN: Tue-Sat. **HOURS:** 12.30-2.00pm and 7.30-10.00pm. **CLOSED:** August. **CREDIT CARDS ACCEPTED:** Access, Visa. **NUMBER OF SEATS:** 38. **SERVICE:** Included. **SET PRICE LUNCH:** £15.95. **SET PRICE DINNER:** £27. Wheelchair access (but not lavatory). **NEAREST TUBE STATION:** Finsbury Park.

Atlantic Bar and Grill

20 Glasshouse Street, W1

071-734 4888

(21)

£40

'Fight your way towards some interesting food'

The almost uniquely generous opening hours for eating and drinking at the Atlantic Bar & Grill has created a success that threatens to become monstrous. There is now a door policy on what was publicized and praised at the outset for not being a club and the crowd that the Atlantic attracts is not everybody's cup of cappuccino. Stories of fights breaking out and other outrages are tough on chef Richard Sawyer who works hard to provide an interesting, skilfully prepared menu for a clientele whose first concern may well not be the consistency of the beurre blanc or whether by Provincial tomatoes the chef really means Provençal (Sawyer is given to spelling mistakes and literals). Since the Atlantic opened in early summer of '94 the menu has evolved and a swings and roundabouts change in pricing applied, the most positive outcome from the customer's point of view being more dishes at two sizes, two prices, examples being Atlantic club salad with smoked chicken, cheese and quail's egg; Innes Farm rocket and pear salad with Roquefort and poppy seed dressing. Antipasti assembled as being typical of the Mediterranean or the Orient are offered as first courses to share and some of the constituent parts are imaginative. There is considerable scope for vegetarians in the soups, salads and pastas. Main courses that typify Sawyer's current style (he trained at the Connaught) are braised lamb shank, spiced butter beans, smoked bacon and spaghetti squash; breast of chicken browned with lemon, thyme, lime and coriander with crisp spatzelli (sic). You would be correct in thinking that such a menu is in excess of the demands of those who go out ogle or be ogled. It certainly deserves better surroundings which claim art deco but convey art dreary. But who knows, queues of the curious or just thirsty may fade away as queues tend to do, the service may become more co-ordinated and Sawyer get an audience who doesn't think Crostini is Moschino's cousin.

OPEN: Mon-Sun. **HOURS:** 12.00pm-3.00am (12.00pm-12.00am Sun). **CREDIT CARDS ACCEPTED:** All major cards. **NUMBER OF SEATS:** 200. **SERVICE:** 12.5%. No-smoking area. **NEAREST TUBE STATION:** Picadilly Circus.   MAP REF: 1,D/2

 # Aubergine

11 Park Walk, SW10

071-352 3449

(22)

£26

'A dazzling newcomer'

Aubergine opened at more or less the same time as the first edition of this guide was published (October 1993). In one year Gordon Ramsay has proved that he is a chef to be counted among the big boys (still all boys sadly) in the capital. His training – with Marco Pierre White in

Wandsworth and with Joël Robuchon and Guy Savoy in Paris – allied with the relatively inexpensive set price menus gives London haute cuisine restaurant customers, in that elegant American phrase, the best bang for their buck. Some dishes on the menu still bear the stamp of MPW, but that is no criticism, and slowly the menu has evolved and become more personal to Ramsay. Cappuccino of haricots blancs with truffle oil is a fabulous soup, earthy and opulent at one and the same time. Salad of red mullet with fried artichokes, sauce Antiboise is also masterly. A main course of brill that was a special of the day was quite simply the best fish dish I can remember. In Guy Savoy manner the sauce was light and subtle, more a mix of oil and stock than a sauce. With the brill came salt cod mash (great idea), fresh peas and spinach. Other much praised main courses are pigeon 'poché, grillé' with purée of swede and wild mushroom ravioli, jus madeira and pot-roasted calves' sweetbreads with creamed watercress, jus of ceps. The vanilla flavour in the sauce with sea bass is, I know, a fashion but like many fashions not flattering. The tempo does not subside in the dessert course. Orange tart with orange sorbet is faultless and a newcomer to the list, a sort of dark brandysnap sandwich with ice cream flavoured with pruneaux, is also great. The wine list is intelligently compiled with enough choice at the lower end of the scale to provide interesting drinking and yet a bill at dinner well under £100 for two, a price now easily achieved elsewhere for nothing very notable to eat. Since we're proud of our Gordon from Glasgow, it seems to me a pity that the context in which he sets himself – in terms of service – is so remorselessly French. The ground-floor dining room is unrecognizable from the days of 11 Park Walk, the Italian restaurant that preceded Aubergine. It is spacious and light, the tables well-disposed, the predominant colour a sort of roughed-up apricot.

OPEN: LUNCH: Mon-Fri. DINNER: Mon-Sat **HOURS:** 12.00-2.30pm and 7.00-11.00pm. **CLOSED:** Bank Holidays. **CREDIT CARDS ACCEPTED:** All major cards except Diner's Club. **NUMBER OF SEATS:** 50. **SERVICE:** Optional. **SET PRICE LUNCH:** £18. **SET PRICE DINNER:** £26. **NEAREST TUBE STATION:** South Kensington.

MAP REF: 2,B/2

Avenue West Eleven

157 Notting Hill Gate, W11   **23**

071-221 8144   LUNCH: £15; DINNER: £23

'A menu not so much eclectic as psychotic'

Notting Hill Gate seems able to absorb any number of restaurants. To add to the array already in place, within about a month of one another in the summer of 1994, W11 and Avenue West Eleven opened. The latter, the second restaurant of Phillip McMullen who owns Brasserie du Marché aux Puces (q.v.), is located at the point where Notting Hill Gate becomes Holland Park Avenue. The look of the place is diverting. Were you to put a label to the theme it might be Santa Fe artist's pad. Earthy colours, rag rugs and locked-in-resin sculptures are features of the decoration. A service bar in the centre of the space is panelled in sheets of beaten tin. Tables are covered in natural hessian and then by brown paper cloths. Downstairs is a bar proper. The menu is not so much eclectic as psychotic. In just one dish – e.g. Dorset crab, Chinese-style egg custard pancake, shiitake mushrooms and bean curd – you can girdle the world. Somehow I get the feeling that some of the ideas were imposed on chef Alan Bird; he is clearly not comfortable handling them, but there is enough, all at admirably restrained prices, that works. Just go with your fancy. It might be for parrotfish, dill and lemon gin sauce, orange, prune and cardamom tea compote. Or it might not. You could settle for soup of the day followed by lamb cutlets Reform and devils on horseback.

OPEN: Mon-Sun. **HOURS:** 12.00-3.00pm and 6.30-11.15pm (7.30-10.30pm Sun). **CLOSED:** Bank Holidays. **CREDIT CARDS ACCEPTED:** Access, AmEx, Mastercard, Visa. **NUMBER OF SEATS:** 60. **SERVICE:** Optional. Wheelchair access. **NEAREST TUBE STATION:** Notting Hill Gate/Holland Park.   MAP REF: 4,C/1

Babur Brasserie

119 Brockley Rise, SE23   **24**

081-291 2400/4881   LUNCH: £10; DINNER: £15

'An Indian restaurant worth a detour'

Babur was the first Mogul emperor and although the cooking here is said to be Mogul style it incorporates regional specialities as far-flung from one another as Nepalese momo (dumplings), and Parsee patrani machli (fish, in this case sole, steamed in banana leaf). In addition this notably upmarket, pastel-painted establishment, with prices and civil service to match, organizes various festivals based on aspects of Indian cookery and culture. These can turn out rather muddle-headed where the menus are concerned – a Parsee event with no dhansak – but show commendable willingness and an alertness to the tools of marketing. From the list of specialities, try lamb cooked with mint, honey and lemon (poodina gosht) and chicken enriched with nuts and seeds (shugati masala). Unusually various species of fish feature; cod is cooked in the tandoor, tilapia is poached in a sauce flavoured with coriander, cumin and fenugreek leaves. You could make a meal from the vegetable dishes and indeed are invited to: any four vegetable dishes served with nan and basmati rice are charged at £8.25. Don't omit from the selection aloo makhani (whole potatoes in a rich masala) or the baingan bhartha (roasted aubergines with spices). Although going out for an Indian meal tends to be something you do locally, anyone truly interested in the cuisine should consider the trek (if trek it is) to Forest Hill.

OPEN: Mon-Sun. **HOURS:** 12.00-2.30pm and 6.00-11.30pm. **CLOSED:** Christmas Day and Boxing Day. **CREDIT CARDS ACCEPTED:** Access, AmEx, Diner's Club, Visa. **NUMBER OF SEATS:** 54. **SERVICE:** Optional. No-smoking area. Wheelchair access. **NEAREST BR STATION:** Honor Oak Park.

Bahn Thai

21a Frith Street, W1   (25)

071-437 8504   **£20-£30**

'A long established Thai restaurant becomes streetwise'

The Bahn Thai has opened itself up to Soho street life quite literally. The ground-floor dining room has been remodelled as a café and in summer there is nothing between you and Frith Street's parade. Some elements are more engaging than others; the cadgers with cans of Special Brew and the irritating roar of testosterone victims on their Harley Davidsons could be subtracted without diminishing the pleasure. Still, the new look gives the restaurant more of a sense of place and pace than before and it is comforting that redecorating also usually means cleaning. Sadly a test lunch on the ground floor chosen from the main menu delivered flavours that were unusually flat. From a meal of Thai dim sum, spiced duck, curried blue swimming crab with herbs and fried rice noodles, only the shrimp paste and garlic dip lingered in the memory. The Bahn Thai's menu is long, painstakingly long andsomehow has the bewildering and off-putting air of a tax return. By the time you have figured out the chapter headings, the sample meals, the symbols including one that looks like a fridge with the door open signifying 'The dish may be spicy but will have a low temperature' and what you would do were you in fact a Thai, you might be ready to welcome the statement contained within the two pages of guidance notes 'We prefer to suggest a different restaurant rather than to disappoint you by being able to allow time for a relaxed meal'. But this would be a pity as Bahn Thai is capable of providing authentic, unusual and sometimes thrilling dishes as well as well-chosen wines that flatter and enhance the food. Go with plenty of time to read and inwardly digest.

OPEN: Mon-Sun. **HOURS:** 12.00-2.45pm (12.30-2.30pm Sun) and 6.00-11.00pm (6.30-10.30pm Sun). **CLOSED:** Christmas, Easter and Bank Holidays. **CREDIT CARDS ACCEPTED:** All major cards. **NUMBER OF SEATS:** 100. **SERVICE:** 12.5% optional. No-smoking area. Wheelchair access (but not ladies' lavatory). Tables outside seat 6. Private rooms seat 20, 30 or 50. **NEAREST TUBE STATION:** Leicester Square/Tottenham Court Road.   **MAP REF:** 1,E/2

The Bedlington Café

24 Fauconberg Road, W4   (26)

081-994 1965   **£15 (Bring Your Own Wine)**

'Bedlam Café on busy nights'

To describe the decor as basic would be a compliment to this popular place, one of the first conversions of caff by day to chilli in the evening. Reasonable verging on cheap prices – chicken with ginger £2.95, pork with sweet basil £2.90 – allied to a BYO policy with a corkage of 50p ensures a crowd determined to enjoy themselves. One table was spotted arriving with what looked like a six-pack of Sancerre. Apart from the Laotian dishes there are no surprises on the menu but the dishes pull no punches with fiery spicing. Dim sum are perhaps the best of the starters; Thai fried rice with shrimp, pork, ham, sausage, spring onions, garlic, peas and egg is hearty and almost a meal in itself. The Bedlington is a cash-only operation – no cheques or credit cards – and while lack of sophistication is its charm it can also be part of its downfall when too many customers spoil the hot and sour broth.

OPEN: Mon-Sun. **HOURS:** 8.00am-10.00pm. **CLOSED:** Christmas Day. **CREDIT CARDS ACCEPTED:** None. **NUMBER OF SEATS:** 38. **SERVICE:** Optional. **SET PRICE LUNCH AND DINNER:** £10-12. Wheelchair access (but not lavatory). Tables outside seat 10. **NEAREST TUBE STATION:** Gunnersbury, Chiswick Park.

Beiteddine

8 Harriet Street, SW1

071-235 3969 or 071-245 6335 £27

An unexpected find in Knightsbridge

Lebanese waiters can be past masters of politeness. 'Where would you like to sit?' the staff at Beiteddine asked when we entered a busy restaurant without a booking. The dining room is decorated with a long fresco on one wall bringing a glimmer of the Levant to this faceless backstreet off Knightsbridge. So does the Château Musar wine on the list and the wide choice among the warm or cold small dishes that comprise a mezze. Most startling in a familiar roll-call is batrakh (dried fish roe) that looks like sliced frankfurter and comes with a positively Spanish garnish of raw garlic. Old favourites such as tabbouleh, warm hummus topped with sliced lamb and pine kernels, chicken livers, moutabal (aubergine purée), and the house special of diced lamb, parsley, onion and tahini, are all skilfully made. The plainness of Lebanese main courses can make them pale by comparison, but here the portions of charcoal-grilled lamb or chicken are generous for the £8 price mark. Beiteddine is a good option in terms of price for those in search of proper cooking in an expensive area.

OPEN: Mon-Sun. **HOURS:** 12.00pm-12.00am. **CREDIT CARDS ACCEPTED:** All major cards. **NUMBER OF SEATS:** 45-50. **SERVICE:** Optional, £2 cover charge. Wheelchair access (but not lavatory). **NEAREST TUBE STATION:** Knightsbridge. **MAP REF:** 2.F/4

Belgo

72 Chalk Farm Road, NW1

071-267 0718 £22

'The place to flex your mussels'

Roped in to help judge a competition sponsored by Muscadet wine to find London's most sympathique restaurant I was sent to assess Belgo. Unable to award the automatic mark allowed for listing Muscadet I was also deflected from finding the place sympathique by the noise, the racket, the thump that sits well with beer and schnapps drinking and with the consumption of kilo pots of mussels with chips inside the time limit of two hours but not, I think, with what the competition organizers had in mind. Belgo has hit on a sound, almost insupportably popular formula. If you hit the place at a quiet moment – late lunch perhaps – there is space enough if not time to appreciate some Belgian cooking apart from mussels. Wild boar sausages with stoemp (Belgian bubble and squeak), rabbit strudel with cherry beer sauce, carbonnade Flamande and five ways with asparagus are good enough to have you laughing out of the other side of your face at that Belgian joke. Shellfish, as in lobster and scallops, tends to be swamped by butter. Bavette, that tough but flavourful cut of steak rarely offered in Britain, is served as part of a deal that includes chips, salad and dessert for £8.95. Alternatively you could at lunchtime, weekdays only, embark on all the moules marinières or Provençales and frites you can eat for £6.95. This would be in the spirit of the establishment whose anarchic approach to life is reflected in the decor. A recent rethink of the latter by architects Ron Arad and Alison Brooks – Belgo near their office is their local canteen – has dramatically added to the space. Andre Plisnier and Denis Blais, owners of Belgo, have bought the premises in Covent Garden that were Smith's. Zentraal – as is the projected name– seating 350 is due to open in March 1995.

BEER IS THE WINE of the north – a truth we British are just salvaging from our collective gastronomic amnesia, but which the Belgians have always held as self-evident. Taste your way around the 35-option Belgo list to see how beer can be more various (and stronger) than you ever thought possible. There are a few wines for wimps; and Belgian schnapps for those not wishing to go gently into the Chalk Farm night.

OPEN: Mon-Sun. **HOURS:** 12.00-3.00pm and 6.00pm-11.30pm (12.00-11.30pm Sat, 12.00-10.30pm Sun). **CLOSED:** Christmas, Boxing Day and New Year's Day. **CREDIT CARDS ACCEPTED:** Access, AmEx, Diner's Club, Switch, Visa. **NUMBER OF SEATS:** 120. **SERVICE:** 15% optional. **SET PRICE LUNCH :** £5. **SET PRICE DINNER:** £10. Wheelchair access. **NEAREST TUBE STATION:** Chalk Farm.

MAP REF: 5,B/2

The Belvedere in Holland Park

Off Abbotsbury Road, W8

071-602 1238   **£30-£35**

'For when the sun has put his hat on, hip, hip, hip, hooray'

Johnny Gold, owner of Tramp as well as the Belvedere, must hang on the words of the weather girl more anxiously than some. It is a pretty day rather than the food, at the time of writing, that is the lure for this most blessedly situated restaurant on the edge of Holland Park. A meal on the terrace of Holland House looking down on people strolling and peacocks strutting – or vice versa – can be one of the best hands London can deal you, or it can be if you are prepared to make only modest demands on the menu. In essence the menu is a similar list to the one devised by Jeremy

Strode, the chef who joined the Belvedere in 1991 when its look was modernized. As good cooks go, so Strode went, but these days you could argue that anyone could put together a salad of rocket, figs and shavings of Parmesan cheese or make cornmeal pancakes to serve with avocado and salmon ceviche. What proves more difficult are the main-course dishes such as 'tournados' (sic) of salmon with seared woodland mushrooms and a warm balsamic vinaigrette. Not only the typos but notions such as the efficacy of searing wild mushrooms are warning signs that the kitchen competence is not much more than mechanical. Trying a chef's special of the day – cyclinders of monkfish wrapped in Parma ham – proved that the problem was not that of the chef being obliged to cook an inherited menu. One very noticeable change in it, however, is the firm divisions of Starters and Main Courses where previously it was a seamless list you could juggle as you pleased. Unless you defiantly order two first courses, this renders bills more substantial than they tended to be before. However, the Belvedere still stands out as one of the better catering operations in the London parks and a natural destination on those rare balmy English days.

OPEN: LUNCH: Mon-Sun. DINNER: Mon-Sat. **HOURS:** 12.00-3.00pm and 6.00-11.00pm. **CLOSED:** Christmas Day and Boxing Day. **CREDIT CARDS ACCEPTED:** All major cards. **NUMBER OF SEATS:** 120. **SERVICE:** Optional. Wheelchair access (but not lavatory). Tables outside seat 20. **NEAREST TUBE STATION:** Holland Park.

Bengal Clipper

Cardamom Building,
Shad Thames,
Butler's Wharf, SE1

30

071-357 9001   **£23**

'A flowering of the spice trade'

Butler's Wharf was once the chief importing wharf for spices when that trade was opened up by the East India Company in the 18th century. This fact cannot have escaped Terence Conran, chief colonizer of Butler's Wharf in the 20th century, but he has left the opportunity of exploiting it to the owners of the Bengal Clipper. The large restaurant on the ground floor of the Cardamom Building has no view of the river but has some compensatory faintly nautical design features, located in the main in an extravagant use of curved wood panelling. There is also a certain cross-Channel ferry feel to the patterned carpet and the gold-braided mess jackets of the waiting staff. The menu exemplifies the restaurant's name and theme only up to a point. The pride of Bengali cooking, the freshwater fish elish (hilsa) is used as a stuffing for a beef tomato and in a kebab and there are dishes based on freshwater catfish and tiger fish, but some of the larger than usual range of fish dishes are based on definitely non-Bengali varieties. Karkar chop, a first-course crab cutlet, is vivaciously spiced to a Goan recipe as are a lentil-based mussel soup, the famous Goan xacuti chicken, a salmon dish and one of giant prawns. On the whole, for Goan you can read hot. Elachi murg, a dish created by chef

Azam Khan to explore and exploit the powerful flavour of cardamom, is a must. Vegetable dishes are sometimes overcooked and consequently flaccid in texture and dun-coloured in appearance. Breads and chutneys are excellent. Where Bengaliness could really come into its own – in the choice of sweet things – the opportunity is missed. This may well be due to a canny estimation of the probable clientele of arbitrageurs crossing over from the City. In the evenings there is a cocktail pianist which is, or is not, an asset depending on your feelings about chansons with your curry.

Open: Mon-Sun. **Hours:** 12.00-3.00pm and 6.00-11.30pm. **Closed:** Good Friday and Christmas. **Credit cards accepted:** All major cards. **Number of seats:** 175. **Service:** Optional, £1.50 cover charge. **Set price lunch:** £12.95. **Set price dinner:** £18.95. Wheelchair access (but not lavatory). **Nearest tube station:** Tower Hill.

Beoty's Restaurant

79 St Martin's Lane, WC2

071-836 8768/8548 £30

'Longevity has a charm of its own'

This guide is not impervious to sentiment. How many West End restaurants have been trading for nigh on 50 years? Very few that you might want to go to – Mon Plaisir and the White Tower being honourable exceptions – but the Greek/Cypriot-owned Beoty's still holds allure. It is a survivor of the restaurant genre labelled Continental, places with long menus that nowadays do not so much impress as pose the question of how a kitchen can turn its hand to so many dishes without recourse to pre-preparation or the freezer. A wise way to prune the choice here is to pick either from the Greek menu or the eminently reasonable set price menus of the day. These might deliver a not particularly exemplary hummus or taramasalata, the last paired with avocado, followed by perfectly good roast duck with apple sauce or grilled chicken kebab served with rice. Lamb cooked to pieces is, of course, on offer and syrup-soaked pastries are the appropriate dessert – to be followed by Turkish delight with coffee. The generously sized, generously spaced tables are laid with olives, radishes and Greek bread. Service from the long-serving retainers tenders a sort of gruff solicitude and will warm up with encouragement. There are one or two not bad Greek wines on the list, e.g. Chateau Carras. Insist on a table on the ground floor.

Open: Mon-Sat. **Hours:** 12.00-3.00pm and 5.30-11.30pm. **Closed:** Public holidays. **Credit cards accepted:** Access, AmEx, Diners Club, Visa. **Number of seats:** 89. **Service:** Optional. **Set price lunch:** £12.50 (2 courses) or £14 (3 courses). **Set price dinner:** £13 (2 courses) or £15 (3 courses). No-smoking area. Wheelchair access. Private room seats 10 to 70. **Nearest tube station:** Leicester Square/Charing Cross. **MAP REF:** 1,E/1

Bertorelli's

44a Floral Street WC2

071-836 3969

32

£28

*'Mid-price Italian opposite Covent Garden
Opera House'*

As Oscar Wilde said, 'The trouble with being up-to-date is that it is bound to go out of fashion.' A couple of years back the modishness of Maddelena Bonino's Italian menu dished up under the venerable name of Bertorelli's (now part of Groupe Chez Gerard Ltd.) seemed considerably more ground-breaking than now it does. The pressure of numbers also tends to fray the edges of the execution of dishes such as rocchetti (pasta spindles) with asparagus, squid, tomato and garlic which turned out to be a less interesting gathering than its invited guests imply; sauté of salt cod with potato, spinach, chick-peas, cherry tomatoes and basil oil where the chick-peas were undercooked. However, there are also more precise renderings. Ziti with merguez sausage, roquette and fresh tomatoes was one and a daily special, pigeon and venison terrine wrapped in pancetta with pickled peach and red onion salsa, another. Desserts are reliable. In Groupe Chez Gerard style what you are given on the one hand – Italian breads with olive oil, olives, and gherkins – you are charged for by the other – £1.50 per person masquerading as a cover charge. The Italian wine list is mostly well sourced. Staff are notably amiable and unfazed by a packed house which can happen post-theatre.

OPEN: Mon-Sat. **HOURS:** 12.00-3.00pm and 7.30-11.30pm. **CLOSED:** Christmas Day and New Year's Day. **CREDIT CARDS ACCEPTED:** Access, AmEx, Diner's Club, Visa. **NUMBER OF SEATS:** 90 in Restaurant, 55 in Café. **SERVICE:** 12.5%. No-smoking area. **NEAREST TUBE STATION:** Covent Garden.   MAP REF: 1,E/1

Bibendum Restaurant and Oyster Bar

Michelin House,
81 Fulham Road, SW3

33

RESTAURANT: 071-581 5817
OYSTER BAR: 071-589 1480

RESTAURANT: £65
OYSTER BAR: £25

'Quite simply, a splendid restaurant'

Simon Hopkinson's cooking at Bibendum is dependably excellent and dependably expensive. However, Alastair Little (q.v.) for one has made his prices more or less comparable and at Bibendum you get in addition to fine – often superb – food a beautifully designed dining room set within the Michelin building, tables impeccably laid, delicious olives to start and intense chocolate truffles to finish, sophisticated service and a sensationally good wine list in the hands of an unintimidating sommelier. Admittedly 15% service charge is automatically added (as is the practice at all restaurants where Terence Conran is involved) but at Little's service is extra too, albeit not a fixed sum. But enough of invidious comparisons – the two chaps are friends. A profitable way to discover whether you want to invest in Hopkinson's cooking is to get hold of a copy of *Roast Chicken and Other Stories* (Ebury Press £17.99), the book of recipes Hopkinson published in the spring of '94. Tellingly the chapters are organized by ingredients. Hopkinson's ability – honed through painstaking repetition – to empathize with and get the best out of certain ingredients distinguishes his deceptively simply cooking. As the blurb says, like any accomplished cook he knows what goes with what, where to start and when to stop. This last is perhaps the most important. Dishes that appear with regularity on an ever-changing menu are Baltic herrings à la creme; escargots de Bourgogne; tarte fine aux cêpes; crab vinaigrette; roast poulet de bresse (for two); grilled rabbit mustard sauce; fillet steak au poivre; crème brulée. They sound plain but they can be near-perfect versions. Oriental spicing and a liking for Italian cooking also inform Hopkinson's dishes and he is gloriously enthusiastic about offal. Choices – that were taken – on one day from a £25 set price lunch this year included a first course of sauté of lambs' sweetbreads and tongues with wilted greens, garlic cream and rosemary and a main course of various pork pieces (fresh and salted) served with mashed potato and mustard sauce. Just in case this makes you tremble, the same menu could have delivered a meal of inventive antipasti, wings of skate with saffron and caper sauce, treacle tart with Jersey cream. Speaking of dessert, my son claims Hopkinson's Pithiviers au chocolat the best thing he has eaten in his entire life. There are good tables and cramped tables at Bibendum. The best way round this is to visit in a party of four or more. Each person could always agree to pay for themselves.

Beside the forecourt to the Michelin building and at the foot of the lift that can whisk you one floor up to the restaurant is Bibendum's **Oyster Bar**. In too small an area for the numbers who want to use it, a simple menu of oysters, crustacea with first-rate mayonnaise, salads and dishes such as crisp pork belly with pickled cucumber and chilli dip and prosciutto with celeriac rémoulade is served. You don't look for bargains at the Conran Shop and you won't find them on the wine list but if you time it right and avoid the crowds, a meal here is the perfect centrepiece to a self-indulgent shopping day.

THIS IS STILL the London list to beat for both avant-garde and classically minded drinking pleasure. Gold-card diners can set about the vintage Krugs, the clutch of DRCs, the 18 lip-smacking Pomerols or the sumptuous range of Sauternes and Barsacs. History is there, at a price: Suduiraut 1899, Noval 1931, Mouton 1945 (£550, £795 and £2,000 per bottle respectively, plus the stiff 15% service charge – that's £300 to have your Mouton '45 served to you). Yet in some respects the byways of this list merit more of a detour than the highways: the choice of six Cornas, for example, or the two fine pages of Italian wines. German wines of the quality listed here qualify as a curiosity nowadays, and if you want a Long Island Merlot or a choice of fine Oregon Pinot Noirs, then you'll find them all at the top of the Fulham Road. Bibendum doesn't consider its list overpriced, yet you'll need £25 to begin choosing with any degree of excitement, and fine wines, too, can be cheaper elsewhere (Trotanoy '70 will set you back £275 here plus £41.25 service, compared with £160 plus £20 service from Harvey Nichols's Fifth Floor Restaurant Big List).

RESTAURANT: OPEN: Mon-Sun. HOURS: 12.30-2.30pm (12.30-3.00pm Sat and Sun) and 7.00-11.30pm (7.00-10.30pm Sun). CLOSED: 25th-28th December and Easter Monday. CREDIT CARDS ACCEPTED: AmEx, Mastercard, Visa. NUMBER OF SEATS: 72. SERVICE: 15%. SET PRICE LUNCH: £25. Wheelchair access (but not lavatory). OYSTER BAR: OPEN: Mon-Sun. HOURS: 12.00-11.00pm (12.00-10.30pm Sun). CLOSED: 25th-28th December and Easter Monday. CREDIT CARDS ACCEPTED: AmEx, Mastercard, Switch, Visa. NUMBER OF SEATS: 45. SERVICE: 15%. Wheelchair access. NEAREST TUBE STATION: South Kensington. MAP REF: 2,D/3

The Big Night Out

148 Regents Park Road, NW1

34

071-586 5768   LUNCH: £9; DINNER: £32

'Or the Sunday Brunch or the Good-Value Lunch

Not one restaurant reviewer, including this one, has failed to mention the stupidity of the name of this relatively new venture belonging to chef Richard Coates and front-of-house Hugh O'Boyle. Indeed in bringing down their lunch prices and establishing an excellent value set price weekend brunch since opening, they themselves continue to undermine with the food and the prices the notion that this is a special occasion venue – with all the attendant horrors implied. However, as I said in my original review, these are the two chaps who called their outside catering company Alakart so we just have to accept that naming businesses is not their strong suit. Running a happy ship is, where O'Boyle is concerned and, perhaps even more importantly, cooking is, where Coates is concerned. It would be hard to imagine a lighter and lovelier brill and crab tartlet with a truffle and thyme dressing or a better gruyère soufflé with rocket and a red pepper oil. Breast of duck served rare with a creamy gratin had a ideal jus, not over-reduced and just fleetingly flavoured with cassis. In a dish of guinea fowl Coates demonstrated that telling ability of a good cook – imbuing ingredients with intense natural flavours. The pastry chef responsible for the superior desserts will have left by the time this guide is published but doubtless another competent or even gifted person will have been found. The proximity of the wine company Bibendum is an asset to the restaurants of Regent's Park Road – c.f. Odettes. Thought has been given to aperitifs and digestifs as well as the main list – try starting the meal with a glass of the chilled sherry-like Vin de Voille de Robert Plageoles – and indeed to the teas and coffees that may complete the event. More thought needs to be given to the interior decoration. The airless dining room is oddly proportioned, the main part a too-tall cube with a glazed pitched roof. Wooden backs to the banquettes taken to head level of a seated customer divide the space horizontally in an uncomfortable manner. Also if this is a big night out, even if we can't have tablecloths, let's have linen napkins.

OPEN: LUNCH: Sun. DINNER: Mon-Sat. HOURS: 12.00-3.00pm and 7.00-12.00am. CREDIT CARDS ACCEPTED: All except Diner's Club. NUMBER OF SEATS: 68. SERVICE: Optional. SET PRICE LUNCH: £8.50. SET PRICE DINNER: £16.50. No-smoking area. Tables outside seat 4. Wheelchair access (but not lavatory). Private room seats 30. NEAREST TUBE STATION: Chalk Farm.   MAP REF: 5, A/1

Billboard Café

222 Kilburn High Road, NW6 **35**

071-328 1374 £20-£25

'A spot of light relief'

To an area which can seem dour and bleak even in midsummer came a spacious bar and grill drawing its inspiration from Northern Italy and California. That combination works well, and although the lively list of covered toasts, salads, eight home-made pastas and grills holds few surprises, there are enough items – a first course of marinated chargrilled duck breast on lamb's lettuce with feta and bacon; main course breast of chicken rolled around ricotta and sun-dried tomatoes; carrot cake with lemon cream sauce – to demonstrate that here is more than a formulaic expression of modernity in food. An impressive level of commitment emanates from the staff. The ambiance is pitched at the 'yoof' element who appreciate the live jazz on Wednesdays and the selection of ideologically sound newspapers available over brunch at weekends. If you are seeing a play at the Tricycle Theatre, the Billboard is the natural direction to take for something to eat afterwards.

OPEN: LUNCH: Sat-Sun. DINNER: Mon-Sat. **HOURS:** 12.00-3.00pm and 6.30pm-12.30am. **CLOSED:** Christmas Day, Bank Holiday Mondays. **CREDIT CARDS ACCEPTED:** Access, Mastercard, Switch, Visa. **NUMBER OF SEATS:** 65. **SERVICE:** 10%. **SET PRICE BRUNCH:** £6.25. **SET PRICE DINNER:** £10 or £15. Wheelchair access (but not lavatory). Main room may be hired privately. **NEAREST TUBE STATION:** Kilburn/Kilburn Park.

Bistrot Bruno

63 Frith Street, W1 **36**

071-734 4545 £29-£32

'Bruno heads for Regent Street but the legacy lingers on'

Last year's guide saw Bruno Loubet poised to leave the Four Seasons Hotel (q.v.) in order to give his all to the Soho bistro in which he is a partner with Pierre Condou. This year the news is that the deal for a much larger site has at long last been done and L'Odéon in Regent Street opposite the Café Royal is due to open at about the time this edition is published. The new 200-seat restaurant offering fixed price menus and à la carte and the 60-seat bar will give Loubet the scope he deserves to disseminate his particular brand of invention. A hallmark of Loubet's style is a down-to-earthiness, embracing an admirable lack of snobbishness where food is concerned; he sees as much gastronomic potential in sardines as sea bass, as much to praise in pearl barley as pleurottes (and doubtless the healthy financial margins don't escape him either). Combinations are thought through with an intelligent grasp of harmony and counterpoint as can be seen in dishes such as fresh salt cod on split pea purée with a thyme and smoked bacon sauce or wood pigeon breast poached in beetroot consommé and served with soured cream. In common with most modern chefs, he dices with spices, particularly successfully in the dish of seared sea bass with Szechuan pepper and piquant cabbage and in the lime-pickled new potatoes – the tubers first left to soak in salted water as is an Indian practice – that accompany roasted stuffed rabbit leg. Menus change monthly but the spirit is consistent. Before Loubet joined Bistrot Bruno full time, Jason Hornbuckle was working there under his tutelage and guidance. With the opening of L'Odéon, Hornbuckle will assume the position of head chef at the Bistrot. Loubet will have the advantage of premises with space and style, qualities that are not the strong suit of the Frith Street rooms.

OPEN: LUNCH: Mon-Fri. DINNER: Mon-Sat. **HOURS:** 12.15-2.30pm and 6.15-11.30pm. **CLOSED:** Christmas to New Year. **CREDIT CARDS ACCEPTED:** All major cards. **NUMBER OF SEATS:** 40. **SERVICE:** Optional. **NEAREST TUBE STATION:** Tottenham Court Road/Leicester Square.

MAP REF:1,E/2

Bistrot 190

190 Queen's Gate, SW7

071-581 5666

£23

'If you want to know what to be seen to be eating'

Here is a contrast: a large, light room attractively cluttered with junk shop *objets* (all well dusted on last inspection) and a menu positively bubbling with up-to-the-minute ingredients. Caponata toast, caraway croûtes, olive and spring onion rosti, horseradish butter, parsnip crisps, whisky zabaglione; all bear witness to the fertile imagination of Antony Worral-Thompson and his cohort here, chef Harry Greenhaugh. And although you have to pay £1.45 each for a good selection of bread, you then have a vehicle for consuming lavish amounts of the Normandy butter and fine olive oil which are set on the table. Start to play the restaurant critic and pick on things you sense will be difficult to get right and you will probably be rewarded by being proved correct. A first course of chargrilled Serrano ham with fresh figs followed by a fennel risotto was a perfect example of the second school of decision-making. Of course, the ham would have been nicer uncooked and the figs were not ripe while the risotto had failed to bring out the milder flavour of thoroughly cooked fennel (there is a Marcella Hazan recipe which explains exactly how this is done) and did not have the texture bestowed by diligent stirring. Grilled Toulouse sausage with the Mediterranean chutney and linguine with olives and basil were more satisfying. A spicy apple, cinnamon and raisin brioche outdid the zabaglione. Wines, chosen by a series of different suppliers, are offered by the small pitcher as well by the bottle; sound practice. Note that there is a creative breakfast menu served between 7 and 11am and also a slightly less febrile brunch menu offered on Sundays. Bear in mind the no-bookings policy when timing your visits.

OPEN: Mon-Sun. **HOURS:** 7.00-12.30am (7.00am-11.30pm Sun). **CLOSED:** 3 days at Christmas. **CREDIT CARDS ACCEPTED:** AmEx, Access, Mastercard, Diner's Club, Visa. **NUMBER OF SEATS:** 55. **SERVICE:** 10%. **SET PRICE LUNCH:** £12.50 Sun. Private room seats 28. **NEAREST TUBE STATION:** Gloucester Road.

Bleeding Heart
Restaurant & Wine Bar

Bleeding Heart Yard,
off Greville Street, EC1

071-242 2056   **£23**

'Yours will be if you fail to find this tucked-away restaurant'

'Difficult to find' is a criticism – or perhaps just an observation – levelled at the Bleeding Heart Restaurant & Wine Bar but in my experience Americans tourists manage it easily enough and there are several good reasons for seeking out this unprepossessing yard with its beastly name reached from the part of Greville Street just before Saffron Hill coming from Hatton Garden. The yard's name, it is said, is attached to a tale concerning the death in the 17th century of the socialite Lady Elizabeth Hatton torn limb from limb by her European ambassador lover. Charles Dickens refers to the place, and obliquely to the incident, in *Little Dorritt*. A satisfied (English) customer remarked to me that, given the location of the yard near what was the Bishop of Ely's palace, the name is more likely to be a reference to the medieval devotion to the Sacred Heart of Jesus. But that might bring fewer American tourists. The premises are divided into a restaurant and a wine bar/brasserie, both sections serving reasonably priced and carefully prepared French food expressed as good-value set price menus as well as à la carte. In the summer months the terrace is also used. Staff are French and service has been described as 'impeccable. Approved – and characteristic – dishes from the restaurant menu are marinated roasted peppers, artichokes and fennel with garlic croûtons; grilled calves' liver with a sweet and sour sauce; salmon pie with potato crust and watercress sauce; iced nougat soufflé with blackcurrant coulis. It is mainstream cooking happy to let wine take centre stage if that is what you want. The clientele in the wood-panelled, leather-upholstered restaurant tends to be 'suits' with colleagues (some female) and it has been noted that printer's reps, notoriously canny judges of restaurants, tend to gather in the wine bar. A jarring note that should be dispensed with is the injunction displayed on tent cards to have 'A Bleeding Good Evening for £12.95' (price of the fixed cost menu).

ROBERT WILSON IS (unlike many restaurateurs) a wine enthusiast, and his enthusiasm rubs off in a longish, fairly priced list; the bottles themselves are available for ogling behind bars in the restaurant. France (especially Burgundy and the Rhône) and a well-researched New Zealand selection furnish the specialities, while there's good choice under £15 (including Mexican Petite Syrah, Provençale Viognier, sound clarets and Australian varietals). Magnums, dessert wines and rosés are all plural.

OPEN: Mon-Fri. **HOURS:** 12.00-3.00pm and 6.00-11.00pm. **CLOSED:** 24th Dec to 6th Jan. **CREDIT CARDS ACCEPTED:** Access, AmEx, Diner's Club, Visa. **NUMBER OF SEATS:** 90. **SERVICE:** Optional. **SET PRICE DINNER:** £12.95. Tables outside seat 28. Wheelchair access (but not lavatory). Private room seats 45-50. **NEAREST TUBE STATION:** Farringdon.   MAP REF: 8,D/1

Blue Elephant

4-6 Fulham Broadway, SW6

39

071-385 6595   **£35**

'Trader Vic's on Ecstasy'

The Sissinghurst of tropical house plants is one description of this 240-seater Thai extravaganza. Potted palms, little pools, rustic bridges, thatched roofs, sprays of orchids, bamboo furniture, brass plates, bronze cutlery and 'beautiful' (their description) Thai staff dressed in what looks like the uniform of an exotic airline bring the photographs of a holiday brochure to life – and all for a ride to Fulham Broadway tube station. Food is better than theme-park however, and the several Blue Elephants – branches in Brussels, Paris and Copenhagen – make viable an efficient system of the direct importation of Thai ingredients. As with most Thai restaurants the menu is long. In terms of finance, a balanced assembly of dishes and lack of tedious introspection the set-price Royal Thai Banquet is the sensible way to order – at least on first acquaintance. A wide range of dishes, all carefully differentiated, is included. Homok talay, an earthernware pot of fish stew of mussels, prawns, crab and scallops flavoured with krachai root (a key ingredient in Thai curry pastes), lemon grass, sweet basil and mint; and massaman, a Muslim dish from South Thailand of slow-cooked lamb in a hauntingly spiced sauce are two of the highlights. Only the dessert is a let-down, spoiled by cheap vanilla ice-cream. The Blue Elephant also offers a separate vegetarian menu featuring an ingredient, yod phaeng made from soya beans, which they claim as their chef's creation. Yod phaeng appears in many guises including as a soufflé with coconut milk, red curry pasta, lemon grass and makrude (citrus) leaves steamed inside banana leaves. The Royal Siam Promenade is an intricate and chilli-hot set-price vegetarian menu. The wines are ambitiously priced and a cover charge (not applicable to set-price menus) and 15% 'suggested' service charge all take their toll, but a night at the Blue Elephant is a big night out.

OPEN: LUNCH: Sun-Fri. DINNER: Mon-Sun. **HOURS:** 12.00-2.30pm and 7.00pm-12.30am (7.00-10.30pm Sun). **CLOSED:** 24-27 December. **CREDIT CARDS ACCEPTED:** Access, Visa, AmEx, Diner's Club. **NUMBER OF SEATS:** 240. **SERVICE:** 15%, cover charge £1.50. **SET PRICE LUNCH AND DINNER:** £25 and £28. Wheelchair access. **NEAREST TUBE STATION:** Fulham Broadway.

Blue Print Café

Design Museum,
Butler's Wharf, SE1

40

071-378 7031   **£30**

'The design module for modern eating'

A modern urban conversation might be a discussion of the relative merits of the restaurants at Butler's Wharf. The grouping is no longer entirely the province of Terence Conran and his henchman Joel Kissin; someone chattering along these lines might put in a word for an Indian meal at the Bengal Clipper (q.v.) However, the knotty question of which view of the river, gastronomically speaking, you would want to head for often comes down in favour of Blue Print Café and the cooking of Lucy Crabb who, like nearly all the chefs in Conran's orbit, has trained with Simon Hopkinson, chef of Bibendum. Her thoroughly modern menu is cheaper than Le Pont de la Tour, the execution sounder than at Cantina del Ponte or the Chop House. Dedicated practice – the Hopkinson approach – tends to make almost perfect terrines, salads – try the Caesar salad – and pasta dishes which, bowing to the inevitable, are listed as main courses. With pasta, shortcomings in ingredients cannot be concealed and spaghetti putanesca was notable for the pasta itself, the fresh oregano and high-quality pine kernels (so often rank and rancid). Spinach and ricotta gnocchi seemed practically starch-free and in appearance beautifully marbled. A tendency noted last year to put cream in soups has not been stamped out. A dollop found its way into roasted tomato soup with wild garlic pesto. Typical main course fish and meat dishes are baked brill fillet with a herb crust and beurre blanc; pan-fried calves' liver with caremelized onions; roast duck breast au poivre. The kitchen is strong on desserts. Praise has been lavished on caramelized banana and cinnamon ice cream and pistachio and banana parfait layered with Amaretto biscuits 'resembling the wall of a house in the Abruzzi'. When the weather is kind the somewhat protected terrace running the length of the restaurant is where you will want to sit but reservations will only note that a seat outside 'has been requested'. The interior has been described as Bauhaus banal with an air of underfunding that fits in only too well with its host the Design Museum.

OPEN: Lunch: Mon-Sun. **DINNER:** Mon-Sat. **HOURS:** 12.00-3.00pm (12.00-3.30pm Sun) and 7.00-11.00pm. **CLOSED:** Christmas Day. **CREDIT CARDS ACCEPTED:** All major cards. **NUMBER OF SEATS:** 85. **SERVICE:** 15%. Wheelchair access. Tables outside seat 76. **NEAREST TUBE STATION:** Tower Hill.

Bodali

78 Highbury Park, N5   **41**

071-704 0741 or 071-359 3444   **£14 (Bring your own wine)**

'Indian food cooked domestically carefully'

This small, family-run establishment remains worth seeking out if you are interested in Indian cooking. The style is Gujerati (non-vegetarian) and more specifically has some reference to the cooking of the Muslim Bohris. Before you get too excited, a large part of the menu is pretty standard stuff but daily specials on the blackboard deliver insights into the domestic tradition of food preparation, i.e. greater care taken with spicing, sauces and choice of ingredients. A subtle sauce containing cashews, aubergines, coconut, dried apricots, red peppers, onions, tomatoes and cream – the inclusion of cream being the Bohri clue – is served with prawns and with chicken and lamb tikka. Vegetable assemblies are interesting, particularly the glancingly sweet combination of cabbage, carrot, green pepper and peanuts that makes up sambaro. Also good is red kidney bean curry. Rice with onion and dill is a fine acccompaniment but breads can be disappointing. The £1.50 cover charge seems less of an imposition when you try the homemade chutneys, the carrot-based one being particularly delectable. Service is optional, a phrase that the waitress seems to interpret rather too literally.

OPEN: Mon-Sat. **HOURS:** 6.00-11.00pm. **CLOSED:** Bank Holidays and 4 weeks in August. **CREDIT CARDS ACCEPTED:** None. **NUMBER OF SEATS:** 26. **SERVICE:** Optional, £1.50 cover charge. Wheelchair access (but not lavatory). **NEAREST TUBE STATION:** Finsbury Park/Arsenal.

Bombay Brasserie

Courtfield Road
(opposite Gloucester Road Tube), SW7

42

071-370 4040 or 071-373 0971   **£32**

'A spicy definition of grandeur'

This still most stylish and, in terms of its clientele, most cosmopolitan of all London Indian restaurants, has been flourishing now for near on a dozen years. The pleasure of the grand sweep of space remains constant and although the standards of cooking have been variable over the years, they are, at time of writing, really rather good. A meal that started with aloo tuk – a dish that demonstrates what happens when deep-fried potato skins achieve nirvana – and crab bhujanee – a presumably Southern Indian dish of crabmeat flaked with coconut, mustard, tamarind and other spices – and went on to an intensely, resoundingly, peppery lamb Chettinad, with which various subtle vegetable and potato assemblies were offered, was highly satisfactory. The one disappointment in the order was the Parsi dish of jardaloo ma margi where tomatoes and dried apricots used in a sauce for chicken contrived to taste like tinned tomato soup. An excellent new arrival in the vegetable section of the menu is bhindi Jaipuri, crackling fried okra and onion mixed with ground spices. The vegetarian thalis – set meals presented in small dishes on a tray – are good and relatively good value. At lunchtimes there is a buffet where new dishes are occasionally tried out. The wine list is short and short on bargains but there is a rather touching note on the menu suggesting fruit juices with the meal – pear with white meat and cherry juice with red. Service tends to be nicer – and being seated happens more quickly – if you are known to them, but this too is authentically Indian.

OPEN: Mon-Sun. **HOURS:** 12.30-3.00pm and 7.30pm-12.00am. **CLOSED:** Christmas Day and Boxing Day. **CREDIT CARDS ACCEPTED:** Diner's Club, Access, Mastercard, Visa. **NUMBER OF SEATS:** 175. **SERVICE:** Optional. **SET PRICE LUNCH:** £14.95 (buffet lunches). No-smoking area. Wheelchair access. **NEAREST TUBE STATION:** Gloucester Road.   MAP REF: 2,B/4

Boyd's Restaurant

135 Kensington Church Street, W8

43

071-727 5452   **£35**

'Mostly everything in the garden is lovely'

If the English treated eating out as a more natural occupation, then I suspect that Boyd's would do better. It is the sort of restaurant that in France would have a strong local following based on its general competence and, in culinary terms, good taste; in England we seem to need more. Unfortunately for Boyd's the 'more' might be found just a few doors up at Kensington Place or across the street at Clarke's. However, both calm (not on offer at K.P.) and a wide choice (not on offer at Clarke's) are provided here by former professional musician Boyd Gilmour who plays his 'piano' – as French chefs like to style their stoves – with considerable skill. Some tunes are so simple as to be almost chopsticks e.g. a first course of garden salad with fresh herbs, but there is a lightness and brightness to the cooking that fits well with the decor and its newly emphasized conservatory style. The outdoorsiness of bare, green-stained, rather small wooden tables might not appeal to some. It grates with me when prices seem pompous – £2.25 for coffee with a couple of chocs – or grasping – no financial credit given if you deviate in any one course from the set price menu; the full price of the alternative choice is added on.

The pattern of the menu tends towards first courses of a soup, salads that might feature chargrilled vegetables or marinated fish, a terrine and a pasta dish served in two sizes at two prices. The one fish-based main course changes daily according to supply and much of the rest of the main course – and sometimes the fish too – depends for emphasis on the thrill of the charcoal grill. Cheeses are well chosen. Follow your own instincts when choosing dessert rather than settling for the sampler plate entitled Boyd's Choice at £8.50. Boyd seems able to spin a cage of sugar rather better than he can bake a cherry pie.

THIS PRETTILY beribboned wine list has a strong New World showing (Sauvignon Blanc addicts are well-served, with New Zealand's Oyster Bay offering best value of the five on offer, while the Cabernets of Stag's Leap and Cape Mentelle, and the Cape Mentelle Shiraz, both offer similar flavour impact in red). Europe is listed to balance, with deft pluckings from Spain (including the lovely and rounded Vina Ardanza Reserva '85), Italy and France. The five vintages of the rarely electrifying Château Boyd-Cantenac remain for the proprietor's amusement. A good selection of half-bottles and spirits (especially whisky) add further depth.

OPEN: Mon-Sat. **HOURS:** 12.30-2.30pm and 7.00-11.00pm. **CLOSED:** 2 weeks over Christmas and Easter Bank Holiday. **CREDIT CARDS ACCEPTED:** Access, Diner's Club, Mastercard, Visa. **NUMBER OF SEATS:** 40. **SERVICE:** Optional. **SET PRICE LUNCH:** £14. **NEAREST TUBE STATION:** Notting Hill Gate.   **MAP REF:** 4,C/1

The Brackenbury

129-131 Brackenbury Road, W6

081-748 0107 ⓸⓸ **£23**

'Still the very model of a neighbourhood restaurant '

The Brackenbury is that rare thing; the unspoiled success. Praise – well deserved – did not turn its head or cause its kitchen manners to become slipshod or let it make the assumption that a hike in prices runs in tandem with bookings made days ahead. The Brackenbury has retained the spirit of what it is; an unpretentious neighbourhood restaurant with chef/proprietor Adam Robinson the ideal boy next door for any keen eater. Estate agents may christen the area of artisan dwellings Brackenbury Village. They would do better to print on their property details attractions such as pappardelle, broad beans, mustard and bacon (£3.50); fried goose egg and duck livers on toast (£5); lambs' sweetbreads with peas, onions and mint (£7.75); soufflé beignets with poached apricots (£3.00); (Dishes and prices all taken from one late-spring lunch menu.) Emulating his one-time boss Alastair Little (q.v.), Robinson changes his menus at each meal, capitalizing on what is seasonal and, in palate terms, sensational. The kitchen understands what goes with what and why. The 'exoticism' of, say, marinated scallops, black bean dressing and coriander will always be offset by something as down-home as boiled leg of lamb, butter beans and caper sauce. Surroundings are wine-bar simple with a satisfactory amount of spillage onto the wide pavement when the weather invites it. Service may crack under the strain of more people wanting this sort of food at this sort of price than there are tables to provide it, but it means well. The list of wines roams the world as confidently and almost as economically as does the menu with 26 of the choices, including sherry and port, offered by the glass. Equally considerate is the offer of excellent cider and ginger beer.

OPEN: LUNCH: Sun-Fri. DINNER: Mon-Sat. **HOURS:** 12.30-2.45pm and 7.00-10.45pm. **CLOSED:** Bank Holidays and 10 days over Christmas. **CREDIT CARDS ACCEPTED:** All. **NUMBER OF SEATS:** 55. **SERVICE:** Optional. Wheelchair access (but not lavatory). Tables outside seat 20. **NEAREST TUBE STATION:** Hammersmith.

MAP REF: 7,A/1

Brady's

513 Old York Road, SW18

081-877 9599 ⓸⓹ **£14**

'Where Guppys might go for fish and chips'

Those who contemplate their navels and ponder the worth and identity of British food should take themselves off to Brady's in Wandsworth. This modest little place provides the ideal definition of a fine British meal based on fish. Luke and Amelia Brady previously ran an hotel in Suffolk which had a notable dining room. Here they have defined their terms more precisely and within them produced something excellent. The mainstay of the menu is fish and chips but Brady's is not a chippie; frying takes place out of sight (and smell) and there is no takeaway. Cod, plaice and haddock are cooked without their skins in a light, even batter. Grilled fish, including dishes of the day such as tuna, are also available. Potted shrimps are homemade and are not the usual commas embalmed in butter but a mass of shrimps flavoured with mace and pepper. Salmon fishcake is generous with the fish. Half a pint of prawns with which you could try out the range of herb-flavoured mayonnaise sauces is another option in the first course. Fish and chips are fried without a trace of grease. Desserts include homemade apple crumble and a great treacle tart with the filling given added texture by grated coconut. The cream-painted room is narrow and crowded but service is brisk and those waiting are usually seated quite quickly. The good news for those, like me, for whom Wandsworth is a long haul is that a new restaurant, probably in Fulham is mooted.

OPEN: LUNCH: Sat. **DINNER:** Mon-Sat. **HOURS:** 12.30-2.30pm and 7.00-10.45pm. **CLOSED:** Bank Holidays, 1 week in August and Christmas. **CREDIT CARDS ACCEPTED:** None. **NUMBER OF SEATS:** 38. **SERVICE:** 10%. Wheelchair access. **NEAREST BR STATION:** Wandsworth Town.   MAP REF: 3,D/2

Brasserie du Marché aux Puces

349 Portobello Road, W10   **46**

081-968 5828   **£23**

'Easygoing place in an entertaining area'

Since Phillip McMullen opened Avenue West Eleven (q.v.) the menu at his agreeable little café-restaurant at the far end of Portobello Road – when travelling north – seems a little calmer. It is arranged as a list with no divisions, just a gradual price increase as you move from soup of the day through, for example, sautéed salmon fillets with samphire and raspberry beurre blanc, down to lamb chump with roasted garlic mash. Cream of carrot soup has been described as unassailable; a salad of crab and mango with a chilli dressing approved of, and main course of beef onglet (flank steak) with celeriac mash and root vegetable chips much enjoyed. Salads and vegetables are priced separately but reasonably. Desserts are typified by blueberry and gooseberry fool and chocolate truffle cake. The room has tables making a right-angle turn around a long bar. Windows on two sides give a view onto the shabbier end of Portobello market, a scene obviously livelier at weekends than early in the week. Note the easygoing hours; champion if you feel like some grilled goat's cheese with beetroot and walnuts for your tea.

OPEN: LUNCH: Mon-Sun. **DINNER:** Mon-Sat. **HOURS:** 10.00am-11.00pm (11.00am-4.00pm Sun). **CLOSED:** Bank Holidays. **CREDIT CARDS ACCEPTED:** None. **NUMBER OF SEATS:** 38. **SERVICE:** Optional. Wheelchair access (but not lavatory). Tables outside seat 8. Private room seats 32. **NEAREST TUBE STATION:** Ladbroke Grove.

Le Cadre

10 Priory Road, N8

47

081-348 0606

£20

*'If the French accents are sometimes wrong,
it's not grave'*

Groups like Café Flo bringing off quite well approximations of French bistros make it more difficult these days for independent ventures effectively to woo with intimations of those holidays across the Channel spent ever on the qui-vive for a Relais Routier. 'Good Food, Good Wine and a Good Time!!' is the sub-heading on the à la carte menu of this small neighbourhood restaurant where French accents are scattered through the dishes with an insouciance bordering on ignorance and spellings such as feuillte and pleurettes instil only a modicum of confidence in the authenticity of the cooking. Authenticity of atmosphere is attempted through reproduction period French posters, bare boards and blackboards chalked with additional wine choices. First courses in the fixed price menu follow the layout of soups, a terrine and a mousse, mussels, a feuilleté and a composed salad. Duck terrine was fine, mousse of smoked salmon was insipid, both were tricked out with garnishes more fiddly than you tend to find in France. Perhaps to confirm the English distrust of French cooking, sauces in the main course tend to be strident. Vegetables are included in the price of the main course and perhaps because of that seem cooked without much love. Life looks up in the dessert course with a particularly fine ile flottante au caramel and various other excuses to order glasses of dessert wine and digestifs. Port which makes an appearance in various dishes is offered by the glass. Service is friendly and efficient. Le Cadre is handy – and popular – in the locale.

OPEN: Mon-Sat. **HOURS:** 12.00-2.30pm and 7.00-11.00pm. **CLOSED:** Bank Holidays and 25th-30th December. **CREDIT CARDS ACCEPTED:** Access, AmEx, Diner's Club,Visa. **NUMBER OF SEATS:** 55. **SERVICE:** Optional. **SET PRICE LUNCH:** £11.50 (2-course) and £13.50 (3-course). **SET PRICE DINNER:** £13.50 Mon-Thur, £15.50 Fri-Sat. Wheelchair access (but not lavatory). Tables outside seat 14. **NEAREST TUBE STATION:** Highgate/Turnpike Lane.

Café Delancey

3 Delancey Street, NW1

48

071-387 1985

£15

'A European refuge in Camden Town'

Easygoing opening hours and attitudes make this café/restaurant, and most recently bar, popular in the neighbourhood. There is an authentically European – as opposed to cod-French – feeling to eating here and the food is on the whole more carefully prepared than any of the foregoing might make make you think. A salade gourmande which in some circles is called Cobb salad (spinach, bacon and croûtons) was well done and gravad lax elegantly presented complete with side salad, sweet mustard sauce and black rye breadroll. The various sausages are excellent and come accompanied by rosti. Specials of the day are presented on a blackboard. A central courtyard provides an agreeable space for outdoor eating away from traffic fumes. Service at a test meal was extremely pleasant but apparently the level of geniality can fall on occasion.

OPEN: Mon-Sun. **HOURS:** 8.00am-12.00am. **CLOSED:** Christmas Day, Boxing Day and New Year's Day. **CREDIT CARDS ACCEPTED:** Access, Visa. **NUMBER OF SEATS:** 150. **SERVICE:** Optional. No-smoking area. Wheelchair access (but not lavatory). Tables outside seat 36. Private room seats 50. **NEAREST TUBE STATION:** Camden Town. MAP REF: 5,D/1

Café dell'Ugo

56-58 Tooley Street, SE1 ⓭

071-407 6001 **£23**

'Underneath the arches, we'll dream our dishes up'

The irrepressible Antony Worrall-Thompson, when landed with premises near London Bridge station – and, some would wistfully point out, the London Dungeon – via the convolutions of a deal done by the company of which he is part, promptly labelled the area South City. No one was fooled; but Woz has succeeded with his hallmark energy, invention and patchwork quilting of ingredients to attract a clientele both night and day. Some of the dishes that were said at the time of opening to be originals, i.e. not having made an appearance at any other of his establishments, exemplify the style: chargrilled figs with prosciutto and taleggio cream; lamb shank tagine with root vegetables and couscous; roast stuffed suckling pig with baked squash and celeriac mash. Those wise in the ways of eating may seek out the simpler combos on the menu – say chicory and rocket salad with flakes of Parmesan – but the ability of young chef Kille Enna minimizes the dangers inherent in culinary overload. On the ground floor of what was originally a railway arch, a cheaper menu is served which, as well as oysters, salads, fishcakes, burger, and sausages and beans, offers nicely elaborate sandwiches such as roast Mediterranean chicken with plum tabbouleh, herb mayo and watercress in pitta. And what else would you expect as accompaniment other than root vegetable crisps? The tempo never stops. There are specialist coffees, specialist breads, and a dozen takes on espresso including Bargain Café Ole; a large milky espresso without froth served with croissant and preserves. Many of the staff, like many of the wines, are New World.

OPEN: LUNCH: Mon-Fri. DINNER: Mon-Sat. **HOURS:** 12.00-3.00pm and 7.00-11.00pm. **CREDIT CARDS ACCEPTED:** AmEx, Diner's Club, Mastercard, Switch, Visa. **NUMBER OF SEATS:** 76. **SERVICE:** Optional. Tables outside seat 12. **NEAREST TUBE STATION:** London Bridge.

Café des Arts

82 Hampstead High Street, NW3

(50)

071-435 3608   **£25**

'Thoroughly modern food in listed surroundings'

The quintessentially Parisian name belongs to a restaurant whose food is Anglo-Mediterranean or, if you prefer, modern British. The premises – a seventeenth-century listed building – lend rusticity and charm, the latter also a virtue possessed by the waiting staff. Café des Arts used to be staffed entirely by women but it would seem marriage has changed all that. Chef Sally Holme is now Sally James and her co-chef is Fergus Greer. The menu relies on chargrilling and even scorching – as in scorched broccoli, Puy lentils and roasted red peppers served, in common with several of the items, in two sizes at two prices – and comes up with some tempting ideas such as smoked trout hash with poached egg and dill Hollandaise; roasted lamb fillet with deep-fried minted gnocchi (deep-fried gnocchi are great). Among the desserts warm chocolate brownies with whisky fudge sauce is particularly satisfying. Occasionally menu descriptions are more impressive than the end result but in the extraordinarily arid land that is Hampstead eating, Café des Arts shines out as good deed.

OPEN: Mon-Sun. **HOURS:** 12.00-4pm and 6-11.30pm. **CLOSED:** Christmas Day, Boxing Day and New Year's Day lunch. **CREDIT CARDS ACCEPTED:** Access, AmEx, Diner's Club, Mastercard, Switch, Visa. **NUMBER OF SEATS:** 64. **SERVICE:** 12.5%. **SET PRICE LUNCH:** £4.95. Private room seats 28. **NEAREST TUBE STATION:** Hampstead.   MAP REF: 6,A/2

Café du Jardin

28 Wellington Street, WC2

(51)

071-836 8769   **£25**

'A menu worth digging into'

Restaurant reviewers always feel happier when chefs get their own restaurants; they (the chefs) are less likely to do a flit. Tony Howorth who has done stints at Le Caprice (q.v.), the Ivy (q.v.) and Soho Soho (q.v.) is now a co-owner of Le Café du Jardin in Covent Garden. Defying the restaurant's plodding, tourist-baiting name, Howorth's menu is lively and inventive even if the titles of dishes are sometimes more exciting than the dishes themselves. Coca de trempo is by another name bruschetta, this one of grilled peppers and garlic on toasted black onion brioche. Free and easy movement between languages – Spanish, French and Italian – suggest a sort of culinary Esperanto but on the whole Howorth's abilities avoid gobbledegook on the plate. Sometimes one or two fewer ingredients would be to the good, as in removing sautéed turnips from the mashed potato that accompanies grilled calves' liver with black butter and capers (maybe the capers too come to think of it). Prices are more restaurant than café and subject to a 'recommended' 15% service charge. The wine list is also peripatetic, much of it still wet behind the ears. The decorative theme of the ground-floor corner site is black and white. Since Howorth's arrival the basement has been revamped and made a more seductive, private place.

OPEN: Mon-Sun. **HOURS:** 12.00-3.00pm and 5.30pm-12.00am. **CLOSED:** Christmas Day. **CREDIT CARDS ACCEPTED:** AmEx, Diner's Club, Mastercard, Visa. **NUMBER OF SEATS:** 120. **SERVICE:** 15%, optional. **SET PRICE DINNER:** £9.95. Wheelchair access (but not lavatory). Tables outside seat 25. Private room seats 60. **NEAREST TUBE STATION:** Covent Garden. **MAP REF:** 1,F/1

Le Café du Marché

22 Charterhouse Mews,
Charterhouse Square, EC1

52

071-608 1609 £35

'The market is Smithfield, the café is a restaurant'

Hercule Poirot – at least in his David Suchet television incarnation – might have used Le Café du Marché. The art deco block of flats in which Poirot is seen to be living in the TV series is on the east side of Charterhouse Square, one of London's more charming architectural assemblies. Le Café du Marché (referring to next-door Smithfield) is a converted meat warehouse in a passageway to the north of the square. The mustachioed owner is English, his wife Austrian, the staff – like the menus – mainly French. The advice given last year to stay with the familiar French dishes such as boudin blanc, côte de boeuf grillé, lapin rôti and jarret d'agneau printanière which feature on the set-price menus still holds true. Test meals have proved that the incursion of Middle European creations such as beetroot and horseradish with hard-boiled eggs are to be skirted around. Le vrai Cornish pasty au jus de l oignon sounds like a joke that should only be played on a Hooray from the City. The first-floor dining room, Le Grenier, functions as a grill room at lunchtimes and either as overflow – and an escape from the piano and double bass playing – or a room for private functions in the evenings. The historic-London nature of the location and the design references to the bistros of France render Le Café du Marché a candidate for the description romantic, but an uneven quality to the cooking, ebullient pricing and a 15% 'optional' service charge can make the bill a rude shock.

OPEN: LUNCH: Mon-Fri. DINNER: Mon-Sat. **HOURS:** 12.00-2.30pm and 6.00-10.00pm. **CLOSED:** Christmas, New Year and Bank Holidays. **CREDIT CARDS ACCEPTED:** Access, Visa, Switch. **NUMBER OF SEATS:** 110. **SERVICE:** 15% optional. **SET PRICE LUNCH AND DINNER:** £19.75. Wheelchair access (but not lavatory). Private room seats 66. **NEAREST TUBE STATION:** Barbican. **MAP REF:** 8,D/2

Café Fish

39 Panton Street, SW1

071-930 3999

53

£25

'Fish and vegetarian dishes on some scale'

There is a formula at work in Café Fish which recognizes the need amongst West End customers for variety coupled with brisk service; on both counts it fits the bill. The impressively long menu listing some 50 items offers fish, shellfish and seafood prepared both in traditional ways (chargrilled, steamed, meunière and fried) and with some innovation and embellishment. The result is reliable, if somewhat workmanlike, food served in an atmosphere of mock-Parisian bistro and bustle. The essentially French theme is borne out by the plateaux de fruits de mer and dishes such as cotriade de poissons et moules safranes (assorted white fish and mussels in a saffron broth), and a Provençal casserole that is perhaps more Margate than Marseilles. The more exotic approach to flavouring and spicing – usually best exemplified in the plats du jour – was vindicated in the standard menu dish of truite en papillotte (boned trout cooked in a paper envelope with shredded vegetables and lemon grass). The English approach to fish is acknowledged in fish cakes, haddock and chips, 'gourmet' scampi and an uncanonical, not altogether successful kedgeree. Effort goes into making vegetarian dishes attractive if even fish is meeting with your suspicions these days. The Groupe Gerard (the owners) approach to cover charge (£1.25) is here illustrated by a fish pâté being served with your bread and butter. The quite interesting wine list, divided by grape variety, is reasonably enough more eloquent on the subject of white wine. The volume of sound in the usually animated atmosphere of Café Fish is increased by live piano music. The cheaper wine bar downstairs, open throughout the day and evening, is worth keeping in mind when going to the movies in and around Leicester Square.

OPEN: LUNCH: Mon-Fri. DINNER: Mon-Sat. **HOURS:** 12.00-3.00pm and 5.45-11.30pm. **CLOSED:** Christmas Day. **CREDIT CARDS ACCEPTED:** All major cards except Switch. **NUMBER OF SEATS:** 92. **SERVICE:** 12.5%, cover charge £1.50. No-smoking area. Wheelchair access (but not lavatory). Tables outside seat 6. **NEAREST TUBE STATION:** Leicester Square/Piccadilly Circus.   MAP REF: 1,D/1

Café Royal Grill Room

68 Regent Street, W1

071-437 9090

54

£40-£45

'Time to recognize again one of London's most ravishing rooms'

The Michelin star awarded this year to Herbert Berger – who last twinkled with one many years ago at Le Connaisseur in Golders Green – is well deserved. The recently appointed restaurant manager, David

Arcusi, has brought the service and also the wine list into line with both Berger's judicious mix of modern and traditional cooking and this ravishing rococo room now ready for a new influx of lovers of food and the romance of restaurants. They have to negotiate a glum entrance hall but it could be argued that it only makes the Grill's interior the more glorious. It is possible to eat totally straightforwardly – which has a romance of its own – for example starting with asparagus or Scottish smoked salmon and moving on to roast rack of lamb with truffled potatoes or roast Bresse chicken, both served for two to share, or simple grills. But Berger's dishes in a contemporary vein are equally gratifying. The first course of a warm salad of calves' sweetbreads garnished with deep-fried slices of celeriac and dressed with pistachio oil demonstrated a mastery of the cooking of sweetbreads, which require a surface crust to emphasize their yielding nature. An equally fine warm salad is one of wood pigeon with sweet and sour chicory, beetroot and juniper berries, constructed with an artist's eye as well as palate. Typical of the fish and meat main courses are supreme of turbot with a crispy potato crust in sorrel and grain mustard sauce; sauté of scallops and red mullet with tapenade, basil and orange zest; tournedos of beef with a gratin of parsnips and truffles in Madeira sauce. The individual desserts such as caramelized pastry leaves with bitter chocolate, poached pear and Williamine sauce tend to be more satisfactory than the assiette gourmande. This last comes as part of the good-value set price dinner menu. The wine list offers some well-chosen bottles that will not take your bill into the stratosphere. This is a place to take someone you love.

OPEN: Mon-Sat. **HOURS:** 12.00-2.30pm and 6.00-11.45pm. **CLOSED:** Telephone for advice. **CREDIT CARDS ACCEPTED:** All major cards. **NUMBER OF SEATS:** 80. **SET PRICE LUNCH:** £19.50. **SET PRICE DINNER:** £28. Wheelchair access. Available for private hire, seats 80. **NEAREST TUBE STATION:** Piccadilly Circus.

MAP REF: 1,D/1

Calabash

The Africa Centre,
38 King Street, WC2

071-836 1976   **£15**

*'Real ethnic food close to pizza-piazza
of Covent Garden'*

Anyone familiar with student union bars and restaurants will feel at home in this basement restaurant beneath the Africa Centre. But African fabrics embellish the plain furnishings, the staff are friendly, the food comes in good quantity and prices are reasonable. All in all, it is a find within an ersatz area, provided that you like African food. A short list of first courses includes fried plantain with hot sauce (aloco); salads including a fiery tomato and chilli combination; excellent hot sambusas which resemble samosas. Main courses are either substantial stews of meat and vegetables served with something starchy, such as (Ethiopian) ingera bread or pounded yam, or fried dishes of fish or chicken served with plantain and salad. There is evidence of a sensitive palate in charge, creating dishes of delicacy. Wines are available but African beer seems to be the thing to drink. Service is of the sort to whom the word deadline is completely without meaning.

OPEN: LUNCH: Mon-Fri. DINNER: Mon-Sat. **HOURS:** 12.30-3.00pm and 6.00pm-11.30am. **CLOSED:** Bank Holidays. **CREDIT CARDS ACCEPTED:** All major cards. **NUMBER OF SEATS:** 80. **SERVICE:** 10%. **NEAREST TUBE STATION:** Covent Garden/ Leicester Square/Charing Cross.   MAP REF: 1,F1

Camden Brasserie

214-216 Camden High Street, NW1   (56)

071-482 2114   £15-£20

'Bewilderingly unpretentious'

Anyone wandering in from the leather-clad, body-pierced excesses of Camden High Street risks being taken aback by the very straightforwardness of this restaurant (not, in either menu or opening-hour terms, a brasserie). Babylon is expected, not a placid bistro. Yet what's done is done well: three decent little merguez sausages with horseradish and a parsley leaf on a plain white plate; good fresh tuna, dressed orientally; charcoal-grilled swordfish retaining tenderness by dint of an oil-rich marinade. Bowlfuls of matchstick chips come with everything, though you must pay for (warm) bread. Desserts are unflamboyant and generously dosed with cream. The waiting staff seem selected for comeliness, and patrol with pleasant efficiency; the customers are perplexingly un-leather-clad, un-body-pierced, un- marginal. Wines are sound and simple. As we go to press, the Brasserie is fusing with its subterranean neighbour The Underground Café: the new menu is a greatest hits of both, with an increased emphasis on lightness.

OPEN: Mon-Sun. **HOURS:** 12.00-3.00pm and 6.00-11.30pm (11.00am-10.30pm Sun). **CLOSED:** Christmas Day and Boxing Day. **CREDIT CARDS ACCEPTED:** Access, Mastercard, Visa. **NUMBER OF SEATS:** 110. **SERVICE:** Optional. Wheelchair access (but not lavatory). **NEAREST TUBE STATION:** Camden Town.

MAP REF: 5,C/2

The Canteen

Unit 4G Harbour Yard,
Chelsea Harbour, SW10   (57)

071-351 7330   £30

'Not your everyday nosh'

The guiding hand of co-owner Marco Pierre White would seem to be conducting here as energetically as that of the late Leonard Bernstein.

Aficionados of White's food – on display at the Dorchester (q.v.) and to some extent at Aubergine (q.v.) can here sample versions at £6.50 for first courses and £10.50 for main courses plus £1 cover charge. This 'imposition' of menu style and content may have contributed to the abrupt departure in the late spring of '94 of chef Steve Terry. His position has been taken by former sous-chef Tom Paine. Since the restaurant's name, even if only the name alone, implies casualness, it seems odd that the menu is so fixed. There is sometimes a special of the day but the rest seems engraved in stone. There is a Provençal slant to the dishes and some suggestion that somebody has spent time at Roger Vergé's Moulin de Mougins. You could start with a fish soup with saffron and rouille or a tian of crab and avocado – actually bearing no relationship to a Provençal tian and served colder than the weather gets in those parts – and then have fillet of red mullet with ratatouille Provençal and sauce tapenade or even roast rack of lamb Niçoise with pomme fondante, ratatouille (again) and jus of olives. On a sunny day at a table with a view, this might help fade memories of the checkpoint charlie who stopped you at the entrance to the complex and the underground car park with its spaces inhospitable to anything larger than a Reliant Robin.

Cappucino of mushrooms with crayfish and chervil is a brilliant, rich froth but the intensity of fungi obliterates any flavour of shellfish beyond a sort of brininess. Risottos of squid ink and roasted calamari or simply of saffron are usually extremely well done and if richness is required in the first course there is the well-rehearsed papillote of smoked salmon 'Albert Roux'. The main course of cod Viennoise with its light tomato crust and unctuous, almost cheesy, sabayon based on grain mustard is a high-class rendering of a domestic staple; what mass manufacturers of frozen fish dinners must hope for if they ever get to heaven. The aforementioned turbot is spread with a luxurious shellfish mousse and served with candied root vegetables. Meat dishes have classic accoutrements such as sauce bercy, Vichy carrots, pommes Anna, pomme fondante, essence of cèpes; the valuable and these days quite rare fruits of training in serious, traditional kitchens. The execution of desserts is equally poised. David Collins' design, which has fun with the theme of playing cards, introduces an idea of gambling. You might be taking chances with the suavity or speed of the service but not with the quality of the dishes; they are, for the most part, a dead cert.

THIS TERSELY worded list is satisfyingly eclectic, with most countries and most grape varieties getting a peek at the action (try Zind-Humbrecht's dry Turckheim Riesling or Ravenswood's punchy Zinfandel for worthwhile sorties off the beaten track). Prices, though, still grate in a restaurant whose banner is value.

OPEN: Mon-Sun. **HOURS:** 12.00-3.00pm and 6.30pm-11.45am. **CLOSED:** Christmas. **CREDIT CARDS ACCEPTED:** Access, Visa. **NUMBER OF SEATS:** 130. **SERVICE:** Optional. Wheelchair access. **NEAREST TUBE STATION:** Fulham Broadway.

La Capannina

24 Romilly Street, W1

071-437 2473 or 071-734 9630   **£25**

'A bit of old Soho to cherish'

Under the same family ownership for nearly 35 years – and with some staff who have been there nearly as long – La Capannina, just a few yards away from the burgeoning cafés of Old Compton Street, is a reminder of old Soho days when being gay was synonymous with merry. There are some restaurants better for one mealtime than another: La Capannina is a lunch place. The clientele at that time is drawn from the media businesses of the area. The waiters bustle enthusiastically. Regulars, and indeed anyone with any sense, will address themselves to the dishes of the day presented as a typed list or the produce displayed on the trolley. The best balance is obtained from something light to start, say bresaola or marinated fresh anchovy fillets followed by something robust such as cotechino with lentils, braised beef in barolo or bollito misto when available. Pasta to start, fish to follow – you can inspect the gleam in its eye on the trolley – is another approach but pasta dishes tend to be swampingly sauced. The short wine list has improved but sometimes you are better off combing the shelves of the vaguely hunting-lodge interior to see what you can find. Regulars complain about prices creeping upwards; bills totalling more than anticipated can to some extent be explained by the old-fashioned practices of cover charge, and vegetables separately priced, so be aware. La Capannina belongs to the pre-espresso machine age. It is a treasure; try it.

OPEN: LUNCH: Mon-Fri. DINNER: Mon-Sat. **HOURS:** 12.00-2.30pm and 6.00-11.15pm. **CLOSED:** Bank Holidays. **CREDIT CARDS ACCEPTED:** All major cards. **NUMBER OF SEATS:** 90. **SERVICE:** Optional. No-smoking area. Wheelchair access (but not lavatory). Private room seats 25. **NEAREST TUBE STATION:** Leicester Square/Piccadilly Circus.   MAP REF: 1,E/2

Capital Hotel

22-24 Basil Street, SW3

071-589 5171   LUNCH £25 ; DINNER £40

'Small and perfectly formed hotel dining'

Because Philip Britten is not the sort of chap to go off in a submarine forty thousand leagues under the sea to cook for the crew or some such ploy in order to titillate the audience of the *Food and Drink Programme*, he is perhaps not as celebrated a chef as – based on cooking skills – he should be. Only the fourth chef to work at the relatively small, family-owned Capital Hotel since its opening about 23 years ago, Britten has held on to the Michelin star the hotel was awarded. Having been the chef with Nico Ladenis at Chez Nico in Battersea when Ladenis was given two, it would seem not unreasonable or unlikely that in the future he might get another.

His dishes are inventive and singular but based on intuition and understanding about what might compliment what. I have not tried tuile of forest mushrooms, pancetta and caramelized onions on a cep and cocoa sauce but I can see – or in my mind's eye taste – why it would work. He is fond of using a judiciously chosen wine as an ingredient, as in the soup geminy (meaning twinned) of Jerusalem artichokes and girolles with riesling d'Alsace; soufflé fruits de mer with morels in vin jaune and crème fraîche; braised black leg chicken in Madeira with spinach and garlic ravioli. Simpler versions and simpler dishes are presented on the good-value set price lunch menus where Britten's liking for the impact and uncomplicated saucing of flavoured oils is apparent. His desserts are usually one of the highpoints of a meal. Service is formal and assiduous. A radical overhaul of the, to my mind, frumpy dining room is planned. It should give Britten's cooking the setting it deserves. See also the review for Le Metro (part of the Capital hotel) where you now can find bargain basement Britten.

THIS REMAINS A good address at which to drink fine wine (you could save a total of £153 by drinking a bottle of Palmer '83 plus one of Latour '78 here for dinner rather than at Bibendum). Some attempt has been made to provide options in the middle and lower price brackets, but the list is still fundamentally a top-heavy one, with feeble choice for those with less than £20 to spend. Le Vin de Levin, a genuine vin du patron, is, alas, unenticing, even at £10.50. What it needs is a wine transfusion from Le Metro's excellent little list.

OPEN: Mon-Sun. **HOURS:** 12.00-2.30pm and 7.00-11.15pm. **CREDIT CARDS ACCEPTED:** Access, AmEx, Diner's Club, Mastercard, Visa. **NUMBER OF SEATS:** 40. **SERVICE:** Included. **SET PRICE LUNCH:** £25 and £28. **SET PRICE DINNER:** £40. Wheelchair access. Private room seats 24. **NEAREST TUBE STATION:** Knightsbridge. **MAP REF:** 2,F/4

Le Caprice

Arlington House,
Arlington Street, SW1

60

071-629 2239   **£35**

*'When you have eaten out a lot you want to go
to Le Caprice'*

What do Sir Claus Moser and Peter Stringfellow have in common? They both include Le Caprice on their list of favourite restaurants. Le Caprice appeals to anyone who enjoys eating out. It is impeccably run, the menu is shrewdly compiled and confidently executed, it is reasonably priced and almost invariably you see faces to which you can put names, a factor which most people will admit ups the ante in the pleasure of going out. And if you don't, there are David Bailey's photographic portraits to look at which become more intriguing by the year. Open every day, last orders midnight is another reason why Le Caprice springs to so many minds when people start to think about where to go to eat. The menu manages to satisfy various moods without coming across as a rag-bag or a breathless global tour. Feeling restrained – or feeling you should be – you might start with Thai spiced shrimp broth or seared scallops and trompettes with sorrel and move on to grilled yellow fin tuna with grilled vegetables or grilled breast of free-range chicken with spiced aubergine and coriander pesto. Feeling self-indulgent you could start with sautéed foie gras with Sauternes jus, go on to deep-fried cod with pea purée and chips and finish with tarte Tatin of pears. Le Caprice appeals to people whose life involves a lot of eating out. That is quite a significant accolade. The wines, including the house wines, are well chosen. Sunday brunch is a nice time to visit.

Open: Lunch: Mon-Sat. Dinner: Mon-Sun. **Hours:** 12.00-3.00pm and 6.00pm-12.00am. **Credit cards accepted:** All major cards. **Number of seats:** 70. **Service:** Optional, £1.50 cover charge. Wheelchair access (but not lavatory). **Nearest tube station:** Green Park.   MAP REF: 1,C/1

Caravan Serai

50 Paddington Street, W1

071-935 1208   **£19**

'The last outpost in London for Afghan food'

The Putney branch (Buzkash) of this Afghan restaurant has become a Nepalese restaurant called Everest Tandoori, leaving the Paddington Street premises your one opportunity for Afghan food in London. If you are wondering whether this is something you would want to seize, it might be useful to know that Afghan food is (unsurprisingly) not dissimilar from Northern Indian, has some Nepalese touches apparent in the filled pasta dumplings and refers to Persian food in the use of tart fruit and the importance attached to rice. Rather like someone asked the same question too often, the management has devised a brisk and formulaic approach to meals which starts with the presentation to each customer of a slice of potato in rather greasy batter with a herb and yogurt sauce, interrupts the first and main courses with a dab of apricot sorbet and at the last visit, finishes by presenting the table with a small Afghan carpet smelling firmly of camphor. Needing a little rug for your hall might be one reason to visit Caravan Serai. Culinary ones are best found in first courses of ashak (pasta parcels of leek and lamb); bonjon (an emphatic way with aubergine slices) and kebab nanee, a well-seasoned sausage of lamb (or chicken or veal) wrapped with salad and yogurt in soft bread. Main courses tend towards the mild and creamy rather than chilli hot. Indeed, a notable use of adverbs – 'lamb chops *cautiously* spiced', fillet of veal *'marinated very carefully'* – conveys the tone. Best of the assemblies tried was shahi korma, king prawns cooked in a *delicately* prepared sauce served with chalaw (Afghan-style) rice. Don't omit to order narenge chalaw, basmati rice with orange peel and almonds, and the nan breads. If you had an ulcer, you'd appreciate the dessert of firnee, a sort of junket made from ground rice scattered with pistachios. The wine list is perfunctory and ridiculously expensive. A bottle of Fleurie, no vintage, no pack drill, was charged at £19.95. Despite service charge automatically added on, you are left free to add more to reward the slightly charmless attention.

OPEN: Mon-Sun. **HOURS:** 12.00-3.00pm and 6.00-11.00pm (6.00-11.30pm Sat-Sun). **CLOSED:** Christmas Eve, Christmas Day and Boxing Day. **CREDIT CARDS ACCEPTED: Access, AmEx, Diner's Club, Visa. NUMBER OF SEATS: 66. SERVICE:** 10%. **SET PRICE LUNCH:** £9.95. No-smoking area. Private room seats 16. **NEAREST TUBE STATION:** Baker Street. MAP REF: 1,B/4

Caviar House – 'La Brasserie'

161 Piccadilly, W1

(62)

071-409 0445   LUNCH: £29; DINNER: £35

'For those whose hearts skip to the chant Sevruga,
Beluga, Imperial or pressed'

Given the regular announcements from the government that we are coming out of the recession, it is perhaps timely to be seen sitting behind large plate glass windows in Piccadilly spooning up caviar. La Brasserie is the restaurant arm of Caviar House, an outfit only recently established in central London. The conversion of what was some form of financial institution has been carried out only up to a point; there remains a numismatic sobriety in the atmosphere in the dining room and a feeling that deals are being done behind closed doors on the mezzanine floor. However, prices for the black jam are more reasonable here than at Caviar Kaspia starting at £13.75 for 30g of Iranian Sevruga or pressed caviar and rising to £194.00 for 125g of Imperial. The caviar is served with blinis and new potatoes. The à la carte menu incorporates caviar as a garnish into some dishes. An ingredient that is a Caviar House speciality is the Balik salmon smoked to a 'secret recipe' in the mountains outside Zurich. The menu otherwise is a modern list, but it seems rather to miss the point to come here and eat asparagus or Caesar salad even if baby artichokes make an uncanonical appearance as part of it. The set price menu at £19.50 for three courses and coffee is excellent value. Wines are not voraciously marked up and are well chosen for their job. Service is not at all grandiose which is a relief. A huge amount of caviar and vodka followed by the news that you booked a room at the Ritz next door might, I think, be an effective wooing technique.

OPEN: Mon-Sat. **HOURS:** 12.00-3.00pm and 6.45-11.00pm. **CREDIT CARDS ACCEPTED:** All major cards. **NUMBER OF SEATS:** 40. **SERVICE:** Optional. **SET PRICE LUNCH AND DINNER:** £19.50. Private room seats 12. Wheelchair access (but not lavatory). **NEAREST TUBE STATION:** Green Park. MAP REF: 1,C/1

Chada Thai Cuisine

208-210 Battersea Park Road, SW11

⑥③

071-622 2209 or 071-627 2059   LUNCH: £13; DINNER: £21

'Where the middle classes deem it fit to be Thai'd'

As you enter Chada, mahogany wood panelling provides a polish that you can also assume for the cooking and the smiling service. Selecting from the long menu, organized like a filofax with tabs describing each section, requires a determined palate or an appeal for guidance – graciously supplied. One way to deal with the first course is to order the combination platter of satay, Thai pancakes, spring rolls, dumplings, won ton and fish cakes. The use of chilli in the main courses is relatively restrained. A curry – perhaps the quite unusual roasted duck in red curry – a stir-fried dish of beef or pork, seafood presented in an earthenware pot, some steamed rice, vegetables and a noodle assembly would provide a cross-section of the menu and balance in terms of cooking methods. There is a comprehensive vegetarian menu also worth studying. Ice cream or fresh fruit are the best dessert options, Singha beer the only sensible beverage.

OPEN: LUNCH: Sun-Fri. DINNER: Mon-Sun. HOURS: 12.00-2.30pm (12.00-3.00pm Sun) and 6.30-11.00pm (6.30-11.30pm Fri-Sat; 7.00-10.30pm Sun). CLOSED: Bank Holidays. CREDIT CARDS ACCEPTED: Access, AmEx, Diner's Club, Visa. NUMBER OF SEATS: 50. SERVICE: Optional, 70p cover charge. SET PRICE LUNCH: £10.95. Wheelchair access. NEAREST TUBE STATION: Sloane Square.

Chapel Lafayette

374 North End Road, SW6

⑥④

071-362 0021   £18

'We're going to the chapel and we're going to get . . .'

Had any restaurant opened in a converted church hall at the Fulham end of North End Road, it would have got the accolade 'useful in the area'. As it is, Chapel Lafayette has as one of the partners Adrian Linssen, who was responsible for the success of Bar Escoba in Old Brompton Road, and some effort is being made to offer a reasonably authentic Cajun and Caribbean menu which jacks the joint up into a slightly more compelling category. As is the case with many new restaurants, the bar, the cocktails, and in this instance, the bourbons, are a significant part of the operation. Tables for eating take a back seat and they work better for groups out to party rather than couples wanting to have meaningful exchanges. Dishes that give a flavour of the menu are: Caesar salad; crabcakes with balsamic dressing; seafood and okra gumbo; jerk chicken with candied yams; baby back ribs; strawberry and clotted cream alaska. It has been noted that the yams were authentically sweetened with grilled mini-marshmallows. This may have been the influence of the chef who has worked at Euro Disney. Chapel Lafayette is quiet at lunchtimes, loud in the evenings and gospel at Sunday brunch.

OPEN: Mon-Sun. **HOURS:** 11.00am-1.00am. **CLOSED:** Christmas Day and Boxing Day. **CREDIT CARDS ACCEPTED:** Access, AmEx, Visa. **NUMBER OF SEATS:** 100. **SERVICE:** 12.5%. **SET PRICE LUNCH AND DINNER:** £5.50.Wheelchair access. Tables outside seat 16. **NEAREST TUBE STATION:** Fulham Broadway.

Chester's

359 Upper Street, N1

071-359 1932   £27

*'Where Islington person discovers the paysanne
(s)he is at heart'*

To Islington, already abundantly supplied with places to eat, comes Ian Loynes to be chef of Chester's, a first-floor restaurant in a listed building that houses some of the antique stalls of Camden Passage. Loynes has put in time at The Square and The Lexington (see entries) and may well be the creator of the salad that has appeared in all three of these places and is known as the Paysanne. A mixture of leaves flat and frilly, lentils, root vegetable crisps, softly boiled quails' eggs and pieces of duck confit, it is served in two sizes and, if not quite as healthy as the generic name salad would imply, can be diverting and delicious as a first or main course if not over-oiled by the cooking methods and dressing. Loynes handles well the rest of the menu which bristles with contemporaneity. A score of at least three buzz words is achieved by mousse of goat's cheese and roast red peppers on a tapenade blini. Pastas read temptingly, for example open ravioli of porcini mushrooms with Welsh pecorino cheese. Main courses can be as right-on nursery as baked cod with saffron mash and basil jus or as full of Eastern promise as breast of duck with Chinese spices and a baked plum jus. In the appropriate season you can get a practically perfect summer pudding. A lively bar scene within the creamery-greenery conservatorily decorated premises tends to obscure the fact that here is something considerably better than bistro cooking. Someone likes jazz. It is live for Sunday brunch and well chosen on tape at other times.

OPEN: Tue-Sun. **HOURS:** 12.00-2.15pm and 6.00-11.15pm (6.00-11.15pm Sat; 11.00am-5.00pm Sun). **CLOSED:** Bank Holidays, Easter and Christmas. **CREDIT CARDS ACCEPTED:** All major cards. **NUMBER OF SEATS:** 65. **SERVICE:** 12.5%. **SET PRICE LUNCH AND DINNER:** £11.95-£14.95. **NEAREST TUBE STATION:** Angel.

Chez Gerard

8 Charlotte Street, W1

071-636 4975   £30

'Meat to eat'

The Carnivores Club which specializes in defiant rallying calls from the likes of Digby Anderson and Auberon Waugh meets to eat meat at Chez Gerard in Charlotte Street. In some large part this must be due to Neville

Abraham and Lawrence Isaacson of Groupe Chez Gerard plc sponsoring the club . . . but the côte de boeuf served at Chez Gerard is also justification. It is excellent beef and the chef a master of timing the cooking of it. Cuts such as onglet and chateaubriand are also served as, indeed, are other dishes including fish and vegetarian dishes, but the pride of place goes to côte de boeuf served for two with unputdownable chips and sauce béarnaise. Other sauces seem to me otiose. First courses can be a bit mechanical, as if assembled according to a manual. Cheese is a much better option than dessert and an excuse to go on with red wine from the creditable list. The redesign of the Charlotte Street branch as a modern French bistro is one of the best jobs Virgile and Stone have done and their influence will apparently be spreading. Also at 31 Dover Street W1 (071-499 8171) and 119 Chancery Lane WC2 (071-405 0290).

OPEN: LUNCH: Sun-Fri. DINNER: Mon-Sun. **HOURS:** 12.00-3.00pm and 6.00-11.00pm. **CREDIT CARDS ACCEPTED:** Access, AmEx, Diner's Club, Visa. **NUMBER OF SEATS:** 84. **SERVICE:** 12.5% optional, cover charge £1. **SET PRICE DINNER:** £15 and and £17.95. No-smoking area. Wheelchair access (but not lavatory). Tables outside seat 12. Private room seats 12. **NEAREST TUBE STATION:** Goodge Street/Tottenham Court Road.   MAP REF: 1,E/3

Chez Max
168 Ifield Road, SW10   **67**

071-835 0874   LUNCH: £28; DINNER: £35

'Twinned with France'

The twins Max and Marc Renzland, who in their working clothes look as if they have stepped out of a book of nursery rhymes illustrated by Mabel Lucy Atwell, have expanded to Fulham. Their new premises complete with liquor licence, a bar and loos in which there is room to swing a cat, should you want to do such a thing, were previously the first French fish restaurant of Pierre Martin (see Le Suquet). Gone are the Provençal prints and paintings of Cannes to be replaced with peppermint-green walls and framed menus from great restaurants, some apparently purchased in the sale of Elizabeth David's culinary effects, the sale that made us look with new respect at our wooden spoons. It is great to be able to sit in relative comfort and enjoy the cooking which I would put almost on a level with that of their friend and mentor Simon Hopkinson (see Bibendum). It is even more fidele to the classics of France than is Hopkinson's and shares that feeling of absolute rightness; this is how eating should be. The menu is priced at dinner at £23.50 for three courses with coffee or tisanes a fair £1.25 extra. On the bare wooden tables are Kalamata olives and butter from Charentes and handed round are slices of vigorously salted homebaked olive oil bread. For food of this calibre it is incredibly good value and remains so even with supplements added in as you might have to for a dozen rather than half a dozen oysters, or filet of Aberdeen Angus beef hung to perfection. The menu changes in part weekly but elements will always be traceable to E. D.'s *French Provincial Cooking*. (Much to the twins' delight Elizabeth David came to their restaurant when it was located in Richmond and apparently ate and, more particularly, drank with gusto).

The meticulous way in which, say, a sauce tartare is made can lift a first course of deep-fried baby squid into gourmet class. Imam bayeldi, a dish often more interesting for its spurious-sounding legend than its flavours, is here a confection humming the warm notes of cumin and coriander that might indeed make someone faint with pleasure, or at least nigh. The innate sweetness of scallops which caramelizes upon meeting a red-hot pan is offset with a thin lemony sauce. The Scottish beef served with shallot purée, red wine sauce and a gratin Dauphinois makes steak-lovers even out of Germans. Adhering to the principle of importance attached to sourcing and shopping, there is one cheese served in its prime. In the dessert course tarte Tatin aux poires, crème brulée, petit pot au chocolat and tarte à la crème point up the wisdom of the French in rarely straying from these perfect, rich finishes. Because customers grew used to supplying their own wine at Le Petit Max, the twins are happy if you bring your own. A corkage charge of £3.50 (£7.00 a magnum) is levied. However, the gentle marking-up policy on some of the bin ends provided by Oddbins means that it is not, financially anyway, necessarily a terrific wheeze.

OPEN: LUNCH: Tues-Fri. DINNER: Mon-Sat. **HOURS:** 12.30-2.30pm and 7.00-11.00pm. **CLOSED:** Bank Holidays, Easter, Christmas. **CREDIT CARDS ACCEPTED:** Access, Visa. **NUMBER OF SEATS:** 70. **SERVICE:** 12.5%. **SET PRICE LUNCH:** £15.50. **SET PRICE DINNER:** £23.50. Tables outside seat 10. Private room seats 12. **NEAREST TUBE STATION:** Earls Court.

 # Chez Moi

1 Addison Avenue, W11 ● 68

071-603 8267 **£35**

'The discreet charm of the bourgeosie'

Some restaurants remind you how hungry you are or can instil appetite where perhaps not much was present. The long established – since 1967 Chez Moi is one. From the moment you walk into the pair of pink candy-striped rooms with their yellow-clothed tables, comfortable green banquettes, shining glasses, formally dressed staff and individual table lamps you know you are in a place that understands profoundly well the business of pleasurable eating; Chez Moi is bourgeois in the best sense. What it is not is old-fashioned. Chef Richard Walton, who with front-of-house Colin Smith is the original co-owner, stays abreast of – and in command of – culinary trends. Proof of his wide reading and his willingness to learn from cooks he employs is revealed not only in the menu section where you might expect to find it entitled Quelque Chose de Different, but also among the Chez Moi Specialities such as coquilles Saint-Jacques minute et sa ballotine Japonaise (the garnish an evolved version of seaweed-rolled sushi) sauté de rable de lièvre émincé sauce au miel. Within this same section are the racks of lamb which for some are the point of coming to Chez Moi. Fish dishes tend towards the overworked and simpler options have disappeared from the menu (although doubtless available on request). Vegetables are treated with consideration and your choice of, say, spinach; cabbage with bacon and shallots; purée of carrots; parsnip gâteau is included in the price of the main course. Prices generally are fair – there is no last ditch attempt, as at some places, to coin it with desserts – and the set price lunch menu at £14 for three courses is dramatically good value. At this meal Walton reworks the familiar (e.g. Boston fish chowder; Caesar salad; spanakopitta; lobster Newburg; fricassée de ris d'agneau) and tries new dishes out, some with an Oriental slant. It is the cooking, he says, that he enjoys most. A test lunch revealed a good adaptation of omelette Arnold Bennett with a covering of hollandaise and parmesan au gratin followed by quickly seared salmon topped with more hollandaise. It was self-confessed foolish ordering but perhaps also bad planning in a short menu. From the à la carte came marvellous marinated raw tuna followed by pot-au-feu de poussin which in its presentation, with vegetables cooked separately, plus the intensity of the stock somewhat belied its title. Service is courteous and appears to have all the time in the world.

OPEN: LUNCH: Mon-Fri. **DINNER:** Mon-Sat. **HOURS:** 12.30-2.00pm and 7.00-11.00pm. **CLOSED:** Bank Holidays. **CREDIT CARDS ACCEPTED:** All major cards. **NUMBER OF SEATS:** 45. **SERVICE:** Optional. **SET PRICE LUNCH:** £14. Wheelchair access (but not lavatory). **NEAREST TUBE STATION:** Holland Park/Shepherd's Bush.

MAP REF: 7,D/2

China Court

Swiss Centre,
10 Wardour Street, W1

071-434 0108 £13

'Heidi goes to Hunan'

The China Court, part of the Swiss Centre, is a happy synthesis of Swiss and Chinese resulting in good food served in a spotlessly clean dining room and loos more from a Swiss canton than Cantonese. Staff are happy to explain, although not entirely comprehensibly, the items on the menus including the one written in Chinese characters. The set dim sum lunch supplies a representative range of the fried and the steamed and you can always add on more recherché items such as tripe and chickens feet. Service is quick, value is good. Outside dumpling hours, after 5.00pm, the main menu also repays study as there are dishes such as egg foo young with crabmeat not necessarily offered elsewhere. Since the report in last year's guide, staff seem to have mellowed. A smile has been seen.

OPEN: Mon-Sun. **HOURS:** 11.45am-11.30pm. **CREDIT CARDS ACCEPTED:** Access, AmEx, Visa. **NUMBER OF SEATS:** 750. **SERVICE:** 10%. **SET PRICE LUNCH:** £4. **SET PRICE DINNER:** £7. Wheelchair access. Private rooms seat 16 and 300. **NEAREST TUBE STATION:** Leicester Square/Piccadilly Circus. MAP REF: 1,E/1

Chinon

23 Richmond Way, W14

(70)

071-602 4082   **£35 (£15 at the bar)**

'A chef ploughing his own fertile furrow'

The move that Chinon made to lighter, brighter (next door) premises divided into basement restaurant giving onto a terrace and garden and a more informal ground floor wine bar/bistro has resulted in a greater volume of business and a wider mix of customers. This must be gratifying to chef Jonathan Hayes because he has not adopted the identikit informal menu with its et tu Caesar salad, prosciutto, parmesan and rocket and obligatory fish and chips. Dishes here are still recognizably his: a purse of goat's cheese with a relish made from celeriac, cream and apple; ravioli of fresh crab; main courses such as roast pigeon breast with a pastry-wrapped spiced pear; roasted baby sea bass with garlic grasses and teryaki dressing; prune and almond tart. Presentation is pretty, with skilful, well-thought-out accompaniments and flavours are true. The upstairs/downstairs division can blur in the evenings with both menus offered on the ground floor should numbers dictate it. Sometimes long waits occur. Having too few pairs of hands on both sides of the kitchen door is a downside that has been observed in several restaurants which, like Chinon, have decided to make their prices and style more accessible. But one cannot quarrel with the aim. The wine list is also not a knee-jerk reaction, in this case to contemporary drinking.

OPEN: LUNCH: Mon-Fri. DINNER: Mon-Sat. **HOURS:** 12.30-2.30pm and 6.00-10.45pm. **CLOSED:** Bank Holidays. **CREDIT CARDS ACCEPTED:** All major cards, except Diner's Club. **NUMBER OF SEATS:** 35. **SERVICE:** 12.5%. Wheelchair access (but not lavatory). 3 tables outside. Private room seats 35. **NEAREST TUBE STATION:** Olympia/Shepherd's Bush.   MAP REF: 7,C1

Christopher's American Grill

18 Wellington Street, WC2

(71)

071-240 4222   **£35**

'Yabba-dabba-dough'

Christopher's still occupies a heavily undersubscribed category; the upmarket American restaurant. Emulating the food of the big city steak houses such as Palm, the point of the place, could be said to be its 14 oz steaks cut from American (USDA) beef, carpetbag steak stuffed with oysters, 3lb Maine lobsters and other examples of brash consumption. However, chef Adrian Searing, who has worked in New York, also introduces a more subtle American influence with dishes such as clam chowder, a Caesar salad with the option of anchovies in or out, crab cakes with red pepper mayo, and, reminiscent of the oyster bar at Grand Central Station, oyster pan roast. Notable specialities of his own devising are smoked tomato soup, lobster guacamole and a chicken and veal sausage served with mash and mustard sauce that bears a strong resemblance to a French boudin blanc. The list of vegetables, expensively priced like everything else on the menu, includes particularly good creamed spinach, fries and celeriac mash. Cavils about Christopher's concern a certain un-American inconsistency to the cooking standards, service that sometimes in its bid to be biddable comes across as gauche, the unflattering lighting upstairs, a male-oriented clientele at lunchtimes and the expense. However, there is now a cheaper way of eating here which is the restructured ground floor bar where a café menu is served and on Sundays, a child-friendly brunch. The premises, a converted neo-Renaissance nineteenth-century building that once housed a casino are, to my mind, the most glamorous in Covent Garden and excitement still mounts when climbing the winding stone staircase around which operatic arias curl. At the time of writing, the eponymous Christopher Gilmour is looking for premises for an American sports bar.

A LIST OF successful compromise – between the cultural affirmation of Californian vinous well-being and the metropolitan Briton's thirst for familiar French flavours. Christopher's Choice has been well-assembled, and ten wines by the glass plus four dessert wines by the glass is what all should offer but few do. The choice includes Fetzer's comfortable Zinfandel and Niepoort's succulent '87 late-bottled vintage port. Californian wines in general have been well-chosen, whereas the antipodean selection could do with a bit more zip. Prices for the fine wines are on par (Palmer '85 is only £1 cheaper at the Capital Hotel).

OPEN: LUNCH: Sun-Fri. DINNER: Mon-Sat. **HOURS:** 12.00-2.30pm (12.00am-3.00pm Sun) and 6.00-11.45pm. **CLOSED:** Bank Holidays. **CREDIT CARDS ACCEPTED:** All major cards. **NUMBER OF SEATS:** 120. **SERVICE:** 12.5% on parties of 7 or more. **SET PRICE DINNER:** £15 pre-theatre. Private room seats 32. **NEAREST TUBE STATION:** Covent Garden.   MAP REF: 1,F/1

Chutney Mary
535 Kings Road, SW10   **72**

071-351 3113   **£30**

'A gastronomic legacy of colonialism'

The Anglo-Indian inspiration and to some extent 'theme' of this extremely popular restaurant – go at lunchtime if you want quiet – to some extent obscures the the real edge it has over most other Indian restaurants. The edge is due to the careful watch over the cooking given by co-owner Namita Panjabi – and her own researches and experiments – and to the fact that the chefs have all been brought directly from India, with each chef a specialist in his region or style. The menu is divided into sections that cover the cooking of the Christian communities in India, Anglo-Indian specialities, vegetarian main dishes – from which the rarely offered Kerala vegetable hotpot with hoppers is a must – and one entitled Unabashedly Indian. It is worth ordering a wider range of first courses. Calamari fried with chilli and other Keralan spices and served with rocket is one of the best squid dishes ever. Prawn balchao demonstrates the pungency of Goan sauces. A recent addition to the main courses, prawn

66

dossa (sic), started as a speciality on the summer menu. The pancake is the one familiar from Southern Indian vegetarian restaurants – a dramatically large, crisp disc made from lentil and rice batter – but is here wrapped round large, lightly spiced prawns and served with the traditional fresh coconut chutney. It seems mildly heretical but, if so, is a worthwhile schism. Masala roast lamb, the Bombay treatment of that meat of the moment, lamb shanks, is an Anglo-Indian speciality as is the Country Captain which displays all the charm of the old-fashioned inauthentic curry. There are various good chicken curries including one from Goa coloured green with herbs. Don't omit from your order some side dishes such as crispy fried okra, spicy cashews (wonderful) and curried potatoes Bombay style. Chutneys are made to house recipes and some of them gratifyingly chilli-hot. As at Bombay Brasserie, the conservatory here is the more desirable part in which to sit. Service is an up-and-down affair. There is an effort made to match wines to the food, with New World bottles tending to score well. Note: Between 3 October and 20 November 1994, Chutney Mary is running a festival featuring 10 dishes from Camellia Panjabi's masterly book, *50 Great Curries of India*. Some of these dishes will then migrate to the main menu.

OPEN: Mon-Sun. **HOURS:** 12.30-2.30pm (12.30-3.30pm Sun) and 7.00-11.30pm (7.00-10.30pm Sun). **CREDIT CARDS ACCEPTED:** Access, AmEx, Diner's Club, JCB, Mastercard, Visa. **NUMBER OF SEATS:** 130. **SERVICE:** 12.5%, £1.50 cover charge. **SET PRICE LUNCH:** £10 (2-course) and £12.95 (3-course). **SET PRICE DINNER:** £10 (2-course) and £12.95 (3-course) after 10.00pm.No-smoking area. **NEAREST TUBE STATION:** Fulham Broadway.

Chutneys

124 Drummond Street, NW1

071-388 0604   **£6**

'Reason enough to turn vegetarian'

An unreconstructed carnivore friend admitted to being happily poori (but not much) and considerably wiser after a meal at this quite chic, inexpensive vegetarian restaurant in Euston's little India; Drummond Street. Dishes from Southern and Western India, Gujarati thalis, plus snacks from Bombay's Chowpatty area combine to demonstrate how intricate and vivacious a pattern can be woven with relatively few basic ingredients but many spices, flavourings and cooking processes including the fermenting of batters based on rice and pulses. Potatoes shoulder a good deal of responsibility in the menu, particularly in assemblies that can serve as first courses, notably ragara pattice; fried potato cakes served with spicy chick-peas and potato bonda; a mixture of mashed potato, lentils and spices deep-fried in a gram-flour batter and served with chutney. Pooris, crisp, hollow spheres or flat discs of pastry, are rendered startling mouthfuls by the sharp/soft and sour/sweet range of ingredients used as stuffing and garnish. Bhel poori or special poori are, to my mind, the best. Among the curries, the tarka dal with its flavourings of fennel and mustard seeds plus a smokiness lent by fried onion and garlic is exceptional. A stylish new look to the decor featuring futuristic light fittings, trance-inducing art and paint shades of burnt orange, toffee, mustard yellow and drab navy is additional explanation for the crowds that pack into Chutneys. The buffet lunch remains one of London's bargains. Organic wines are offered 'for vegetarians and vegans'. I would have thought such bottles would only provide the danger of finding hidden meat protein in a dead bug.

OPEN: Mon-Sun. **HOURS:** 12.00-2.45pm and 6.00-11.30pm. **CLOSED:** Christmas Day. **CREDIT CARDS ACCEPTED:** Access, Visa. **NUMBER OF SEATS:** 120. **SERVICE:** 10%. **SET PRICE LUNCH:** £3.95. **SET PRICE DINNER:** £5.95. Wheelchair access (but not lavatory). Private rooms seat 35 and 60. **NEAREST TUBE STATION:** Euston Square. MAP REF: 1,E/4

Cibo

3 Russell Gardens, W14   **74**

071-371 6271/2085   LUNCH £20; DINNER £25-£30

'New wave Italian becomes more of a ripple'

As one of the new wave of Italian restaurants, slipstreaming in the wake of the incomparable River Café (q.v.), Cibo has impressed restaurant-goers with its spirit of generosity, exemplified in the nibbles beforehand and the petits fours, the air of impulsiveness about both decor and cooking and the fact that there is somewhere in the bleak hinterland of Olympia that provides diverting shelter. However, test meals recently have pointed to a heavy-handedness in the kitchen which can render too many dishes similar; wilting and over-burdened with ingredients. There is an indigestible love of melted cheese and it is interesting to note one week's menu is titled Cibo cucina con i formaggi. That said, you will probably be gratified by the pasta dishes, stuffed pasta often sporting an adventurous ingredient such as cardoons, or apple with a venison sauce, the seafood risotto and the plainer fish dishes such as sea bass in a herb sauce. Service is often slow. I must also warn you that the last time I ate at Cibo at neighbouring (different) tables were Fergie and Michael Winner.

OPEN: LUNCH: Sun-Fri. DINNER: Mon-Sat. **HOURS:** 12.00-2.30pm (12.30-3.30pm Sun) and 7.00-11.00pm (7.00-11.30pm Sat). **CLOSED:** Christmas Eve, Christmas Day and Boxing Day. **CREDIT CARDS ACCEPTED:** All major cards. **NUMBER OF SEATS:** 55. **SERVICE:** 12.5% on parties of 5 or more. **SET PRICE LUNCH:** £12.50. Wheelchair access. Tables outside seat 6. Private rooms seat 12 or 16. **NEAREST TUBE STATION:** Olympia/Shepherd's Bush. MAP REF: 7,C/1

Claridges Hotel – The Causerie

Brook Street, W1   **75**

071-629 8860   £45

'A refuge from the world outside'

The reason that at lunchtime a glass of hock costs £17 and a Manhattan £18.50 at the Causerie at Claridge's is that with them comes the offer of as much as you would like to help yourself to from the smörgåsbord table. The system was instituted during the last war in order to get around the price limit imposed on meals. A sense of period clings to the Causerie. In part this is connected with the impeccable service, an exemplification of what I imagine people mean by the good old days. The smörgåsbord has about 20 dishes, many of them based on fish and, this being a Scandanavian array, pickled fish. Smoked meats and hams are another main constituent part of the display. It is kept in good order; nothing bedraggled at the Causerie. Presumably in order to encourage more evening trade – at lunchtimes there seems to be plenty of dowagers and their nephews to go round – there is a new system: from 5.30pm onwards a charge of £12 per person for either the smörgåsbord or the hot dish of the day followed by cheese or dessert (try the bread and butter pudding). Seating (for about 40) is on small sofas for two arranged in a way that facilitates gossip but also enables a close watch on fellow diners.

Open: Lunch: Sun-Fri. **Dinner:** Mon-Sun. **Hours:** 12.30-3.00pm and 7.00-11.15pm. **Closed:** Good Friday and Boxing Day. **Credit cards accepted:** All major cards. **Number of seats:** 120. **Service:** Included. **Set price Lunch:** £21, £26 and £34. **Set price dinner:** £28 and £32. Wheelchair access. Private room seats 14. **Nearest tube station:** Bond Street. MAP REF: 1,B/2

Clarke's

124 Kensington Church Street, W8   ⑦⑥

071-221 9225   Lunch £30; Dinner £50

'Removes the worry of what to order'

The set prices for lunch and dinner at Clarke's have not changed since last year. That fact viewed alongside the increasingly tortuous schemes of some other restaurants to inflate bills makes the sums (£22, £26 and £37) which are inclusive of VAT, service and coffee, tea or infusion, seem reasonable if only because customers' calculations become so simple. Acting on the observation of a friend that she felt my review of Clarke's last year had been a little crisp concerning the lack of choice on the evening menus, a recent test meal was at lunchtime when there are three choices in each course, the last one being cheese or one of two desserts. One of the first courses illustrates something that is both a strength and a weakness of Clarke's. Potted wild salmon, cod and lobster with herbs was not a success; too stolid, too much of it, too much butter, too much tarragon and not enough other seasoning. The waiter said at the end of lunch that Sally Clarke also thought it wasn't good. I refrained from asking why, in that case, it was on the menu but it was left off the bill. Grilled John Dory sporting branches of dill and grilled baby chicken crowned with a wreath of flowering thyme came with identical vegetables (nice peas, carrots, fennel and butter beans) which lent a slightly mechanical air to the main course. As quite often is the case here, it was the dessert that was the triumph; poached pear with soured cream and biscotti that has the unusual but interesting addition of fennel seeds.

Dinner when there is no choice is presented as four rather fancier courses, although fancy with well-sourced ingredients rather than complex cooking procedures or in-depth sauces. A typical menu is warm sea kale and baby leeks with black truffle oil and shavings of Parmesan, followed by chargrilled fillet of turbot with morels, wild rice and wilted spinach, then cheeses with oatmeal biscuits and apple and finally blood orange and rhubarb trifle with pistachio nuts and notably luscious chocolate truffles with coffee or tea. It is a vivid, well-balanced and satisfying combo as long as you like everything in it. You might suppose the system was introduced in order to be almost febrilely responsive to the shifts of the marketplace but in fact menus are planned a week at a time. This does have the advantage of enabling you to match your visit to a menu that appeals – hoping that it also appeals to your companions. There I am being crisp again and it has to be acknowledged that Clarke's is perennially popular. So it should be based on the sophistication of much of the cooking, the keen service, the cool prettiness of the ground floor and the allure of an open kitchen which bestows equally desirability on the basement dining room, the wine list and its choice by the glass, but not because it suits those too idle to be interested in what they choose to eat.

CLARKE'S HAS a brainy wine list, as you'd expect from Sister Wendy's favourite restaurant (they ply her with champagne). This is the place to come to keep up with Randall Grahm's latest Bonny Doon whims, almost invariably worth a punt; and the best of the Californian rest, with its emphasis on the new and the unusual, also rewards the bold. Good burgundies (Rion, Méo-Camuzet, Leflaive) and Alsace wines from Ostertag; while Domaine de Limbardie makes a great house red. There are lots of interesting eaux de vie and brandies to terminate your day.

OPEN: Mon-Fri. **HOURS:** 12.30-2.00pm and 7.00-10.00pm. **CLOSED:** 2 weeks in August, Christmas and Easter. **CREDIT CARDS ACCEPTED:** Access, Visa. **NUMBER OF SEATS:** 90. **SERVICE:** Optional. **SET PRICE LUNCH:** £22 or £26. **SET PRICE DINNER:** £37. No-smoking area. Wheelchair access (but not lavatory). **NEAREST TUBE STATION:** Notting Hill Gate.**95**   MAP REF: 4,C/2

Connaught Hotel

Carlos Place, W1

071-499 7070   **£45**

'A refuge of classicism and tradition'

The more we crow about the improvement in London's restaurants, the more London's restaurant chefs push out the boundaries of technique and ingredients, the more treasured is the Connaught. This bastion of tradition with its stately- home kitchen in the hands of Michel Bourdin capable of Irish stew, oxtail and treacle sponge pudding as well as sole Jubilee, pintadeau en cocotte grand'mère aux morilles et champignons à la crème and petits legumes Frou Frou has become more accessible, in terms of price through set price menus available in both the Restaurant and the Grill Room which now, incidentally, offer identical à la carte lists. A test meal in the Grill, the more intimate of the two rooms, was 'a treat and no disappointment' to someone who 'has become blasé about eating in restaurants in a way that my parents find shocking'. From the table d'hôte, artichoke Jeanette was a perfectly cooked artichoke heart with tips of asparagus and the lightest of cheese sauces. Zephirs of sole Tout Paris (also listed on the carte as a speciality to be ordered in advance), feathery quenelles with lobster and champagne sauces, set up a yearning for the days when quenelles and grand sauces were still in fashion. Chef Bourdin likes to extend the repertoire of British dishes and promote them in the set price menus. Good cheeses and a chocolate mousse from the trolley as rich as some of the customers completed the meal. Eating à la carte there is more scope to test the French classicism of the kitchen or capitalize on game in season. If you are in that sort of mood – hotel guests may well be – it is possible to eat very simply, for example starting with kipper pâté and moving on to grilled kidneys and bacon with pommes purées. Service is formal, and it may slightly intimidate but remember for this gentlemanly club that isn't, the only conditions of membership are a reservation and, if you are a chap, a tie.

OPEN: RESTAURANT: Mon-Sun. GRILL ROOM: LUNCH: Mon-Fri.DINNER: Mon-Sun **HOURS:** RESTAURANT: 12.30-2.30pm and 6.30-10.30pm. GRILL ROOM: 12.30-2.30pm and 6.00-10.45pm. **CLOSED:** GRILL ROOM: Weekends January-April and Bank Holidays. **CREDIT CARDS ACCEPTED:** All major cards. **NUMBER OF SEATS:** 75 in Restaurant, 35 in Grill Room. **SERVICE:** 15%. **SET PRICE LUNCH:** £25-£30. **SET PRICE DINNER:** £35 (Grill Room only). Wheelchair access (but not ladies' lavatory). Private rooms seat 10 and 22. **NEAREST TUBE STATION:** Bond Street.

MAP REF: 1,B/2

The Cork and Bottle Wine Bar

44-46 Cranbourn Street, WC2

78

071-734 7807

£19

'A real wine bar in the West End wilderness'

At first a sense of gloom descends with the feet going down the stairs. A basement, and one in less than fragrant Leicester Square, does not seem enticing. However, after a survey of the huge range of wines and their moderate mark-ups the place begins to make good sense and its appeal to a better class of after-work drinker and Anglophone tourist is explained. The open-top sirloin sandwich on toasted baguette is recommended. Regulars also praise anything stewed meaning slow-cooked dishes such as lamb shank with lentils or ox tongue with mustard sauce. Although the *Daily Mail* described the food as Provençal-style, the salads and cold dishes displayed show shades of M&S: a love of chicken, prawns, pâté, avocado and rich dressings. Spicy chicken salad with apples and coriander leaves is old-fashioned but unusually subtle as – surprisingly – were prawns grilled with garlic. Salads to go with both were spruce. There are usually several hot fish dishes, a sausage-based dish and one for vegetarians. Service is kangaroo fashion – hop and get it. There is a sister or brother establishment at 25 Hanover Square (071-408 0935).

ONE REASON FOR the perennial appeal of the Cork and Bottle is that owner Don Hewitson actually likes wine. The selections change frequently; basic value for money, enthusiastically trumpeted through the familiar and useful italic-written notes on the list, remains constant. Selections of champagnes and New Zealand are extensive, though certain grandes marques (such as Mumm) are present in greater quantity than their quality would merit. Generally, however, the list is a model of balance, priced from £9.95 up. Try the accurately varietal Tarrawarra Vineyard Pinot Noir (£19.95), the gutsy 1989 Amador County Zinfandel (£14.95) or Château de Fuissés intense 1991 St Véran (£17.95) – if they're still on the list.

OPEN: Mon-Sun. **HOURS:** 11.00am-12.00am (12.00-10.30pm Sun). **CLOSED:** Christmas Day, Boxing Day and New Year's Day. **CREDIT CARDS ACCEPTED:** Access, AmEx, Visa. **NUMBER OF SEATS:** 85. **SERVICE:** Optional. Tables outside seat 12. **NEAREST TUBE STATION:** Leicester Square.   MAP REF: 1,E/1

The Criterion

224 Piccadilly, W1

071-925 0909   **£23**

'Beside Eros but not yet deserving of one'

The Conan Doyle aperçu quoted on the Criterion's menu, 'The sight of a friendly face in the great wilderness of London is a pleasant thing indeed to a lonely man', seems to imply that the visitors to this remarkable restaurant site are expected to be tourists. This is neither flattering to those who are nor to those who are not and Brian Baker's concise modern menu is certainly something Londoners should know about. Baker is a chef who at the age of twenty-one gained a Michelin star at Hambleton Hall and is now the rather unlikely provider of Cal-Ital dishes such as chilled red pepper and cucumber soup; thin-crust pizza; grilled marinated salmon with dill dressing; blueberry granita, in a dramatic, recently lovingly restored 1870s interior owned since 1949 by Forte plc. A test meal brought mixed results gastronomically but the overall feeling that, as a place to enjoy yourself, the Criterion is coming into its own. Asparagus and sorrel salad was all right but mean, even for £4.95. Linguine with smoked chicken artichoke hearts and a dressing of garlic and olive oil proved thoroughly enjoyable. A Pithiviers shaped savoury pastry containing goat's cheese and herbs was a satisfactory vegetarian option. Hock of ham was dry and came with a variety of stewed pulses in an oversweet sauce. Cheesecake was insipid. There is a set price deal whereby choosing dishes starred with an asterisk from the first and main courses means that you will be charged £10 which, if you strike lucky, represents very good value. Service is bonny. Drinks and light meals are no longer served at the tables on the terrace at the back (pity given the proximity to theatres and cinemas) but afternoon tea continues to be offered between 2.30pm and 5.30pm.

OPEN: LUNCH: Mon-Sun. DINNER: Mon-Sat. **HOURS:** 12.00-11.30pm (12.00-15.30pm Sun). **CLOSED:** Christmas Day and New Year's Day. **CREDIT CARDS ACCEPTED:** Access, AmEx, Diner's Club, Switch, Visa. **NUMBER OF SEATS:** 200. **SERVICE:** Optional. **SET PRICE LUNCH AND DINNER:** £10. Wheelchair access. **NEAREST TUBE STATION:** Piccadilly Circus.   MAP REF: 1,D/1

Daphne

83 Bayham Street, NW1   **80**

071-267 7322   LUNCH: £9; DINNER: £15

'For a short Greek holiday in Camden Town'

Camden Market is doing a pretty effective job of changing the face of the neighbourhood, wiping almost completely the connection that always used to be made between Camden Town and the Greek/Cypriot community, complete with its men's clubs, bakeries, general stores and tavernas. Fortunately all of those still flourish in the side streets and back streets, one of which is Bayham Street where Daphne occupies a terrace house. The restaurant attracts a loyal following, mostly the sort of English (I am one) who keep going to Greece in order to there feel themselves more alive. However, probably more fish is on offer here in NW1 than in all the islands of the Cyclades and a canny way to try it is either via the fish meze, a rolling meal of cold dips, squid, shellfish and whatever are the fish of the day or the combination platter of charcoal-grilled fish. The staples of the Greek/Cypriot formula are well done. The sheftalia test was passed with flying colours. At a recent meal only the ortikia (quail) was disappointing. Daphne may be able to change herself into a laurel tree but she can't render succulent that little farmed bird. Drink Greek wines and dream on. In chilly weather the ground-floor room is the one to book.

OPEN: Mon-Sat. HOURS: 12.00-2.40pm and 6.00-11.30pm. CLOSED: Christmas Day and Boxing Day. CREDIT CARDS ACCEPTED: Access, Mastercard, Visa. NUMBER OF SEATS: 85. SERVICE: Optional. Tables outside seat 25. Private room seats 30. Wheelchair access. NEAREST TUBE STATION: Camden Town.   MAP REF: 5,C/2

Daphne's

112 Draycott Avenue, SW3   **81**

071-589 4257 or 071-584 6883   £35

'Diana's been seen at Daphne's, but the food is worth investigating too'

Daphne's is now a fixture on the list of London restaurants Hard to Get a Table At. It has also attracted the dubious tribute of being compared to San Lorenzo, but for the glossy clientele rather than the food. Whether you would want to struggle to get a table in order to sit next to that lot strikes me as a moot point but just as owner Mogens Tholstrup cannot be blamed for his own good looks nor can he be held responsible for jowly men in gilt-buttoned blazers or women who think they have done something thrillingly sinful if they combine a protein with a carbohydrate. One of the strengths of interior designer Emily Tod-Hunter is not lighting (to prove my point go to Christopher's q.v.). Ironically neither the rooms nor their inhabitants are shown to best advantage in the muted electric light of evenings and nor do beams spot on chef Edward Baines' food which has grown more confident and beguiling of late.

At first glance the Italian menu looks predictable but a salad simply described as lobster salad reveals beneath discs and claws of sensitively cooked shellfish, white haricot beans mixed with shredded fresh spinach in a pool of oil which converts instantly to dressing with a squeeze of fresh lemon juice. The kitchen has mastered the trick of producing risotto for the masses and there was masses of risotto nero made sumpy with squid ink. Anolini, pasta half-moons stuffed unconventionally with vegetables, namely zucchini and zucchini flowers, light and trailing stock rather than melted butter bode well for the other pasta options. With fish and meat straightforward roasts and grills are probably the sensible way forward. If a test of a savvy kitchen is how well they make and dress a green salad, then Daphne's passes with flying colours. Desserts are not dull considering they are being proffered to the 'I'll just have a decaffeinated coffee' brigade. Such folk are turning down, among other confections, almond and fig tart with amaretto cream; crostata with apples; and soufflés in chocolate, Grand Marnier or lemon. Given the nature of the menu, the wine list could go further into Italy. Service for which you pay 'a 15% optional gratuity . . . solely at the customer's discretion' (how thoughtful) tries quite hard but can get into a muddle. I have seen a waiter, three loaded plates held high in the air, frozen as if in a tableau vivant, unable, until unlocked by a sympathetic colleague, to dispose of them.

OPEN: Mon-Sun. **HOURS:** 12.00-3.00pm (12.00-4.00pm Sun) and 7.00-11.30pm. **CLOSED:** Christmas Eve, Christmas Day, Boxing Day. **CREDIT CARDS ACCEPTED:** Access, AmEx, Delta, Diner's Club, Switch, Visa. **NUMBER OF SEATS:** 110. **SERVICE:** 15%, optional. Wheelchair access (but not lavatory). 30 seats outside. **NEAREST TUBE STATION:** South Kensington.   MAP REF: 2,D/3

Del Buongustaio

283 Putney Bridge Road, SW15   82

081-780 9361   LUNCH: £9.50; DINNER: £28

'Osteria con cucina is their description'

While its sister restaurant, Osteria Antica Bologna near Clapham Junction (q.v.), concentrates on mainly southern Italian cooking, here the food is firmly planted in the north of Italy. This Putney establishment is equally busy and successful and the mood of the quirkily decorated room similarly casual. A cover charge, however small (it is 80p) is annoying, but at least the bread is good and deserves a dip into the virgin olive oil left on the table. Olives marinated with orange slivers could, however, be fresher. The menu changes weekly and daily additions are always interesting. Some dishes or combinations of ingredients are rarely sighted in London; tagliolini with ardicchio; paidena Romagnola (pan-baked bread folded over proscuitto, spinach and cheese), Bolognese boned turkey stuffed with Italian sausage. There are only a handful of pasta choices but any one will satisfy as either first or main course and the risottos, such as calamari, mussels and prawns, are highly recommended and suitably rippling. An option for those with intrepid appetite is the five-course menu degustazione at £19.50, billed as chef Antonio Strillozzi's selections and a veritable culinary tour; a plate of savouries to start including mussels, cotechino sausage, grilled peppers and borlotti beans then flan di carciofi vecchio Piemonti (artichoke and Grana cheese pudding with a mushroom sauce), a pasta, a main meat dish and a dessert. The last continue a Tuscan theme with zuccotto Toscana (vanilla and chocolate cream semifreddo) or there is the option of a crumbly asiago cheese served with walnuts and celery. The set price lunch menu is excellent value. Sunday lunch served as three, four or five courses is a celebration of family life.

THIS IS A terrifically good Italo-Australian list. It's priced generously, cleverly organized (along what are best described as emotional lines) and informatively annotated. Don't miss Aldo Conterno's Barbera and Barolo, the Aglianico del Vulture and (for dessert) De Bartoli's Bukkuram; while from the other end of the world Petaluma's Rhine Riesling and Shaw & Smith's Sauvignon are two of the country's best for each varietal, and Seppelt's 1987 Sparkling Shiraz is an extraordinary chocolate-and-cherry-like red sparkling wine. Sounds horrible? Just try it.

OPEN: LUNCH: Fri-Sun. DINNER: Mon-Sat. **HOURS:** 12.00-3pm and 6.30-11.30pm (12.30-3.30 Sun). **CLOSED:** 10 days at Christmas. **CREDIT CARDS ACCEPTED:** Access, AmEx, Visa. **NUMBER OF SEATS:** 45. **SERVICE:** Optional 10% on large groups, 80p cover charge. **SET PRICE LUNCH:** £9.50. **SET PRICE DINNER:** £19.50. Wheelchair access (but not lavatory).**NEAREST TUBE STATION:** East Putney . **MAP REF:** 3,A/2

dell'Ugo

56 Frith Street, W1

071-734 8300   **£22**

'Where the eponymous olive oil flows like a river'

The flagship of Antony Worrall-Thompson's on-going Mediterranean odyssey, dell'Ugo is in fact three restaurants in one; a ground-floor bar and café serving meze and tapas, a first-floor bistro and second-floor armchair-and-linen dining room. As we have come to expect from AWT and, here, his henchman chef Mark Emberton, dishes are always one or two jumps ahead of what you might be expecting and combinations of ingredients and their flavours and textures come across as both adventurous and enticing. But the actuality can sometimes fail to live up to the written promise. Certain signature dishes are consistently successful; the kitchen is a dab hand with lamb shanks and whether the accompanying starch is flageolets, garlic and olive oil mash or couscous – evidence of the latest foray which is into Moroccan food – the result is sustaining and satisfying. But curiosities such as risotto cake with four cheeses or chermoula-grilled fishes with orange lentils appear to value novelty above substance and compatibility. However, this relentless faddishness is also the restaurant's greatest virtue and the constantly changing menu rewards the frequent visitor, of which there are many. For those who enjoy colourful variety – once matched only by the waistcoats of the catering trade's answer to Gianni Versace – dell'Ugo offers wide choice in prices as well as in dishes and an array of flavours which – like its Soho clientele – is audacious and often seductive. The selection of wines changes to some extent each month depending on which wine merchant is being allowed to promote his list.

OPEN: Mon-Sat. **HOURS:** 11.00am-12.30am. **CLOSED:** Bank Holidays. **CREDIT CARDS ACCEPTED:** All major cards. **NUMBER OF SEATS:** 180. **SERVICE:** Optional. **SET PRICE LUNCH AND DINNER:** £10 (Café only). Wheelchair access (but not lavatory). 20 seats outside. Private room seats 14. **NEAREST TUBE STATION:** Leicester Square/Tottenham Court Road.   MAP REF: 1,E/2

Diwana Bhel-Poori House

121 Drummond Street, NW1   **84**

07-387 5556   **£6**

'An ideologically and gastronomically sound little place'

Apart from a disastrous bright yellow custardy substance with the taste of nutmeg and the texture of Polyfilla which is served as one ingredient of the thali Annapurna dal and separately as a pudding, the Diwana Bhel-Poori is the sort of useful little restaurant every Londoner would like to have nearby. It is Indian, vegetarian, clean and cheap. It is not the place for a romantic tryst: lights are bright and the pine benches hard and too narrow for even the neatest rump. It is a T-shirt and shirtsleeve clientele, very respectable: on one visit, a Camden social worker, a pipesmoker from the synagogue, a couple from the Transport and General Workers building down the road, girls with girls. Start with dahi poori, lozenges of cucumber, coriander, potatoes, onions, yogurt and spices buried under shredded wheat and panni poori, chick-peas in a cold, sour sauce. Thalis are generous. Dosa, with its antimacassar-like pancake base and spicy topping, is, as always, gratifying to eye and palate.

OPEN: Mon-Sun. **HOURS:** 12.00-11.30pm. **CLOSED:** Christmas Day. **CREDIT CARDS ACCEPTED:** Access, AmEx, Diner's Club, Mastercard, Visa. **NUMBER OF SEATS:** 112. **SERVICE:** Optional. Wheelchair access (but not lavatory). **NEAREST TUBE STATIONS:** Euston/Warren Street/Euston Square.

Dorchester Hotel

53 Park Lane, W1   **85**

071-629 8888   **LUNCH £40; DINNER £50**

'A many-faceted semi-precious gem'

There are many ways to use this opulent hotel. I would recommend a meal in the **Dorchester Bar** where young Italian chef Paolo Sari who comes from Treviso in the Veneto is in charge of the short menu. At lunchtimes, as well as the menu, a carefully prepared range of cold antipasti – in other words a buffet – is offered for £12.50. In the evenings when you might catch the warm tones of a live jazz ensemble, the à la carte list supplies pasta dishes at which Sari excels – try bigoli con l'anatra, a Venetian wholewheat pasta sauced with shreds of duck, or panzerotti con carciofi e salsa al timo, artichoke-filled ravioli in a thyme sauce – or fish and meat dishes. An additional bonus in this bar that time forgot with its mustard-yellow leather bucket chairs and blue and white Delft-style tiles is the list of Italian wines served by the glass – fourteen in all. They are well sourced and, although I noticed that a party at the table next to ours that included two glossily dressed women who seemed to have just met the men they were with and sadly seemed to have discovered little in common did not seize the opportunity, you can explore via several glassfuls the progress that has been made in Italian wine making.

The Terrace restaurant where Dorchester head chef Willi Elsener rather touchingly adheres to the fastidious style of his mentor Anton Mosimann is now open only on Friday and Saturday evenings for dinner-dances. Since there are few places in London where, without membership, you can trip the light fantastic, this is worth noting.

The Grill Room, its Iberian guildhall splendour hardly altered since the day the Dorchester opened in 1931, provides traditional English food based as much as possible on indigenous produce. The straightforward grills of fish and meat are the more expensive options, not least because vegetable garnishes are priced separately at £3 per vegetable. Main courses (fully garnished) include roast Angus beef with Yorkshire pudding; braised oxtail; pot-roast shank of lamb with root vegetables plus dishes of the day in much the same style. Service is formal but amiable and there is pleasure to be gained from watching the dance of the trollies. The Dorchester Grill should not be forgotten if and when you are asked to prove the worth of British cooking.

The Oriental restaurant is of most interest to the average customer (average in bank balance that is) for the list of dim sum (not the tame set lunch) served at lunchtimes. Although each item is twice the price of Chinatown's Cantonese establishments the little parcels are fashioned by a master dim sum chef, Ngan Tung Cheung, and politely served. The à la carte menu is priced at Hong Kong level and for many the dishes seem disappointingly prissy and chaste. The Oriental is always well subscribed at its festivals welcoming chefs from the grand hotels of the East.

A VERY CORRECT WINE list, this, swelling in all the right grand-hotel places (like champagne and claret and cigars), and hitting all the right name and vintage buzzers. (Indeed some might prefer a younger range of Pauillacs than that on offer here, with more 1960s than 1970s, and Pichon-Lalande 1980 the youngest wine on the list.) Prices, given the milieu, are not roof-high (over 40 bottles under £20, for example). Portugal and South Africa have only token representation as yet, while Australia should match California for length if quality is the criterion.

OPEN: Mon-Sun. **HOURS:** 7.00-11.00am, 12.30-2.30pm and 6.00-11.00pm (7.30-11.00am, 12.30-2.30pm and 7.00-10.30pm Sun). **CREDIT CARDS ACCEPTED:** AmEx, Diner's Club, JCB, Mastercard. **NUMBER OF SEATS:** 81. **SERVICE:** Optional. **SET PRICE LUNCH:** £23.50. **SET PRICE DINNER:** £28. Wheelchair access. **NEAREST TUBE STATION:** Hyde Park Corner/Marble Arch. MAP REF: 1,A/2

Downstairs at One-Ninety

190 Queen's Gate, SW7

071-581 5666

(86)

£35

'Where they put the fun into fish'

As we sat down at our table in this basement restaurant reached down a
staircase with a carpet smelling like soupstains – a table ergonomically
unsound but adding two more covers to an already crowded space – a
merry Australian waiter came to scrawl in orange crayon on the white
paper tablecloth the names of the fishes available that day. The waiter
palpably was having more fun than we were and this particular bid for
camaraderie misfired. A pianist adds to the 'jollity' as do voices pitched to
hear one another over the music. This could be forgiven and forgotten or
put down to the crabbiness of the middle-aged were the cooking splendid
but a change of chef since last year's guide has rendered the dishes, how
shall we say, variable in their success. A pity, as the lively menu with many
dishes offered in two sizes at two prices is a sound concept but perhaps too
ambitious in its efforts to be all things to all men and women – those who
want potted shrimps with granary toast followed by steamed turbot with
hollandaise, new potatoes and spinach followed by grilled cod with lemon
confit, roast garlic and couscous and not forgetting those who want to eat
fish in beer batter with chips or meat or be vegetarian. However, the
raucous clientele which includes a Gordon Gecko element obviously find
some things being done right. The wine list certainly is.

A WIDE-AWAKE LIST, this: one of the few in London to get to grips with
the best of America, Australia and New Zealand as comprehensively as it
does with Bordeaux and Burgundy. The selection is extensive and
comparatively inexpensive: most of the wines are under £40, and if you
want to drink Mouton '82 you'll save no less than £298 by drinking it
here rather than at Le Gavroche. You know that you've come across
something out of the ordinary when you find Californian Alicante
Bouschet, historic white Jasnières and inky Spanish Priorato on the same
list. Plentiful halves and dessert wines complete the appeal.

OPEN: Mon-Sat. **HOURS:** 7.00pm-12.00am. **CLOSED:** Bank Holidays. **CREDIT
CARDS ACCEPTED:** Access, AmEx, Diner's Club, Mastercard, Visa. **NUMBER OF
SEATS:** 70.′ **SERVICE:** 10%. Private room seats 28. **NEAREST TUBE STATION:**
Gloucester Road.

The Eagle

159 Farringdon Road, EC1

071-837 1353

(87)

£12

'The pub with crostini rather than crisps'

Some of the patrons of the Eagle do not so much read newspapers over a
pint as write them. A slice of the clientele comes from the nearby
Guardian and *Independent* (at least until the move to Canary Wharf)

offices. Since journalists rate food and drink on a par with scoops it can be construed as a tribute to this revamping of the pub formula which Michael Belben and David Eyre of the Eagle pioneered and others have since copied. One end of the bar remains devoted to drinks, the other is given over to the Mediterranean food prepared in view of the customers. From behind this section of the bar laden with baskets of fresh produce might come dishes such as chorba, a thick Moroccan soup of beef, chickpeas and lemon hearty enough to keep the wolf from door-stepping; caldeirada, a Portuguese fish stew with fennel; clams and courgettes with saffron rice; grilled spicy Italian sausages with spinach and olives; roast duck salad with walnut vinaigrette; pear and almond tart; cheeses, often Spanish cheeses with quince membrillo. The list of dishes changes daily. The owners are keen to hang on to the fact that this is a pub and there is no compulsion to eat anything. Wines find their inspiration in almost as many countries as does the food. Popularity can have its downside; food is served from 12.30pm at lunchtime and by 12.40pm the place is packed. Be prepared to share or wait for a table. Be prepared also to pay for each item you order as you order it; there is no facility to run up a tab.

OPEN: Mon-Fri. **HOURS:** 12.30-2.30pm and 6.30-10.30pm. **CLOSED:** Bank Holidays. **CREDIT CARDS ACCEPTED:** None. **NUMBER OF SEATS:** 50. **SERVICE:** Optional. Wheelchair access (1 step). 4 tables outside. **NEAREST TUBE STATION:** Farringdon.

MAP REF: 8,C/1

Efes Kebab House

80 Great Titchfield Street, W1

071-636 1953 £19

'Good-value Turkish food in a business neighbourhood'

The combination of BBC staffers, rag traders, dark-suited, cigar-chomping Middle-Eastern businessmen and the occasional tourist or shopper straying north from Oxford Street provides a motley clientele for this long-established (since 1974) Turkish restaurant – secure tenure in W1 is attested by the obligatory display of signed celebrity photographs, in this case dedicated to 'The Brothers', co-owners Khazim and Ibrahim. But the atmosphere is relaxed and the waiters juggle deftly with different moods and motives. They are also helpful. A suggestion that we might augment the meze with arnavut cigeri (the tenderest deep-fried diced lamb's liver) was a good one, as was halep kebabi, a main-course mix of chicken and lamb topped with a spicy aubergine sauce. Sticky-sweet Turkish pastries are the obvious dessert but should you for some reason want apple pie you could also precede it with filet mignon and prawn cocktail. Set menus from £14 per person are good value. The premises are deceptively spacious – reaching back a block – and there is another branch, Efes II, at 175-177 Great Portland Street W1 (071-436 0600).

OPEN: Mon-Sat. **HOURS:** 12.00-11.30pm. **CLOSED:** Christmas Day to New Year's Day. **CREDIT CARDS ACCEPTED:** All major cards. **NUMBER OF SEATS:** 200. **SERVICE:** Optional. **SET PRICE LUNCH AND DINNER:** £14 and £15. No-smoking area. Wheelchair access (but not lavatory). 50 seats outside. Private room seats 50. **NEAREST TUBE STATION:** Oxford Circus/Great Portland Street. MAP REF: 1,D/3

Enoteca

28 Putney High Street, SW15

(89)

081-785 4449   LUNCH: £8; DINNER: £23

'A wine store with food from Apulia'

A number of Italian restaurants cluster near the bridges of South-West London. Consider River Café and Riva. Another that could be cited is Enoteca, located on the Putney side of Putney bridge. Chef/proprietor Guiseppe Turi is from Apulia and there is delectable evidence on the menu of dishes from that region located on the heel of the boot of Italy. Pugliese flavours can be found in assemblies such as fave con cime di rape, broad bean purée served with turnip tops, or marinated kid cooked in milk with herbs. Generally the daily specials tend to be more interesting than the dishes on the printed carte. Home-cured loin of pork is an ingredient worth singling out served either with ricotta and rocket or with fresh figs and there are inventive salads such as the one of fresh, near raw tuna with artichokes and quails' eggs dressed with a masterly finely chopped vegetable salsa. Rabbit and suckling pig frequently feature as starting points for main courses tugging this neighbourhood Italian into a more elevated position, gastronomically, than its unaffected decor and familial service might immediately suggest.

THE WINE LIST is not large. It is, though, full of the kind of bottled intrigue, mystery and suspense which makes Italy such rewarding territory for the wine sleuth. Unlike the equally interesting list at, say, the River Café, this one is broken down into wine styles, with each wine given useful descriptive notes: easy access to exciting drinking. Don't scorn the humble Cappello di Prete.

OPEN: LUNCH: Mon-Fri. DINNER: Mon-Sat. **HOURS:** 12.00-3.00pm and 7.00-11.30pm. **CLOSED:** Christmas. **CREDIT CARDS ACCEPTED:** Access, AmEx, Diner's Club, Visa. **NUMBER OF SEATS:** 35. **SERVICE:** Optional. **SET PRICE LUNCH:** £6.50 or £9.50. Private room seats 40. **NEAREST TUBE STATION:** Putney Bridge.

MAP REF: 3,A/2

Esarn Kheaw

314 Uxbridge Road, W12

(90)

081-743 8930   £15

'Northern Thai specialities near Shepherd's Bush'

The bright, busy premises of Esarn Kheaw are a landmark in the grey stretch of Uxbridge Road and the restaurant is also a beacon for food from the north-east of Thailand. Specialities from this area include charcuterie – notably sausages – but also provide particularly generous and pungent flavours achieved with coriander, chilli, lime juice and fish sauce. Proof lies in two of the raw salads; bamboo shoots with tart and hot flavourings and green papaya and peanuts humming with garlic and stinging with chilli. Last year's description of the house sausages as wind-dried Wall's still stands, but as a description rather than a criticism. Another house special is a satisfying dish of chicken poached in broth and aromatized with dill, basil and ground toasted rice. In this same meal, the curry note – one that should be sounded in the compilation of a Thai meal – was provided by a first-rate green vegetable curry. Ox tripe soup and the steamed mud fish of your choice have been noted as dishes to try next time.

OPEN: LUNCH: Mon-Fri. DINNER: Mon-Sun. **HOURS:** 12.00-3.00pm and 6.00-11.00pm. **CLOSED:** Bank Holidays. **CREDIT CARDS ACCEPTED:** Access, Amex, Diner's Club, Visa. **NUMBER OF SEATS:** 44. **SERVICE:** Optional. Wheelchair access. **NEAREST TUBE STATION:** Shepherds Bush.

L'Escargot Restaurant and Brasserie

48 Greek Street, W1   **91**

071-437 6828   **BRASSERIE £35; RESTAURANT £45**

*'A survivor of old Soho brought up to date
(on the ground floor)'*

Although stories in the notoriously gossipy catering trade of, how shall we say?, raised voices have been told about the kitchens of L'Escargot, the two chefs David Cavalier and Garry Hollihead are, at time of writing, continuing to divvy up responsibilities for the different floors at this historic Greek Street restaurant, originally L'Escargot Bienvenue. There is talk of the current owner Jimmy Lahoud looking for a new site for one of these formerly Michelin-starred lads but so far just talk. Upstairs at L'Escargot is the restaurant proper, an immaculate confection of revivalist deco in peppermint green and chrome. The food, however, looks back to the Eighties and, in its exquisite minimalism, seems out of place in the earthy Nineties. Every dish, from the small but perfectly formed bouillon of rabbit, the more robust fillet of beef, morel jus to a minutely decorated ginger parfait was lovingly constructed but however delicious, one feels that the chef's time might be better spent speeding up the appropriately snail-like service than painting culinary pictures. The idiom throughout L'Escargot is more or less consistently French and is actually deployed far more effectively downstairs in what is known imaginatively as the Ground Floor Restaurant. Here, less formal constraints – echoed in the cheerful decor – produce an altogether more appealing and friendly (cheaper) menu. At about two-thirds the price it offers three times the choice of its upstairs counterpart. There are fewer offal dishes about which massed restaurant critics once raved but highlights have included a salad of trotters, fried potatoes with sauce gribiche, hearty and full of flavour; poulet rôti aux truffes (for two), where the truffles did more than signal luxury; a wonderfully fragrant rhubarb compote, crème à la vanille. Menu prose shows an insouciant mix of languages. The wine list is reasonable and makes no bones about acknowledging what the New World can do.

OPEN: BRASSERIE: LUNCH: Mon-Fri. **DINNER:** Mon-Sat; **RESTAURANT: LUNCH:** Tue-Fri. **DINNER** Tue-Sat. **HOURS: BRASSERIE:** 1200-2.15pm and 6.00-11.15pm; **RESTAURANT:** 12.15-2.15pm and 7.00-10.45pm. **CREDIT CARDS ACCEPTED:** All major cards. **NUMBER OF SEATS:** 70 in Brasserie, 42 in Restaurant: **SERVICE:** Optional. **SET PRICE LUNCH AND DINNER:** £16 and £19 (Brasserie);£39 (Restaurant). No-smoking area. Wheelchair access (Brasserie only). Private room seats 48. **NEAREST TUBE STATION:** Leicester Square.   MAP REF: 1,E/2

L'Estaminet
14 Garrick Street, WC2   **92**

071-379 1432   **£25-£35**

'There is a tavern . . . in Covent Garden'

Having been praised, in this guide and elsewhere, for serving the sort of French bourgeois cooking that is becoming increasingly difficult to find in a town ruled by the dictates of food fashion, it seems perverse of the owners of L'Estaminet (meaning tavern) to lose some of the dishes that typifiy the style, or to prepare them carelessly as has been the case with soupe a l'oignon and crème caramel. The inclusion of a first course of tabbouleh could be justified on the grounds of French colonialism (even if nothing much else could) but serving it with smoked salmon? It is left to the smiling French manageress to convey some of the restaurant virtues of her country and to the grillades, a section of the menu in which côte de boeuf and Châteaubriand Béarnaise for two shine out. Preface those with une douzaine d'escargots en cassolette, or salade de harengs or some fresh asparagus and choose cheese afterwards – sensibly priced at £1.40 a piece – and you will probably be getting the best out of this agreeable, spacious establishment. The wine bar, La Tartine, in the basement where the eponymous open sandwiches and assiettes of charcuterie and cheese are served is useful to know about pre- or post-entertainment. The interest in its wine list shown by L'Estaminet mirrors that of the average restaurant in France located outside the country's wine-producing areas. In other words it is minimal.

OPEN: Mon-Sat. **HOURS:** 12.00-2.30pm and 5.45-11.30pm. **CLOSED:** Bank Holidays. **CREDIT CARDS ACCEPTED:** Access, AmEx, Visa. **NUMBER OF SEATS:** 60. **SERVICE:** 12.5% optiona, cover charge £1.50. No-smoking area. Wheelchair access (but not lavatory). Private room seats 25. **NEAREST TUBE STATION:** Leicester Square/Covent Garden.   MAP REF: 1,E/1

Feng Shang Floating Restaurant

opp. 15 Prince Albert Road, NW1

071-485 8137 **£20**

'A Chinese junk on Regent's Canal '

Floating restaurants have a fairly dismal history – with the one bright barque in 1994, Sylvain Ho Wing Cheong's Bateau Gourmand on the Thames, closing after only a few months – but Feng Shang with its upmarket Chinese menu and its enticingly gaudy craft on the canal in Regent s Park brings off the stunt. Owner Mr Wong seems to manage to be ever-present. His agreeable staff are unusually loyal and long-serving. Prices are relatively high – as seems inevitable when there is an aqueous Unique Selling Point – and efforts to make the food seem special through use of kiwi, strawberry and orange slice garnish can fall flat, but there are dishes well worth ordering: from the hot appetizers moushou pork with crunchy, gelatinous, dark mushrooms often tastes as if sautéed to order and steamed mussels, cockles or scallops with ginger, spring onions and chilli seem the right sort of thing to be eating as you look out on a passing duck or a moored houseboat. Steamed sole or bass are usually very good but establish the price when ordering. Pomegranate chicken is ironically one of the few dishes not to sport pieces of fruit and is an interesting mixture of chopped chicken wrapped in an egg-white skin (either steamed or deep-fried). Noodle assemblies are well done, particularly shredded chicken fried noodles. Should you be planning a treat for a north London vegetarian who likes to eat on the water (this is the sort of request I get constantly) note that Feng Shang has some Buddhist Zhai dishes of chicken and duck fashioned from wheat gluten.

OPEN: Mon-Sun. **HOURS:** 12.00-3.00pm and 6.00pm-12.00am (12.00pm-12.00am Sat-Sun). **CLOSED:** Sundays of Bank Holiday weekends and 4 days at Christmas. **CREDIT CARDS ACCEPTED:** All major cards. **NUMBER OF SEATS:** 130. **SERVICE:** Optional. **SET PRICE LUNCH AND DINNER:** £15, £20 and £25. Private room seats 50-80 **NEAREST TUBE STATION:** Camden Town. MAP REF: 5,B/1

The Fifth Floor Restaurant

Harvey Nichols,
Knightsbridge, SW1

071-235 5250 **£35**

'Not your average department store restaurant'

Reports on the finesse of Henry Harris's cooking in the restaurant that triumphantly completes the stylish food market of Harvey Nichols have been varied. Reason for this can be discovered in a lunch: a brilliant first course of sautéed lambs' sweetbreads and tongues with broad beans, mint and fresh tagliatelle made the other choice of a badly conceived, poorly executed salad of grilled Poilane bread, broccoli, piquillo peppers and gorgonzola dressing seem all the more disappointing. And the person who drew the short straw with that then had to contend with greasy roast poulet de Bresse with lemon and thyme while the winner of the first round went on to enjoy hugely roast wing of skate served with wilted vegetables (some wonderful spring onions) and a mustard and dill beurre blanc. Both did well with desserts of macadamia nut tart with thick, sunshine-yellow Jersey cream and apple and raisin crumble with ice cream. Harris has worked with Simon Hopkinson at Bibendum (q.v.) but has not yet developed his mentor's assured touch which allows risks to be taken in the realm of utter simplicity, as in serving a piece of roast chicken tout court. However, he shares Hopkinson's enthusiasm for capitalizing on the innate virtues in ingredients and when it works, as it does with Henry's black bean soup; native oysters with spicy sausages; langoustine frittata with crème fraiche and caviar; it is thrillingly unlike department store restaurant eating. Fifth Floor is a fortunate restaurant in its lack of bad tables; it is as diverting to be looking out at Knightsbridge and the eyries of the Hyde Park Hotel as it is to be watching food shoppers and the fashionably dressed long queue for the ever-popular, now-extended café section. Service seems to be trying harder these days and the women who check you in seem to resist hanging your coat according to the impact of its label. Look out for the promotions that enable you to buy wine at   wine shop prices. Other restaurants would do well to buy their coffee here; the blend served in the restaurant and the way the coffee is made is admirable.

DRAWING, AS IT DOES, on the stock squeezed into the pantry-like wine department of Harvey Nichols, the 'Big List' on the Fifth Floor is actually one of London's best. And most innovative, since shoppers are readier to risk all than diners are – on 11 wines from Penedès, seven from Chile, or 55 from Australia. English (two from the exemplary Thames Valley Vineyard), Moldovan and Israeli wines (the fine Yarden Cabernet Sauvignon is well worth its £25 tag) give the minnows of the wine world a well-deserved outing. This being Knightsbridge, of course, the list's heart beats in champagne: the 58 stocked here (including a dozen rosés) are definitive. Mark-ups in general are modest (though watch out for the 12.5% service surcharge). There are plenty of halves, too. Hours of happy drinking as you gaze down on ant life at street level.

OPEN: Mon-Sat. **HOURS:** 12.00-3.00pm (12.00-3.30pm Sat) and 6.30-11.30pm. **CLOSED:** Christmas Day and Boxing Day. **CREDIT CARDS ACCEPTED:** All major cards. **NUMBER OF SEATS:** 110. **SERVICE:** 12.5%. **SET PRICE LUNCH AND DINNER:** £18.50 and £21.50. Wheelchair access. **NEAREST TUBE STATION:** Knightsbridge. MAP REF: 2,F/4

Fire Station, The

150 Waterloo Road, SE1

95

071-620 2226 or 071-401 3267   LUNCH: £6; DINNER: £15

'Rings bells for a lot of people'

The Fire Station is one of those places that has so palpably filled a gap that you cannot understand why no one did it before. It is a large, noisy casual wine bar-cum-restaurant with good, inventive, food serving the Waterloo area and the South Bank. (Bar Central more or less opposite, a few doors down from the Old Vic, opened by chaps from Joe Allen and Orso has come along after.) The premises adjacent to Waterloo Station that were indeed once a fire station have been filled with an ad hoc collection of tables and chairs and the kitchen sited centre stage but little else has been added by way of 'decor'. Chef is Dan Evans who has proved his worth at Odette's and 192 Kensington Park Road (see entries). His menu not only changes constantly but might do so within a mealtime. (Alterations can easily be made on the blackboard list.) Late in the evening when demand has outstripped supply it has been known for food to run out altogether. You must be prepared to screech out your order above the din in the bar and wait for it to arrive which it might do in no particular order. Successes have been rabbit and prune pâté; skate on lentils in a vinegary dressing; casseroled lamb shanks. It would be a pity if the anarchic quality of the Fire Station that manages to support and celebrate, rather than thumb its nose, at the area were to be lost in increased efficiency. So far there no signs that this will happen. I have heard that Dan Evans is looking for his own premises but the cooking style should by then be firmly set.

OPEN: Mon-Sat. **HOURS:** 12.00-11.00pm. **CLOSED:** Public holidays. **CREDIT CARDS ACCEPTED:** AmEx, Diner's Club, Switch, Visa. **NUMBER OF SEATS:** 80. **SERVICE:** 10% on parties of 8 or more. Wheelchair access (but not lavatory). Private room seats 40. **NEAREST TUBE STATION:** Waterloo.

First Floor

186 Portobello Road, W11

071-243 0072 **£30**

'Groovy grows up'

'First rate' was the verdict of a test meal at Sunday lunchtime. First Floor, above a pub in Portobello Road, from originally being a happening hang-out, seems to have picked itself, up, shaken itself down and become a serious place to eat. Even the clientele now look like 'models for the Racing Green catalogue'. However, the decor still conveys a sense of anarchy. The high-ceilinged room has a dirty paint job, a crystal chandelier, garden furniture mixed with Victorian chairs, sculpted heads and torsos, the odd drift of river gravel and some dried (dead?) flowers in Italianate baskets. Were you to pigeonhole the menu, it would be under that graceless phrase Cal-Ital but just as you might make a farinaceous start to a meal with polenta stuffed with marinated goat's cheese and sun-dried tomatoes with roast garlic and olive oil or spinach gnocchi with cumin-braised radicchio and watercress dressing, so you could with blini with soured cream, beluga caviar and smoked salmon. At £6.50, the beluga must be little more than emblematic. The main courses at that Sunday lunch were shellfish platter with saffron tapenade, peppered lime dressing and croûtons; pan-fried sturgeon with potato, sun-dried tomatoes and seaweed salad. Particularly impressive culinary legerdemain was shown in ricotta chocolate and strega fritters, a dessert I have only had in other place in Britain, the Walnut Tree Inn near Abergavenny. The recipe for these little deep-fried balls of delight is in *Leaves from the Walnut Tree* by Ann and Franco Taruschio (Pavilion £15.99). Note that live jazz is played on Sundays and also note that there is a cover charge of £1.50 per person.

OPEN: Mon-Sun. **HOURS:** 10.00am-4.00pm and 7.30pm-1.00am (12.00-10.00pm Sun). **CLOSED:** Christmas Day and New Year's Day. **CREDIT CARDS ACCEPTED:** Access, AmEx, Diner's Club, Visa. **NUMBER OF SEATS:** 100. **SERVICE:** Optional, £1.50 cover charge. **SET PRICE LUNCH:** £24.50. **SET PRICE DINNER:** £30. Private room seats 45. **NEAREST TUBE STATION:** Ladbroke Grove. **MAP REF:** 4,A/1

Florians

4 Topsfield Parade,
Middle Lane, N8

97

081-348 8348   **£24**

*'One of the reasons for the gastronomic reputation
of Crouch End'*

To the passer-by, Florians looks much like any local wine bar. The menu, however, is as refreshing as the decor is generic and offers an appealing choice of what once represented the Italian new wave. In a weekly-changing menu recurrent themes are chargrill, risotti of which a particularly delicious variation is made with artichoke and Parmesan, and the inevitable balsamic vinegar put to fine use in, for example, a warm salad of chicken livers, grapes and pine kernels. There are more elaborate dishes such as Roman-style artichoke with grilled scamorza (provolone-type cheese) and caponata. Desserts are somewhat less adventurous and have a discernible English accent to them, although the dessert menu is accompanied by a dizzying list of grappe. There are three eating areas – the front bar (with its own simpler menu and set-price special), a small, bright mezzanine and a larger painted- brick rear dining room. All three enjoy informed and friendly service from people who clearly care about the food and wines and are justifiably proud of them.

THIS ALL-ITALIAN list is full of well-selected and (for once) usefully annotated wines: best buys include Cavalchina's Bianco di Custoza, Candido's Cappello di Prete and D'Angelo's Aglianico del Vulture, all of them under £13.50. Six amari (including the deliciously herbal Averna from Sicily) will settle the most disputatious stomach. The fearless hold something in reserve for the 21 grappe, succinctly described as 'a sort of human central heating'. Keep your eye on the thermostat.

OPEN: Mon-Sun. **HOURS:** RESTAURANT: 12.00-3.00pm and 7.00-11.00pm. BAR: 12.00-11.00pm. **CLOSED:** Christmas Day, Boxing Day and New Year's Day. **CREDIT CARDS ACCEPTED:** Access, Visa. **NUMBER OF SEATS:** 65 in restaurant, 30 in bar. **SERVICE:** Optional. **SET PRICE LUNCH AND DINNER:** £5.95 (bar only). Wheelchair access. 25 seats outside. Private room seats 25. **NEAREST TUBE STATION:** Highgate.

La Fontana

101 Pimlico Road, SW1

●98

071-730 6630/3187   **£30-£33**

'The flavour of white truffles all year round'

La Fontana is a long-established Italian restaurant which you might not choose for the decor – a Fifties interpretation of rustic – or the prices which are high (plus cover charge, separately priced vegetables and exuberantly marked-up wines) or the sometimes exigent service, its overbearing quality exaggerated when equipped with a spirit lamp, a sauté pan and some alcohol to flame, but which is worth seeking out for the food. Owner Signor Pavesi goes to considerable lengths to procure white truffles each year – in season late autumn/early winter – and out of season presents them according to his own recipes as a sauce (for carpaccio, bresaola and vegetables) or as a purée (suited to risotto or taglialerini). The dishes of the day, presented as a typed list, are worth investigating. Cooking in salmi involves marinating and then part-sautéeing, part casseroling the meat, usually game of some kind. L'osso bucco alla Milanese is excellent, avoiding – which is rare in Italian restaurants – an overdose of tomatoes. I must admit never straying outside the list headed Oggio Abbiano but cooking standards can be presumed not to fall apart for the printed menu. The dessert Il Nostro Zabaglione, sounding suitably godfather-like, is another opportunity for a waiter to stand nearby and get up to a lot of meaningful whisking. But it is to delicious effect.

OPEN: Mon-Sun. **HOURS:** 12.00-2.30pm and 7.00-11.30pm. **CLOSED:** Bank Holidays. **CREDIT CARDS ACCEPTED:** All major cards. **NUMBER OF SEATS:** 40. **SERVICE:** Optional, cover charge £1.50. Wheelchair access (but not lavatory). **NEAREST TUBE STATION:** Sloane Square.   MAP REF: 2,E/2

Four Seasons Restaurant

Four Seasons Hotel,
Park Lane, W1

●99

071-499 0888   **£57**

'The Four Seasons holds on to its reputation for interesting hotel dining'

That *grand luxe* hotels should try hard with their restaurants has become axiomatic but the Four Seasons (formerly the Inn on the Park) has, in terms of chefs, done it with with more élan than usual; playing for higher stakes, they persuaded Bruno Loubet (see Bistrot Bruno) to join them from Le Petit Blanc in Oxford and having lost him to his vision of feeding more of the people more of the time, invested in another relatively quirky young chap, Jean-Christophe Novelli. Right from the start Novelli has coped well and his menu grows in confidence, creativity and sheer choice.

Menus, naturally enough, change according to season. From a summer list typically enticing dishes are (in the English translation) langoustine escabeche, coriander seeds, light beetroot oil and spring onions; warm poached lobster sausage, couscous with peppers, ginger and cardamom; supreme of Bresse chicken poached in asparagus juice, served with leeks and tomato; spit-roast quail stuffed with sage, served with creamy Swiss chard and grapes. Novelli's passion for offal has been muted somewhat, doubtless a function of his current target audience, but for those who want it there is the butcher's plate of veal sweetbread, poached ox tongue and ox tail with potato and celeriac purée. Contrarily it is the most expensive main course at £27. Certain dishes marked with an asterisk are advertised as being low in calories, cholesterol and fat, but if you have calories to spare there are delectable desserts such as a crisp mango and almond tart served with passion fruit sorbet or hot bitter chocolate cake served with white chocolate ice cream. To some extent Novelli is still feeling his way and there can be disappointments – a dull, salty tartare of cured, marinated and smoked wild trout is one I can name – but the Four Seasons is the place to keep in mind for an adventurous meal in staid over-stuffed surroundings (guest chef at the Four Seasons Jean-Georges Vongerichten asked me in wide-eyed innocence, 'Why can't London hotel eating be fun?'). Service is well-drilled and pleasant with it.

THIS IS A SOUND but unexciting wine list: all the numerical choice you expect from a grand hotel, with a recognition that there is grape life beyond France's classical quarters. Yet the selections are often sleepy, safety-first ones: large producers lord it over the small fry whose wines are often more interesting and better value. The Italian zone is particularly disappointing. Bottles worth trying include the burgundies of Jadot and Leflaive, Wynns' and Penfolds' wines from Australia, and the single Cabernet Sauvignon from Ridge. Prices are as you feared.

OPEN: Mon-Sun. **HOURS:** 12.30-3.00pm and 7.00-10.30pm. **CREDIT CARDS ACCEPTED:** Access, AmEx, Diner's Club, Visa. **NUMBER OF SEATS:** 55. **SERVICE:** Included. **SET PRICE LUNCH:** £25 (Mon-Sat); £28 (Sun). **SET PRICE DINNER:** £45. Wheelchair access. **NEAREST TUBE STATION:** Hyde Park Corner/Green Park.

MAP REF: 1,A/1

Four Seasons

84 Queensway, W2   (100)

071-229 4320

'A wham-bam Chinese in multi-cultural Bayswater'

Maybe it's the queues at the door, maybe the high-velocity service, or maybe it's the 'Thank you' with which the colourful, glossy dishes are slammed down on to the green tablecloths, but there's a sense of frenzied excitement about this slightly cramped restaurant on Bayswater's street of many cultures. Chinese favourites such as anise-spiced crispy duck and a wide range of hot-plate 'sizzling' dishes are larded with others which show a Malaysian influence. Beef, unusually, can be enjoyed in as many variants as pork; and there's a range of bean curd dishes: the stuffed bean curd (which simply means it has a little minced pork grafted into it) served in a hot pot with simmered vegetables is one of the house specialities. Fresh cuttlefish, combining the look of squid with the texture of mid-life octopus, is served in a doctrinal black bean sauce; if you opt for one of the Kong Po dishes (diced chicken, diced port or bean curd), prepare for temporary taste-bud eclipse. Good Japanese Sawanotsuro sake partners food of these firework flavours better than the workaday wines of the list. It's back to earth with a bump at the end: the towels are cold, the orange segments occasionally mouldy. But the main attraction is sound, as the preponderance of Chinese customers indicates.

OPEN: Mon-Sun. **HOURS:** 12.00-11.30pm. **CREDIT CARDS ACCEPTED:** All major cards. **SERVICE:** 12.5%. **SET PRICE DINNER:** £10.50, £13.50, £16 (for minimum of 2). Wheelchair access. **NEAREST TUBE STATION:** Bayswater.

 # The French House Dining Room

49 Dean Street, W1

071-437 2477 **£22**

'A gem of a restaurant'

I can't think of a restaurant to compare with the French House Dining Room, except, presumably, chef/proprietors Margot and Fergus Henderson's new venture St John in Farringdon (26 St John Street EC1, 071-251 0848) which opens after this guide goes to press, but I wish there were many like it all over London. It is unpretentious in look but because it is above a famously louche Soho pub carries a sort of frisson, due in some part to a brothel-y decor involving mirrors and a dark red tortoiseshell pattern wallpaper. On a Saturday in summer a lunch of freshly boiled whole crab served with an upstanding mayonnaise and excellent salty brown bread, tender grilled ox tongue with a salad of dandelion leaves and strips of sautéed red onions and peeled fresh broad beans as a side dish followed by blackberry ice cream was pretty well faultless. There is always a soup, for example greens and wild garlic, usually an assortment of grilled vegetables such as rocket, olives, sweet potato and tomato, an imaginative salad, say leeks with caper and gherkin vinaigrette, and in the main course grilled fish, a casserole, a roasted bird, a vegetarian assembly and often something based on homemade sausages. Cheeses are well chosen and served in their prime. There is Welsh rarebit as well as puddings like boiled orange cake, black bottom tart and Hokey Pokey ice cream. The wine list is short, French and fairly priced. Service manages the delicate balance of professionalism and friendliness.

OPEN: Mon-Sun. **HOURS:** 12.30-3.00pm and 6.30-11.30pm. **CLOSED:** Bank Holidays. **CREDIT CARDS ACCEPTED:** AmEx, Diner's Club, Mastercard, Switch, Visa. **NUMBER OF SEATS:** 30. **SERVICE:** Optional. **NEAREST TUBE STATION:** Piccadilly Circus/Leicester Square. **MAP REF:** 1,E/2

Fulham Road

257-259 Fulham Road, SW3

071-351 7823

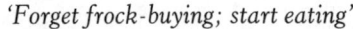

LUNCH: £27; DINNER: £40

'Forget frock-buying; start eating'

The prosaically named Fulham Road is the most recent establishment of restaurateur Stephen Bull who having named a restaurant and a bistro after himself (see entries) had to turn to an address. He is joined in the venture by chef Richard Corrigan who has worked before with Bull at his Marylebone restaurant and also at the Irish restaurant Mulligan's (Corrigan is himself Irish) and at Bentley's in Swallow Street where his inventive meat dishes rather robbed the traditional fish restaurant of its finniness. Much has been made in the gastronomic press of the number of offal dishes on his Fulham Road menu as if it is lèse-majesté to expect a clientele who might hail from Chelsea and South Kensington to eat anything less than a prime cut. In fact there are plenty of alternatives to cheek and tongue, kidneys and sweetbreads, pig's head faggots and black pudding, eye of newt and toe of frog, wool of bat and tongue of dog. A pasta-wrapped bundle of chard – called canneloni – and field mushroom confit – a slightly meaningless description – accompany the daube of ox cheek and tongue bathed in rich, heady juices. Corrigan is a master of black pudding and pig's head faggots, shredded red cabbage and porcini round it out to a eminently satisfactory plateful. But try also monkfish wrapped in cured ham with globe artichokes and crab juices or just a rump steak burger with bacon and marjoram brioche where in place of a melted cheese slice is slowly dissolving foie gras butter. First courses that have found approval are salad of marinated skate with Jerusalem artichokes and mint; tartare of veal; roast langoustines with lemon couscous. Corrigan's heart seems less in desserts, but I might be confusing his heart with mine. The chocolate truffles and biscuits glazed with orange icing that come with coffee are sweetness enough to complete the meal. The premises that in one incarnation before last were the restaurant Le Français have been designed by David Collins, orchestrator of La Tante Claire, The Canteen, The Square and Harvey's in Wandsworth. The jury of restaurant writers seems out on this one, but I like the soft painted squares on the wall that range in tone from cream to beige, the black and white photos of local architectural furniture, the playful jungle-book fabric that covers the banquettes, the strange linen blinds that pull up from below, and the comfortable Starck-influenced chairs. Service is elegantly and efficiently led by Marian Scutton.

LIKE ALL THE LISTS in which Stephen Bull has had a hand, this is eclectic, intelligent and well-ordered, its fine wine selections (like white burgundy from Dauvissat, Sauzet and Blain-Gagnard, and red from Michelot, Pousse d'Or and Mongeard-Mugneret) as astute as its New World souvenirs (from Ca' del Solo, Shaw & Smith and Qupé among others). Reds from Languedoc provide some of the best value under £20 (try Domaine de Limbardie's lively Vins de Pays des Coteaux de Murviel or the appropriately stony Corbières of Château Les Ollieux).

Open: Mon-Sun. **Hours:** 12.00-2.15pm and 6.30-12.00pm. **Closed:** Christmas Day and Good Friday. **Credit cards accepted:** Access, Amex, Visa. **Number of seats:** 80. **Service:** Optional. **Set price lunch:** £14.50 or £17.50. Wheelchair access (but not lavatory). Private room seats 20. **Nearest tube station:** South Kensington. MAP REF: 2,B/3

Fung Shing

15 Lisle Street, WC2 ⬤103

071-437 1539 or 071-734 0284 **£18**

'The most consistently good Cantonese restaurant in Chinatown'

A long-serving Cantonese chef who is a partner in the business is one of the clues to the success and steadiness of this deservedly popular Chinatown restaurant. The manager known as Jimmy Jim also goes to unusual lengths to cherish his clientele, both Oriental and Occidental. Faithful, interested and appreciative diners at Fung Shing are occasionally invited to special banquets held on the first floor where, it has to be said, the heights of Cantonese cooking are scaled. One way to organize this for yourself is to ring the restaurant and discuss a menu based on what you want to spend and what you like and don't like to eat. However, a casual visit ordering from the à la carte (forget the set menus) can also be extremely rewarding. My inclination is to skip the appetizers, except perhaps spicy jelly fish with chicken and pickles, and go straight into an array of main courses. Many of the most interesting ones can be found under the heading Chef Special. The cost might deflect you from whole abalone or double-boiled fluffy supreme shark's fin – flavours as subtle and fugitive as they are expensive – but try crispy spicy eel; stewed duck with yam in pot (provided you like the flavour of fermented bean curd); grilled minced pork with salted fish. A hokey dish that everyone loves (as much as they secretly love sweet and sour pork) is barbecued beef. A bean curd dish introduces a nicely bland note; I like the bean curd with prawns. Ask for the daily green vegetable and enjoy it made smoky with garlic. Under Miscellaneous is stir-fried milk with scrambled egg white; wonderfully soothing and serene. Service usually manages to deal nimbly with the crowds and if you are left to drink in the bar area while waiting for a table, at least the wine list is way above average for Chinatown.

Open: Mon-Sun. **Hours:** 12.00-11.30pm. **Closed:** Christmas Eve, Christmas Day and Boxing Day. **Credit cards accepted:** All major cards. **Number of seats:** 85. **Service:** Optional. **Set price lunch and dinner:** £12.50. Private room seats 28. **Nearest tube station:** Leicester Square/Piccadilly Circus.

MAP REF: 1,E/1

El Gaucho

125 Sydney Street, SW3

104

071-376 8514   £12 (Bring Your Own Wine)

'Eat up your meat like a big boy'

In Chelsea Farmers' Market, El Gaucho lassoes the notion of Argentinian food with theme-park brio. Sited in a Tudor-revival hut decorated with cartoons depicting gauchos and insulated with remorseless salsa music on tapes, it conveys that you are here for the beef or, as they put it, bife (imported chilled from Argentina as at the Gaucho Grill q.v. but no relation). On the rotisserie next to the grill are chickens. These two items form the core of the menu. To start there is a creditable empanada (pastry stuffed with chopped beef) or chorizo (spicy sausage) or choclo (corn on the cob). This last can be overcooked rendering the corn's innate sugariness as very palpable starch. The steaks are are good meat and the cook gauges grilling times skilfully. Baked potatoes, mixed salad and a rather tame salsa are as fancy as the accompaniments get. There is a risk of chicken being rendered dry by twirling on the rotisserie and really the point of El Gaucho is sitting in what seems like an unlikely spot for SW3 and affirming your masculinity by sawing up 300 grams of red-blooded meat from the pampas presented on a plank. A soothing conclusion to this activity is eating the house pastry layered with that friend of the sweet tooth, dulce de leche. El Gaucho is unlicensed but next door at Les Caves de Guillotine are bottles of robust Argentinian red wine on sale.

OPEN: Tue-Sun. **HOURS:** 12.00-3.00pm and 7.00-11.00pm. **CREDIT CARDS ACCEPTED:** None. **NUMBER OF SEATS:** 50. **SERVICE:** Optional. Wheelchair access (but not lavatory). Tables outside seat 50. **NEAREST TUBE STATION:** South Kensington/Sloane Square.   MAP REF: 2,C/2

The Gaucho Grill

19 Swallow Street, W1

105

071-734 4040   LUNCH: £15; DINNER: £23

'Argentinian beef grilled in the restaurant'

For a long time, steak has been the favourite main course for the British customer eating out. Doubts about the wisdom these days of ingesting good old British beef has doubtless done no harm to the restaurants springing up featuring Argentinian beef. The Gaucho Grill, owned by the same company as runs Calzone pizza parlours and the neighbouring Down Mexico Way, imports not only the beef (aged in vacuum packs) but the assado (grill) with its concave bars that are apparently beneficial to the process. If you like steaks you can sit on cowhide-covered chairs in dimly lit but deliberately designed basement premises watching your choice of cut – rump, sirloin, fillet or rib-eye – cooked on the grill at one end of the room. It is good meat and there are various salsas and sauces to cheer it on. Other meats, chicken and fish are also available. Start with black bean soup, grilled sweetbreads (mollejas) or empanadas and finish with flan con dulce de leche. Drink South American wines.

Open: Mon-Sun. **Hours:** 12.00-3.00pm and 5.00pm-12.00am (12.00pm-12.00am Sat; 12.00-10.30pm Sun). **Closed:** Christmas. **Credit cards accepted:** All major cards. **Number of seats:** 120. **Service:** Optional. **Nearest tube station:** Piccadilly.   MAP REF: 1,C/1

La Gaulette
53 Cleveland Street, W1

071-580 7608 or 071-323 4210   £28

'Miles away from a British fish restaurant'

Fish, household or exotic, cooked French-style or the way they might in Mauritius is the unique selling point of this lively restaurant located in a quiet street in Fitzrovia (as the area now likes to be known). Chef/proprietor Sylvain Ho Wing Cheong is related to the more simply styled Chez Liline (101 Stroud Green Road, N4; 071-263 6550) but unless business or domestic life keep you close to Finsbury Park, this is, to my mind, the preferable place, in terms of atmosphere and service, for trying bourgeois, vacqua, red snapper, capitain and other warm-water fish (according to availability) galvanized with spicy sauces or the more familiar varieties such as salmon, sole and sea bass which appreciate creamier, more stealthy accompaniments. Shellfish plays a large part in the menu. A treat is lobster plainly grilled with herbs or prepared à la Mauricienne, a phrase that you can take to mean involving ginger, chilli, tomatoes, herbs, spices and pickled lime. Crab comes this way too or Chinoise, with ginger and spring onion. Requests to inspect a fish before cooking are cheerfully met and the creature will be brought from the kitchen located downstream from a stuffed and mounted marlin. Last year's report noted the high price of separately priced vegetables. Rice, salad or vegetables are now included in the main-course prices. Jolly good show. Set price lunch is a relative bargain.

Open: Lunch: Mon-Fri. **Dinner:** Mon-Sat. **Hours:** 12.00-3.00pm and 6.30-11.00pm. **Closed:** Bank Holidays exc Good Friday. **Credit cards accepted:** Access, AmEx, Diner's Club, JCB, Mastercard, Visa. **Number of seats:** 70. **Service:** Optional. **Set price lunch:** £13.25 (2 courses) and £14.95 (3 courses). **Set price dinner:** £18 (3 courses) and £24 (menu gastronomique). Private room seats 30. **Nearest tube station:** Goodge Street/Warren Street/Great Portland Street.   MAP REF: 1,D/3

 # Le Gavroche
43 Upper Brook Street, W1

071-408 0881 or 071-499 1826   £70

'The luxury of culinary skill and good service'

Michel Roux, in some ways literally embodies the achievement of the Roux Brothers with regards to eating out in this country. Zee bruzzairs who opened Le Gavroche in Sloane Street in 1967 not only brought a new style of French cooking and of menu – short and personal – to a grateful public (they had both previously worked in private service) but headed up and trained a network that gradually spread through the upper reaches of British catering. The young Michel with a London accent that slips effortlessly into perfect French seems to symbolize the achievement. His presence at Le Gavroche has kept this stately liner at a steady pace, perhaps even accelerated it slightly, and the removal of one Michelin star (from three to two) that marked his ascendance seems a formality rather than a judgement. In view of the high prices often charged these days for simplistic food, the bargain of the set price lunch at Le Gavroche assumes even greater lustre. If two people confine themselves to a bottle of one of the invariably remarkably good wines that are included in the menu, they eat canapés, three courses, coffee and petits fours and drink for £72 tax and service included. The service is as balletic as for à la carte, the tables as widely spaced, the seats as comfortable; it is one of London's best deals. A set price lunch recently enjoyed included a dish, cuisse de lapin grillé et confite sur pommes sautées a l'ail et cêpes, that brought to the plate the sort of gastronomic romances you read about a French maman's home cooking and a (shared) bottle of Chateau Clerc Milon '83 (listed at £57 on the restaurant's wine list). For dessert there were perfect sorbets of strawberry, lemon and melon, the last proving it by far the best way to eat melon. It is however, well worth eating à la carte. The cooking and presentation moves up in gear but without necessarily becoming ostentatiously rich, as can be gathered from the sublime essence of tomato that surrounds charred langoustine in a first course; the startling appearance and incredible flavour of Bresse pigeon cooked en vessie with celery and celeriac in the main course. Service is impeccable and I have seen small children charmed. The tendency of French Michelin-starred establishments to flog souvenirs has not been resisted – you can buy a Gavroche gold badge for £10, a statuette for £70. I would rather have lunch.

THIS IS A LIST of magnificent dimensions, and magnificent expense, for French fine wines. The big names lie so thickly scattered in the cellar that it's tempting to think that some among them are purchased on name alone – such as the two vintages of Château Grillet, a single-property AOC rarely justifying its celebrity; or the largely disappointing white wines of the top Médoc properties. Most of the clarets, however, and (since the arrival of Thierry Tomasin as sommelier) an increasing number of the burgundies do merit their place on the list; the spread of vintages for a wide range of single properties is particularly impressive. What does the Gavroche, though, offer those unable to pay three-figure prices? Less consequential Bordeaux châteaux and Burgundy vineyards, in the main, though the Loire, Alsace and the Rhîne offer fair choice. There are good vintage ports and half bottles.

OPEN: Mon-Fri. **HOURS:** 12.00-2.00pm and 7.00-11.00pm. **CLOSED:** Bank Holidays, 23 December-3 January. **CREDIT CARDS ACCEPTED:** Access, AmEx, Eurocard, Mastercard, Visa. **NUMBER OF SEATS:** 60. **SERVICE:** Optional. **SET PRICE LUNCH:** £36. **SET PRICE DINNER:** £48. Private room seats 20. **NEAREST TUBE STATION:** Marble Arch. **MAP REF:** 1,A/3

The Gay Hussar

2 Greek Street, W1

108

071-437 0973 £30

'Hungarian soul food'

The immutability – more or less – of the Gay Hussar becomes ever more precious as Soho mutates. Inevitably its current ownership by a company called Restaurant Partnership plc rather than by the workers co-operative (of a sort) organized by its founder Victor Sassie removes some of the singularity from the place but mercifully no health nut has been allowed to reduce the high levels of animal protein, goose fat and soured cream that course through the Hungarian menu. Those who perceive gender preferences in food would label the dishes 'masculine' but my contention is that we all, girls included, have moments of need for smoked breast of goose with the baked beans called scholet; pancakes filled with goulash; egg dumplings (galuska) and sweet cheese pancakes (turos palacsinta). It is nurturing, comforting food served in old-fashioned quantity. There are lighter items to balance a meal. There is even a vegetarian dish presented in very small print. Lunchtime trade, however, tends towards the chaps with still some evidence of the original faithful clientele of left-wing politicians and publishing types bolstered now by affluent Eastern bloc refugees. The dining room remains cosy and cramped, the red-plush cushions of the banquettes plump with whispered indiscretions.

Open: Mon-Sat. **Hours:** 12.30-2.30pm and 5.30-10.45pm. **Closed:** Bank Holidays. **Credit cards accepted:** All major cards. **Number of seats:** 70. **Service:** 12.5%. **Set price lunch:** £16. Wheelchair access (but not lavatory). Private room seats 12. **Nearest tube station:** Tottenham Court Road. **MAP REF:** 1,E/2

Geales Fish Restaurant

2 Farmer Street, W8

071-727 7969 £14

'Purveyors of high-class fish and chips to the gentry'

Geales was established in 1919, a date which most Notting Hill Gate residents would believe was BNHG (before Notting Hill Gate). It has not deviated from its aim to sell sparklingly fresh fish (and chips) and not a great deal else, but you could make a three-course event of eating here (if appetite allows) starting with the good homemade fish soup or deep-fried clams (tartare sauce 40p extra), choosing one of the fishes of the catch delivered that day, chips and mushy peas and finishing with the cinnamon-spiced apple crumble (served with cream but crying out for custard). When you have to queue for a table as usually you have to – no bookings taken – it is tempting to go ahead and make a real meal of it. Both clientele and decor are a mix of the plain and showbizzy, the wall ornamentation of the cosy rooms being an eccentric collage of nautical prints and gold discs. The admirably reasonably priced wines must be paid for separately and in cash.

OPEN: Tue-Sat. **HOURS:** 12.00-3.00pm and 6.00-11.00pm. **CLOSED:** 2 weeks at Christmas, 2 weeks end of August and Tuesdays after Bank Holidays. **CREDIT CARDS ACCEPTED:** Mastercard, Visa. **NUMBER OF SEATS:** 100. **SERVICE:** 10% on parties of 5 or more, optional. **SET PRICE LUNCH:** £6.95. Wheelchair access (but not women's lavatory). 14 seats outside. Private room seats 30. **NEAREST TUBE STATION:** Notting Hill Gate. MAP REF: 4,C/1

Gilbert's

2 Exhibition Road, SW7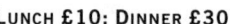

071-589 8947 LUNCH £10; DINNER £30

'A wine list to write home about – where you might find the food'

Competent home cooks sometimes get praised by the recipients of their food saying 'You should open a restaurant'. If more of them did there might be more restaurants like this one but about Gilbert's it must be said that it has endured – about six years now. Any restaurateur will tell you inspiration is rarely the problem; reliability, consistency, and tolerance of the quotidian nature of the work is. The female owner here simplifies life somewhat by offering a short fixed price menu with five options in each course. Some choices, inevitably the more interesting-seeming ones, attract a supplementary price; £2 for starters, £3 for main courses. It must occur to others beside myself that a slightly increased fixed price would be a more congenial way of dealing with the swings and roundabout of, say, avocado with coriander and lime and hot goat cheese soufflé (£2 sup.) or blanquette of veal and roast duck breast with caramelized red wine sauce (£3 sup.) Included in the overall price are olives, homemade bread (by no means exceptional), vegetables (well cooked) or salad. Since the simple, rust-coloured room and the no-nonsense service imply lack of folderol and affectation, it seems a pity that the kitchen decorates fine, simple dishes such as dressed crab with sprigs of parsley and quartered tomato or feels that 'colour' in the shape of more parsley finely chopped must be added to items such as saffron-flavoured fish stew. As with much English cooking a good deal of the enthusiasm is reserved for the dessert course (£4). Walnut meringue with strawberry purée was outstanding. Wine buffs would maintain that exemplary wines need only straightforward food which, given Gilbert's list, to some extent explains the menu. To capitalize on visitors to Albertropolis (the museums of South Kensington), a light menu with no minimum charge is on offer between 6 and 7pm – the reflective hour.

THE WINE LIST remains a compelling reason to visit Gilbert's: it's clearly laid out, fully annotated (with descriptions of unbaroque concision) and inexpensive. Moreover, almost all the wines on it (with prolific halves for the 'less is more' brigade) are there for the right reason: taste-appeal. How many other London restaurants would think to scatter a Clare Valley Riesling, a Galician Albarino, a Condrieu and a '64 sweet Vouvray on to a single page of ten whites? The selection of bottled beers make this even more appealing as a drinker's den, and there are tutored wine-tasting dinners for those who like their pleasure leavened with learning.

OPEN: Mon-Fri. **HOURS:** 12.00-2.00pm and 6.00-10.00pm. **CLOSED:** Bank Holidays, 1 week in February, 1 week in June. **CREDIT CARDS ACCEPTED:** All major cards. **NUMBER OF SEATS:** 32. **SERVICE:** Optional. **SET PRICE LUNCH:** £9.50. **SET PRICE DINNER:** £14.50. 8 seats outside. **NEAREST TUBE STATION:** South Kensington.
MAP REF: 14/B2

Il Goloso

204 Fulham Road, SW10

071-352 9827 £22

'All the trat values including good value'

This narrow, slightly cramped establishment seems emblematic of the Sixties trattoria we used to know and – some of us – love. It calls out to that corner of our hearts where forever a table is laid with a pink cloth and a swarthy man hovers with a pepper mill. However, Il Goloso which actually opened recently – the name means glutton – is as au fait with current culinary trends as any restaurant critic and has latched on to perhaps the most important trend of all; giving value for money. There is a set lunch of two courses (a choice of three dishes in each) and coffee for £5.95 and a similar deal in the evenings for £9.95. From the à la carte tagliatelle with wild mushrooms and rocket salad, calamari in umido (squid slowly stewed in a reduced sauce) and spatchcocked spring chicken kicked into life with spices have all been approved. There is a cover charge in the evenings (some things never change) but at 85p a head it does not stop the bill being eminently reasonable.

OPEN: Mon-Sat. **HOURS:** 12.15-2.45pm and 6.15-11.30pm. **CLOSED:** Bank Holidays, Easter and Christmas. **CREDIT CARDS ACCEPTED:** All major cards. **NUMBER OF SEATS:** 50. **SERVICE:** 12.5%. Cover charge 80p (evenings only). **SET PRICE LUNCH:** £5.95. **SET PRICE DINNER:** £9.95. Tables outside seat 10. **NEAREST TUBE STATION:** Earl's Court/Fulham Broadway. MAP REF: 2,C/3

Gonbei Restaurant

151 King's Cross Road, WC1

071-278 0619 £20

'You're more likely to say au revoir than sayonara'

King's Cross Road has more than its fair share of greasy spoons and sandwich bars. Sandwiched between two of them is this tiny Japanese pearl. Do not expect the lacquered formality of a West End establishment but the food is cooked and presented with care and attention. The menu offers the familiar options of tempura, sushi, sashimi, suki-yaki and yakitori with comprehensive set menus from £16. Worthy of mention is the grilled salmon listed under the heading yakizakana, agedashi, a surprisingly delicate deep-fried bean curd and the staple miso soup, which is exceptional, relying more on flavour and less on seasoning than most of its counterparts around the capital.

OPEN: Mon-Sat. **HOURS:** 6.00-11.00pm. **CLOSED:** Bank Holidays. **CREDIT CARDS ACCEPTED:** Diner's Club, JCB, Mastercard, Visa. **NUMBER OF SEATS:** 45. **SERVICE:** 10%. **SET PRICE DINNER:** £15-£20. Private room seats 18. **NEAREST TUBE STATION:** King's Cross.

Gopal's of Soho

12 Bateman Street, W1

071-434 1621/0840 £17

South Indian dishes in a Soho hideaway'

Gopal Pittal's peaches-and-cream restaurant (the walls are cream, while the waiters and tables dress in peach) brings a touch of Southern Indian romanticism to one of Soho's drabber addresses: the spices proclaim themselves rare, fish comes from the seashore, cocktails usher you on a journey to the end of the rainbow, the muzak is ingratiatingly sub-continental, and the dishes themselves wear the exotic regional badges of Mangalore, Malabar, Karnataka, Goa and Hyderabad. Any scepticism is quickly defused by appetizers rich in the plainly differentiated flavours and textures which elude run-of-the-mill ethnic restaurants: finely minced lamb with herbs and spices, wrapped and steamed in soft, faintly acidulous colocassia leaves (Hyderabad); or richly flavoured and spice-darkened crabmeat with shards of coconut (Mangalore). The sub-headed menu is well-balanced and comprehensible, with clay oven (tandoor) dishes and house specialities providing many of the brightest flavours. Southern Indian fish traditions, hard to replicate Thames-side, are sensibly explored through a lightly spiced, pomfret-based menu curry, cod with fresh fenugreek, and prawns in various guises. Coconut is copious, almost to the point of ubiquity; black onion seed, curry leaf and fresh coriander are preferred to big-gun chilli. Desserts (such as gulab jumun, a pleasingly curdy pistachio-stuffed milk-and-flour cake, or close-textured milk-and-nut ice kulfi) strike the true lactic note. The wine list (compiled by consultant David Wolfe) shows thought and effort, though the Rouge de la Mauricière house red is best avoided (better still replaced); Kingfisher and Cobra beers may be old hat now, but they wear well; while the non-alcoholic Alfonso quencher cocktail (mango, pineapple and lemon juice) is hard to beat as an all-purpose match. Service may be world-weary at times.

OPEN: Mon-Sun. **HOURS:** 12.00-2.45pm and 6.00-11.15pm (6.00-11.00pm Sun). **CLOSED:** Christmas and Boxing Day. **CREDIT CARDS ACCEPTED:** Access, AmEx, Visa. **NUMBER OF SEATS:** 50. **SERVICE:** Optional, £1 cover charge. No-smoking area. Wheelchair access (but not lavatory). Private room seats 30. **NEAREST TUBE STATION:** Leicester Square/Tottenham Court Road/Piccadilly Circus.

MAP REF: 1,E/2

Grahame's Seafare

38 Poland Street, W1

071-437 0975

114

LUNCH: £15; DINNER: £25

'Where to go for some Jewish mothering'

At a test meal at this long-established – 'over thirty-five years' – kosher fish restaurant it was decided to rate out of ten the dishes sampled, marking for overall goodness (OG) and Jewish authenticity (JA). The average score was 6.34 OG and 6.66 JA, scrupulously leaving out of the calculation any JA score for a dish like sole Véronique. This mathematical approach to gastro-criticism was sound in the sense that the meal was strongest on traditional items such as matzoh-crumbed fried gefilte fish (better than the boiled), the borsht served cold but without the hoped-for boiled potato that can make a hot island in a sea of soup, the superior potato lutkas (sic) and the cheese blintzes. In the sole Veronique, a 'chef's speciality', the grapes quarrelled distressingly with a heavy layer of melted cheese over the fish. Better by far is plainly cooked haddock (or indeed salmon, sole, halibut or plaice) grilled, steamed or fried in matzoh meal. The fish is delivered fresh each day from Billingsgate. Motherly waitresses encourage a clientele of regulars. Since Grahame's Seafare is the last remaining Jewish restaurant in the Soho area, an even greater commitment to its ethnicity would be welcomed.

OPEN: Mon-Sat. **HOURS:** 12.00-3.00pm and 5.30-10.00pm. **CLOSED:** Bank Holidays. **CREDIT CARDS ACCEPTED:** Access, AmEx, Diner's Club, JCB, Visa. **NUMBER OF SEATS:** 84. **SERVICE:** Optional. Wheelchair access (but not lavatory). **NEAREST TUBE STATION:** Oxford Circus. **MAP REF:** 1,D/2

Granita

127 Upper Street, N1

071-226 3222

£25

'Islington persons' favourite '

Press attention this year for Granita was in part due to the fact that Tony Blair was seen dining here. Certainly you might be hard put to come up with a more politically correct restaurant right down to its prices which are reasonable, but the dour phrase must not discourage you from visiting. Like the dream party manifesto, what it states on the menu is exactly what you will get. For example: chargrilled mixed vegetables, red pepper, aubergine, zucchini, bruschetta, balsamic vinegar, extra virgin olive oil; tagliarini, new potatoes, French beans, pesto (one of the best pasta garnishes); braised shank of lamb, couscous salad, lemon, mint, red onion, lamb jus; fresh chargrilled swordfish, salsa verde, roasted potatoes, green beans, aragula; plum crisp, cornmeal cinnamon streusel. Chef and co-proprietor Ahmed Kharshoum cooks these and similar modern dishes with a light touch and usually the only disappointment is the discovery that something you wanted has run out that evening. Details such as homemade sultana bread, the tub of unsalted butter left on the table, the choice of drinks both alcoholic and non-alcoholic, teas as well as coffees attest to the sort of care and attention that results in success – and the necessity of booking ahead.

OPEN: LUNCH: Wed-Sun. DINNER: Tues-Sun. **HOURS:** 12.30-2.30pm and 6.30pm-12.00am. **CLOSED:** 10 days at Christmas, 5 days at Easter and last 2 weeks of August. **CREDIT CARDS ACCEPTED:** Access, Mastercard, Visa. **NUMBER OF SEATS:** 62. **SERVICE:** Optional. **SET PRICE LUNCH:** £11.50 and £13.50. Wheelchair access (but not lavatory). **NEAREST TUBE STATION:** Highbury & Islington/Angel.

Great Nepalese

48 Eversholt Street, NW1   ⓶⓵⓺

071-388 6737/5935   £13

'An accurately named restaurant'

The family-run Great Nepalese near Euston station soldiers on delivering sound and frequently superior Indian food, but more to the point a wider range of Nepalese specialities than you are likely to find elsewhere – many of the soi-disant Nepalese restaurants in London serving only one or two identifiably Nepalese dishes. Start a meal with masco-bara (thick, crisp black lentil buns with curry sauce), mamocha (dumplings with a filling resembling spicy sausage), kalezo ra chyau (chicken livers sautéed with mushroom and spices) and if your appetite will run to it haku choyala (vigorously spiced barbecued mutton). From the list entitled Special Nepalese Cuisine the set lunch or dinner (£10.50) gives a guideline as to how you might compose the rest of the meal. Along with a chicken or meat curry – note that mutton means mutton and has an agreeable combative quality – order a potato assembly, a pickle, preferably the coriander pickle, black dal and perhaps the pickled dry vegetable curry, a necessary part of the Nepalese diet in the harsh winter months. Breads are notably good. Service is friendly and responds well to a show of interest. The decor is slightly garish but Kumari, the living goddess, smiles benignly from one wall. Toast her in Nepalese rum.

OPEN: Mon-Sun. **HOURS:** 12.00-2.45pm and 6.00-11.45pm. **CLOSED:** Christmas Day and Boxing Day. **CREDIT CARDS ACCEPTED:** Access, AmEx, Diner's Club, Visa . **NUMBER OF SEATS:** 48. **SERVICE:** 10%. **SET PRICE LUNCH:** £5.50. **SET PRICE DINNER:** £10.50. Wheelchair access (but not lavatory). **NEAREST TUBE STATION:** Euston. MAP REF: 1,F/4

Green's Restaurant & Oyster Bar

36 Duke Street, St James's, SW1

071-930 4566 £52

'A club you can join for the price of a crab sandwich'

Green's is one of the surprisingly few restaurants in London that offers as part of its menu unabashedly British food, much of it reliant on first-rate ingredients such as native oysters, Scottish smoked salmon, lobster, crab, Dover sole, lamb cutlets, sausages, Suffolk ham, Aberdeen Angus beef and so on. The restaurant is lit in a way that flatters its clientele (not as common as you might think) and the bar provides some tables tucked away that are ideal for exchanging confidences and champagne. But when addressing dishes that are more than assemblies (presented on the left-hand side of the menu) the kitchen, perhaps like England itself, seems to have lost a grip on its identity. Listening to a Japanese couple order fish and chips while eating an ineptly composed and sauced 'Japanese chicken salad' seemed all too ironic. Prices are high, so much so that you start to wonder if there is quite enough fish in the dish of roast sea bass with leeks, ginger and lemon butter sauce for £18.50 (vegetables, cover charge and optional service extra). The way to enjoy Green's seems to be to keep your eyes right – on items like smoked cod's roe, salmon fish cakes with fresh tomato sauce, bangers and mash with onion gravy, or the dish of the day such as shepherd's pie, roast chicken, Irish stew and fish pie. There is a good wine list.

OPEN: Mon-Sun. **HOURS:** 11.30am-3.00pm and 5.30-11.00pm. **CLOSED:** Christmas Bank Holidays. **CREDIT CARDS ACCEPTED:** Access, AmEx, Diner's Club, JCB, Visa. **NUMBER OF SEATS:** 80. **SERVICE:** Optional. **SET PRICE LUNCH:** £16.50 (Sun only). Wheelchair access (but not lavatory). Private room seats 36. **NEAREST TUBE STATION:** Piccadilly Circus/Green Park. MAP REF: 1,C/1

Green Street Restaurant

3 Green Street, Mayfair W1

071-409 0453 LUNCH: £16; DINNER: £25

'No membership required for a spiffing lunch'

A club for (mostly) young things at night, Green Street opens its restaurant to non-members for lunch. Useful in the area (which it is) would be describing with much too faint praise the cooking of New Zealander Peter Gordon who more successfully than most takes on the world's markets. In so doing he is informed not only by his own heritage but a concentrated walkabout when in one year he visited Indonesia, Burma, Thailand, Malaysia, Nepal and India. However, in his menu he employs proper restraint, not jumbling together items with different cultural identities. Dishes that are typical – and that have been liked – are spicy mussel, chicken and sea palm laksa; chick-pea, sweet potato and fennel soup with pesto; baked cod with lentils, watercress and salsa verde;

Jaffa cake with Brazil nuts and honey cream. Dishes change in detail, in emphasis or in their entirety on a regular basis - pleasing to regulars. The dining room is in a basement, but one with a conservatory roof. Colours used in the decoration – peppermint green and face-cream pink – are doubtless supposed to be making a statement but it's one you can easily ignore.

OPEN: Mon-Fri. **HOURS:** 12.30-3.00pm. **CLOSED:** Bank Holidays. **CREDIT CARDS ACCEPTED:** All major cards. **NUMBER OF SEATS:** 40. **SERVICE:** Optional. **NEAREST TUBE STATIONS:** Marble Arch/Bond Street.   MAP REF: 1,B/3

The Greenhouse
27a Hay's Mews, W1

071-499 3331   **£30**

'Where Our Gary struts his stuff'

Round about the time this guide is published, chef Gary Rhodes should be overseeing the restaurant at the Festival Hall, a typically canny yet inspired move by his boss hotelier David Levin and a chance, at long last, for some creditable food within the South Bank arts complex. However Rhodes' spectacularly sucessful reign at the Greenhouse will no doubt live on via his courtiers. It has had to when Rhodes was running round Britain for the television series of more or less that name. Although a certain amount of fame has attached to the cheeky chappie for his espousal of traditional English dishes there has been a gradual diminution on the menu of the nostalgia nosh and an increase of a less showbizzy but more sensible appraisal of how tried and true British ideas and ingredients might be adapted to a modern palate. Thus cockles appear with chilli in a relish that accompanies grilled tuna fish; grilled herrings are served on spinach and horseradish crumble; homemade piccalilli is the condiment for boiled bacon and new potatoes. What might be called Rhodes' signature dish – braised oxtail – remains firmly in place and there are other menu stalwarts such as chicken liver pâté (a Spam-coloured – very D-Day – over-lightened mixture); salmon fish cakes; bread and butter pudding. Finesse in the execution of the dishes varies quite considerably so that a soup plateful (as is the fashion) of fillet of cod with peas, smoked bacon and onion sauce can be sublime while a not dissimilar (in concept) dish of pan-fried skate with potato, red pepper and Bayonne ham can seem clumsy and, despite the ham, bland. There are enough successfully executed good ideas to keep the Greenhouse packed out. Getting a table is something you must think about in advance. A part of this popularity may be invested in the myth that persists that the Greenhouse is cheap. It is not and furthermore with cover charge and separately priced vegetables bills can come to more than you might imagine at first glance at the menu. The short but wide-ranging list rises in price in leaps and bounds. A new rendition of the interior desperately trying to convince that the ground floor of a block of flats reached through a courtyard is a greenhouse is not much better than the old. On a low ceiling, overhead fans feel threatening.

Open: Lunch: Mon-Fri, Sun. Dinner: Mon-Sun. Hours: 12.00-2.30pm and 7.00-11.00pm. Closed: Christmas and Bank Holidays. Credit cards accepted: All major cards. Numbers of seats: 95. Service: Optional, £1 cover charge. Wheelchair access. Nearest tube station: Green Park.   MAP REF: 1,B/2

Halcyon Hotel – The Room

129 Holland Park, W11   ⑫⓪

071-221 5411   **£30**

'Where Bienvenida might choose to eat'

The location of this discreetly sited hotel contributes to one element of the restaurant's clientele – the well-heeled of Holland Park and the high-flyers from the BBC – the fact that it has found favour as a place to stay with American rock stars (including Snoop Doggy Dog) contributes another. The Room, as the basement restaurant is called, has these days an anodyne modern chic with the strongest design element remaining the terrace where you may sit outside in pretty weather sheltered by the surrounding mansions. Chef Martin Hadden has worked for, among others, Shaun Hill when he was at Gidleigh Park and for Nico Ladenis. Ladenis has remarked that Hadden left (to go to the Halcyon) a year too soon and based on some of the dishes tried that either lack definition or come over-burdened with ingredients I would say he has a point. The menu is thoroughly modern with all the requisite incursions and accessories – Thai spicing, Japanese horseradish, wonton leaves, balsamic vinegar, wild mushrooms and so on – but in some instances national boundaries are respected. On the whole the best bet is to stay with these simpler assemblies. Soups seem reliable. In deference to the style of clientele there is a vegetarian menu and for business lunchers a business lunch. Service is eager. Piped music is, to my mind, a drag.

Open: Lunch: Sun-Fri. Dinner: Mon-Sun. Hours: 12.00-2.30pm and 7.00-10.30pm (7.00-11.00pm Fri-Sat, 7.00-10.00pm Sun). Credit cards accepted: AmEx, Diner's Club, Mastercard, Switch, Visa. Number of seats: 50. Service: Optional. Set price lunch: £12.95. Set price dinner: £17. No-smoking area. 25 seats outside. Nearest tube station: Holland Park.   MAP REF: 7,D/1

The Halkin

5-6 Halkin Street, SW1   ⑫①

071-333 1234   **Lunch £33; Dinner £40**

'Designerly dishes in polished surroundings'

Metropolitan chic shimmers from this soigné Belgravian hotel, though the metropolis in question is more Milan than London. A harpist, wrestling with the ignominy of American Pie, may waft you through the black-furnished lobby to the dining room. Space and spareness are not simply an effect of the languidly draped windows and the formal Italian gardens pictured on the wall; table spacings are generous, the settings minimalistically elegant. Of course the refusal to complicate matters is one of the hallmarks of Italian cooking, so it comes as no surprise to refind space and spareness again on the plate. Stefano Cavallini's cooking follows the super-deft line left by the departed Gualtiero Marchesi: small scraps of home-made raw duck ham, pine kernels, sultanas and pink grapefruit (rather than the pomegranate promised by the menu) are laid like jewels on frisé lettuce; a main course of breaded red mullet is served, almost austerely, with braised celery alone. Even those main dishes which, like pigeon casserole, would seem to promise rusticità hide behind a sheen of finesse – the unctuous port sauce, the gestural sprinkling of truffle. Yet ingredients are good, false notes are rare, and technical expertise brings its own pleasures, particularly evident in the sensitive cooking of both meat and fish, and a range of precision desserts: mango tart, Tatin-style, served with coconut ice cream, or a grainy robbiola cheesecake with a thick and unctuous white chocolate sauce. Service combines suavity with bustle. The demise of the set price dinner menu may be lamented at the bill-paying stage, but note that on the menu and in the smallest of small print at the bottom of the bill, service is included. The wine list is tailored to impress, with grand bottles at grandiose prices from both Italy and France. There is very little for under £20, and the Chianti Classico Riserva from Isole e Olena, mildly encouraging at £22, proved not to be a Riserva at all but the ordinary cuvée – which the waiter contrived to suggest was the customer's mistake rather than the wine list's.

OPEN: LUNCH: Mon-Fri. DINNER: Mon-Sat. **HOURS:** 12.30-2.30pm and 7.30-11.00pm. **CLOSED:** Bank Holidays. **CREDIT CARDS ACCEPTED:** All major cards. **NUMBER OF SEATS:** 45. **SERVICE:** Included. **SET PRICE LUNCH:** £19.50. Wheelchair access. Private room seats 28. **NEAREST TUBE STATION:** Hyde Park Corner/Victoria.

MAP REF: 1,A/1

Harbour City Chinese Restaurant

46 Gerrard Street, W1

122

071-439 7859   **£18**

'A very civilized Cantonese restaurant'

I am always game, no, extremely keen, to go to the latest Chinese restaurant to open in Chinatown, but the four I find blessedly constant and to which I return with regularity are Fung Shing, Mr Kong, Poon's in Leicester Street and Harbour City. Harbour City is my favourite for dim sum and I like it too for the dishes listed under the headings Chef's Special Selection and Special Authentic Cantonese Hot-Pot. This last embraces the tastes and textures that only true lovers of Cantonese food appreciate. Well, how do you feel about taro with marinated fatty belly-pork in a bean sauce or braised duck-web with fish lips in oyster sauce? Anyone who likes fragrant, resonant stews would like braised beef goulash, or, indeed, baked crab in ginger and spring onion sauce with vermicelli and also chef's specials such as steamed whole prawn in shell with garlic; stir-fried scallop with asparagus in a creamy wine sauce and baked chicken in spicy salt. The unusually long and varied list of dim sum (served only during the day until about 5pm) includes a section called exotic dim sum. Don't miss the comparatively expensive (£1.80) shark fin dumpling in soup, a bowlful for which you could pay five times the price and not get anything nearly as good in a Western restaurant. Remember to stir into the faintly sweet stock a dash of the red vinegar and julienne of ginger served on the side. Seating is more spacious and staff more courteous here than at most other Chinatown places.

OPEN: Mon-Sun. **HOURS:** 12.00-11.30pm. **CLOSED:** Christmas Eve and Christmas Day. **CREDIT CARDS ACCEPTED:** AmEx, Diner's Club, JCB, Mastercard, Visa. **NUMBER OF SEATS:** 160. **SERVICE:** 10%. **SET PRICE DINNER:** From £10.50. Wheelchair access (but not lavatory). Private rooms seat 40 and 50. **NEAREST TUBE STATION:** Leicester Square/Piccadilly Circus.   MAP REF: 1,E/1

Harveys

2 Bellevue Road, SW17

081-672 0114   **£33**

'Luminous cooking south of the river'

Mark Williamson, chef at Harveys when it opened in a new guise in early 1994 is, so to speak, back where he started. Sous-chef to Marco Pierre White when White opened Harveys in 1987, Williamson has in the meantime been working at the Walnut Tree in Abergavenny and in Australia and the Far East. These experiences inform his cooking which is original, daring and skilled. Bright ideas abound. Fashioning lobster 'ravioli' from sheets of filo pastry puts into your head the suggestion – and then confirms it – that what ravioli has been missing all this time is an element of crispness. Ballotine of chicken, essentially a soft-sounding assembly, Williamson sears, thereby infiltrating a nice smoky flavour which is well matched by marinated pulses strewn with deep-fried threads of spinach. Of the ten main courses half feature fish. Halibut is served with a fricassée of shrimp and artichoke in a Creole sauce made fittingly punchy with chilli. Deep-fried Malaysian rice noodles, broken and scattered, provide a contrasting texture. Typical meat dishes are roast rabbit, braised fennel and endive, mustard and tarragon sauce; duck breast cassoulet, caramelized garlic and shallots. Desserts, for example pecan nut zucotta, espresso semi freddo keep up the style and tempo. Oddly, desultory service also seems to have come with the package but Harveys remains, as always it was, one of the best bets south of the river.

OPEN: LUNCH: Tues-Fri. DINNER: Mon-Sat. **HOURS:** 12.00-2.30pm and 7.00-10.30pm. **CREDIT CARDS ACCEPTED:** All major cards. **NUMBER OF SEATS:** 55. **SERVICE:** Optional. **SET PRICE LUNCH:** £13.50 (2 courses). **SET PRICE DINNER:** £17.50 (2 courses). Wheelchair access (but not lavatory). **NEAREST BR STATION:** Wandsworth Common.

Hilaire

68 Old Brompton Road, SW7

071-584 8993

£39

'Handy after Christie's sales; do I hear £12.50? do I hear £70?'

At time of writing Hilaire is undergoing a refurbishment which will provide six to eight additional covers in the ground-floor dining room and – one trusts – a more enticing colour scheme than of old. Bryan Webb has been chef here for nearly eight years, since 1990 as a co-owner. Onto his Welsh roots – nourished to some extent at Franco Taruschio's Walnut Tree Inn near Abergavenny – have been grafted the various influences that add up to that description of cooking, 'modern European'. This can, as we know, admit Oriental influences as exemplified in a long-running favourite on the menu, salad of langoustine and carrot with Thai seasoning. It shares its role as a first course with items such as foccacia with terrine of duck liver with onion chutney and brioche; deep-fried calves' brains with chilli and coriander dip and oysters 'au gratin' with laverbread (a kind of Welsh seaweed) and Stilton. In the main course Webb has a sure hand with dishes such as griddled fillet of John Dory with pea mash, dill and mustard, calves' sweetbreads with mashed potato and olives. There are favourite ingredients and items – pigeon, wild salmon, pheasant, Jersey royals, potato pancakes, pancetta, onion chutney, wild mushrooms, rhubarb – that get shuffled and dealt through the à la carte and the various set price menus. These last look like a laudable attempt to keep prices down but a starting point of a £12.50 two-course lunch can all too easily produce a bill of £70 for two by the time the many supplements – one of them for £10, almost the price of the menu itself – coffee, wine service charge etc. have been negotiated. One female tester hopes that the new look to the place will include staff being enlightened on the possibility of a woman taking out a man and wanting to choose the wine and even pay the bill.

WELL-ORGANIZED (by wine style), clearly laid out, with succinct and accurate descriptive notes for most wines, this is the sort of wine list every aspiring restaurant should aim for. Light reds (lots of non-Burgundian Pinots, for example) seem to be a particular speciality, but variety spices the list throughout and many bottles invite an exploratory punt.

OPEN: LUNCH: Mon-Fri. DINNER: Mon-Sat. **HOURS:** 12.30-2.30pm and 7.00-11.30pm. **CLOSED:** Bank Holidays. **CREDIT CARDS ACCEPTED:** Access, AmEx, Diner's Club, Switch, Visa. **NUMBER OF SEATS:** 50. **SERVICE:** Optional. **SET PRICE LUNCH:** £12.50. **SET PRICE DINNER:** £16 and £25.50. Wheelchair access (but not lavatory). Private room seats 30. **NEAREST TUBE STATION:** South Kensington.

MAP REF: 2,C/3

The Hospitality Suite

London Underwriting Centre,
Mincing Lane, EC3

(125)

071-617 0000

£34

'Your very own executive dining room'

This restaurant on the top floor of the London Underwriting Centre run by Roux Fine Dining is open to the public with advance booking. The style of cooking is early Roux more or less coinciding with some of the content of the brothers' first book, *New Classic Cuisine*, published in 1983, but with a few timely touches. The set price menu (£29.50 inclusive for three courses and coffee) changes daily but it is safe to say it plays safe. Dishes tend to centre around prime cuts of first-class protein. Soufflé Suissesse is as good here as at Le Gavroche. The patisserie is also comparable. The Hospitality Suite, subtly less hospitable to women lunching, is almost as interesting for its boardroom spaciousness and the fascinating view of the City as for its conventionally 'fine' food. You could use it to impress.

OPEN: Mon-Fri. **HOURS:** 12.00-2.30pm. **CLOSED:** Bank Holidays. **CREDIT CARDS ACCEPTED:** All major cards. **NUMBER OF SEATS:** 30. **SERVICE:** Optional. **SET PRICE LUNCH:** £29.50. Wheelchair access. Private room seats 40. **NEAREST TUBE STATION:** Monument.

The Hothouse

78/80 Wapping Lane, E1

(126)

071-488 4797

LUNCH: £15; DINNER: £25

'A bit more than useful in the area'

The lure of working at Wapping has never been a gastronomic one and a first glance at the faintly folksy interior of the large barn-like structure of the Hothouse does not suggest seriously considered food. The menu is also unusually short but the cooking of Simon Wills – last offered at Martin's in Baker Street (now Hodgson's) – demonstrates craftsmanship and an understanding of getting the best out of ingredients. Items you might choose as a first course are as down to earth as black pudding with apple purée or sautéed field mushrooms Bordelaise on toast or as nifty as red pepper mousse with crab and virgin olive oil. Risottos and pastas are well turned out. Among the section entitled Roasts and Grills, something that is neither – braised pork knuckle with braised beans, lemon and sage – stands out as the most interesting. The name of the place is not picked up in the cooking – no Texas chilli, vengeful curry or fiery salsas – but on some evenings the sounds of live jazz snake up from the downstairs bar. Long waits for food are not unknown here.

OPEN: Mon-Sun. **HOURS:** 12.00am-12.00pm. **CLOSED:** Bank Holidays and Christmas. **CREDIT CARDS ACCEPTED:** All major cards. **NUMBER OF SEATS:** 200. **SERVICE:** Optional. **SET PRICE LUNCH:** £12.50. Private room seats 25. **NEAREST TUBE STATION:** Wapping/Liverpool Street.

Hyde Park Hotel – The Restaurant

66 Knightsbridge, SW1

071-259 5380 LUNCH: £25; DINNER: £65

'There is no denying the guy can cook'

With unbecoming lack of modesty, Marco Pierre White calls his latest venture set within the Forte-owned Hyde Park Hotel 'The Restaurant' and has his name printed large on the canopy in the street. He charges £60 per person for three courses from the menu and dates the dishes as if they are works of art. The chap – he is no longer such a young rebel – sets himself up for attack, exacerbates the likelihood with bursts of rude and, what my mother would have called unnecessary, behaviour and yet there is no denying his prodigious skills not only as a chef but as a teacher (c.f. the cooking at The Canteen and L'Aubergine). As a restaurant critic it helps if Marco likes you and in one brilliant move – marrying a man who was born in Yorkshire from where Marco hails – I seem to have ensured that he does (although you never can tell). The menu he offers is uncommonly long for this sort of tight-rope walking performance; in itself an achievement although tantalizing to the diner who can afford such a meal once in a blue moon. The lunch menu of three courses and coffee at £25 is another way of trying White's cooking but he has been quoted as saying that cooking the lunch menu bores him (I should think looking through the credit card vouchers from that deal is the boring bit). Despite that, I have had superb parfait of foie gras and chicken livers with toasted brioche followed by an incredibly sensitively timed dish of fillet of smoked haddock with poached egg and grain mustard sauce at a lunch. Eating from the main list, soup of red mullet is sublime in the force of its flavours, the sort of dish that defines what a luxury restaurant kitchen can do that would be impractical or impossible in a domestic setting; salad of potatoes and lobsters with truffles is far more than evidence of no-expense-spared with ingredients, tastes and textures juxtaposed with brilliance; roast Bresse pigeon on cabbage cooked with goose fat, the leg en croute flavoured with quatre épices served with ravioli of ceps, a fondant potato and thyme jus is complex but doesn't lose the plot. There is much more, including earthy dishes of pot-roast pork using pig's head and Pierre Koffmann's braised pig's trotter. Desserts are impeccable. One important point when eating out at this price is widely spaced tables and this there is. Service is led by the smiling Jean Cottard who has worked at Tante Claire.

THIS IS NOT a list of any great originality or daring. Its strength lies in the quality of the selections: the single-minded, consistent and uncompromising are faithfully listed, often on a multi-vintage basis (all the first growths, for example, but also Palmer, Montrose, Cheval Blanc and Ausone; the two Dagueneaux in the Loire; Zind-Humbrecht in Alsace . . .). Prices, alas, are uncompromising, too, the consolation being that even the less expensive wines (like Château Reynon Vieilles Vignes for Sauvignon lovers, or the half-bottle of Leeuwin's '87 Cabernet Sauvignon for those who want to see how near Australia can come to matching Bordeaux) are well chosen, providing some sort of value at under £30. Merlot fans will relish the unusually long flush of Pomerols. The lacuna most urgently in need of filling is that of the Midi's new AOC stars: to list Provençal reds but not those of Corbières is a dereliction.

OPEN: Mon-Sat, **HOURS:** 12.00-2.15pm and 6.30-11.15pm. **CREDIT CARDS ACCEPTED:** All major cards. **NUMBER OF SEATS:** 55. **SET PRICE LUNCH:** £25. **SET PRICE DINNER:** £65. Wheelchair access (but not lavatory). **NEAREST TUBE STATION:** Knightsbridge. **MAP REF:** 2,F/4

Ikkyu

67A Tottenham Court Road, WC1

(128)

071-636 9280   LUNCH: £7; DINNER: £20

'Homely, good-value Japanese food'

The full name of this hidden basement restaurant – but if you can find Goodge Street tube station you can find Ikkyu – is Robotayaki Ikkyu. The qualifier refers to a hearty, country-style of cooking but what it means to the Westerners who make up a considerable proportion of the clientele is a full stomach with still a reasonably full wallet. The portions of sushi served here, ranking among the cheapest sushi to be found in London, are well-prepared and generous. Sashimi is also available plus yakitori (grilled skewers of food), grilled fish, bowls of ramen (noodles) and a long list of small dishes some, like stewed potato with meat, seeming quite odd. Set meals are emphasized only at lunchtimes. You can have a more interesting time grazing on the familiar and the strange itemized on the list called Dishes. Food tends to be delivered by the waiters – mostly European – in haphazard fashion. It is high time a cleaning lady of whatever nationality had a good go at premises. An investment banker acquaintance who has lived in Japan, and speaks Japanese and loves to eat rates Ikkyu and Suntory (q.v.) as best, in their own ways, in London.

OPEN: Mon-Fri. **HOURS:** 12.30-2.30pm and 6.00-10.30pm. **CREDIT CARDS ACCEPTED:** Access, AmEx, Diner's Club, JCB, Visa. **NUMBER OF SEATS:** 57. **SERVICE:** 10%. **SET PRICE LUNCH:** £5.50. **SET PRICE DINNER:** £6.50. Private room seats 10. **NEAREST TUBE STATION:** Goodge Street. **MAP REF:** 1,E/3

Imperial City

Royal Exchange, Cornhill, EC3

(129)

071-626 3437   **£30**

'Come back Ken'

A consultant chef located in a different continent, as is California-based Ken Hom to this stylish (for the most part) Chinese restaurant below the Royal Exchange, might find it tricky keeping the kitchen up to the mark.

A test meal this year revealed less precision, for example in the constituent parts of the first course to share entitled Imperial Cold Platter, less nerve and verve with spicing, inappropriate garnish, and some evidence of enthusiasm with cornflour. Some of the homelier dishes such as the delectable steamed egg custard have disappeared from the menu. I suspect that a City clientele more interested in deals than duck skin must bear some of the responsibility but it would seem that, inevitably, the good resolutions struck at the beginning are becoming somewhat blurred. There are, however, still high spots on the menu. Cantonese pressed duck, a new addition, is brilliant and the braised red pork casserole Shanghai style eminently satisfying. Noodles seem well handled; spicy Szechuan dan dan noodles have a nice mustardy bite. I dare say when Ken Hom makes his next visit he will get rid of the bud vases on the tables with their single roses and sprays of gypsophila. Service from slender Thai girls is polite but mechanical. The wine list is well thought through.

OPEN: Mon-Fri. **HOURS:** 11.30am-8.30pm. **CLOSED:** Christmas Day, Boxing Day, New Year's Day and Bank Holidays. **CREDIT CARDS ACCEPTED:** Access, AmEx, Diner's Club, Switch, Visa. **NUMBER OF SEATS:** 180. **SERVICE:** 12.5%. **SET PRICE LUNCH:** £13.90-£24.80. Wheelchair access. Private room seats 16. **NEAREST TUBE STATION:** Bank.

Inaho

4 Hereford Road, W2

(130)

071-221 8495   LUNCH: £12; DINNER: £25

'A little box of Japanese goodies'

The restaurant is the size of a shoe-box and the kitchen a great deal smaller, making the assortment of tastes emerging from it pretty amazing. And that is not just the food. Red lacquer fan sous-plats vie with a chiming cuckoo clock; dusty mother-in-law's tongues loom over tables set with modern Japanese pottery cups, all different, all beautiful. Advice is readily given on the manageable (in length) menu and on the daily specials, often the most interesting choices. Sashimi has been cut too thick for a fastidious New Yorker but I think that way more flavour lies. Nasuden, aubergine Japanese style, a wonderful smoky, sweet-sour purée inside a crisp aubergine shell, is an ideal hors d'oeuvre as is the age-dofu, deep-fried beancurd. Set lunches are extremely good value. Sushi is served in the evenings Wednesday to Saturday. Don't be deceived by the small size of the premises, this is big cooking.

OPEN: LUNCH: Mon-Fri. DINNER: Mon-Sat. **HOURS:** 12.30-3.00pm and 7.00-11.30pm. **CLOSED:** 4 days at Easter and 10 days at Christmas. **CREDIT CARDS ACCEPTED:** Access, Visa. **NUMBER OF SEATS:** 20. **SERVICE:** 10%. **SET PRICE LUNCH:** £8-£10. **SET PRICE DINNER:** £20-£22. **NEAREST TUBE STATION:** Notting Hill Gate.

L'Incontro

87 Pimlico Road, SW1

(131)

071-730 3663/6327

LUNCH: £20; DINNER: £53

'Italian chic at a price'

The encounter (as it translates from the Italian) is usually between the rich and their rich friends at this stylish restaurant where black and white photographs of famous and/or romantic meetings provide a detail of the restrained decor. Owner Gino Santin, also proprietor of Santini in Ebury Street and Santini in Milan, says that a while back business suffered in Milan due to the fact that some of the putative customers were eating porridge. (Takings have picked up again.) Such depredations were not the problem in Pimlico but the recession has resulted in an amelioration in prices at lunchtime at least – with a set price two- and three-course deal and a menu entitled One Dish Lunch in place – and the transformation of the basement room into a space suited to parties complete with a piano that is a bar. Simplicity, a virtue that can be just that or alternatively a bore, is the keynote of the approach to the cooking here. You could order a meal of bresaola with extra virgin olive oil and lemon followed by langoustines with lime and fresh raspberries where the only difference between it and a shopping expedition would be some play with the charcoal grill. Better to try a risotto of the day or a pasta dish such as bigoli with an anchovy and onion sauce or slender tagliatelle with a fresh crab sauce or a dish from Venice (from whence comes Santin) such as pasta e fagioli Veneta (bean and pasta soup) or cappe sante (baked scallops) or seppie col nero (cuttlefish in ink served with polenta). Telling yourself 'in for a penny, in for a pound' (which you will be; many of them, enhanced by a cover charge of £1.50 per person) pick up on the offer of lobster either served with spaghetti or as a salad where the creature is beautifully prepared for your delectation but unfortunately laid on unsubtle accompaniments; slices of raw red onion, slices of banal fresh tomato and rocket leaves but with a good basil-infused, lemony dressing. Meat tends also to be plainly treated but can be a treat, as in veal kidneys flash-fried with porcini. Sadly, I feel that ambitiousness in the kitchen here has been affected by the tendency of the rich and thin to have got that way by not eating very much. Such is the dilemma for restaurateurs who set out to cater for them.

OPEN: Mon-Sat. **HOURS:** 12.30-2.30pm (12.30-3.00pm Sat) and 7.00-11.30pm. **CLOSED:** Christmas Day and Boxing Day. **CREDIT CARDS ACCEPTED:** AmEx, Diner's Club, Mastercard, Visa. **NUMBER OF SEATS:** 55. **SERVICE:** 12%, £1.50 cover charge. **SET PRICE LUNCH:** £13.50 and £16.80. Wheelchair access (but not lavatory). Private room seats 35. **NEAREST TUBE STATION:** Sloane Square.

MAP REF: 2,F/2

Inter-Continental Hotel – Le Soufflé

Inter-Continental Hotel,
1 Hamilton Place, W1

071-409 3131   **£55**

'A West End hotel restaurant with a chef/patron'

Early in 1994 it was announced by the Inter-Continental that Peter Kromberg was now chef-patron of Le Soufflé restaurant. This title may have been bestowed in order to recognize Kromberg's close on twenty years' service at the hotel – or perhaps it gives him a slice of the action – but that and the fact that Le Soufflé was made restaurant of the year by the Egon Ronay guide '94 drew fresh attention to this classic establishment. In the windowless dining room efforts have been made to jolly the look, a task that falls heavily on a white piano, some mauve-leaved 'trees' and an array of framed twigs. More successfully distinguishing the space are friendly, interested staff anxious to talk up the cooking, and particularly the well-balanced seven-course set dinner menu trimmed fore and aft with canapés and petits fours (£43). Eating à la carte brings the signature soufflés. Soufflé d'epinards et tête de moine (cheese) vinaigrette aux olives et anchois is masterful in appearance (like all the soufflés) but can be slightly disappointing in its milky texture. However, it is a clever conceit – with the vinaigrette spooned around the garnish at the moment of service – and marries stylishly the natural partnership of spinach and anchovy. Large kitchens of this kind can afford staff to prepare turned and tiny vegetables. When more or less the same array of these infant veg. are over-used as a garnish, as happens here as well as in various other fancy restaurants I can think of, it can lead to a sense of lack of precision and creative intent. Fish dishes tend to be more particular than the meat-based ones. On the whole the approach is subtle and occasionally delightfully surprising. A dessert soufflé finishes the meal on a high note. Details are well attended to; bread is good, the cheese board splendid and there is concern for health exemplified by little hearts denoting dishes low in fat and high in fibre. The wine list is sound, better for Bordeaux than Burgundy, with a good selection of half-bottles and wines by the glass.

OPEN: LUNCH: Tues-Fri, Sun. DINNER: Tues-Sat. **HOURS:** 12.30-3.00pm (12.00-4.00pm Sun) and 7.00-10.30pm (7.00-11.15pm Sat). **CLOSED:** August. **CREDIT CARDS ACCEPTED:** All major cards. **NUMBER OF SEATS:** 80. **SERVICE:** Optional. **SET PRICE LUNCH:** £27.50. **SET PRICE DINNER:** £37.50 and £43. No-smoking area. Wheelchair access. **NEAREST TUBE STATION:** Hyde Park Corner. **MAP REF:** 1,A/1

Istanbul Iskembecisi

9 Stoke Newington Road, N16

071-254 7291 £15

'Here we're talking a lot of tripe'

Selecting this Turkish restaurant from the ever-increasing number in the Stoke Newington/Dalston area is of course to do with its food, not least the offal and tripe specialities (iskembecisi means tripe restaurant), but is also connected to a certain level of comfort; many of the newer restaurants, particularly the ocakbasi (barbecue) joints, are tiny and cramped and cannot take bookings. Even if you think you can't abide tripe, try it as soup. Into the rich broth you add salt, vinegar, lemon juice and pepper until it is disguised and delicious. There is an impressive array of mezeler, most of the little dishes vegetarian, comprising a peaceful mix of Greek, Lebanese and Turkish references plus some deep-fried liver Albanian style. If only restaurateurs could run governments. If you like andouillette try kokarec which is the same sort of content (intestines) charcoal-grilled and served as crisp morsels with finely chopped salads, crushed wheat and small heaps of oregano and cayenne. There are many more familiar kebabs and grills and also slow-cooked traditional Turkish casseroles. Sweet creamy desserts, often scattered with crushed pistachio nuts, complete the meal. Ayran is the Turkish rendition of lassi. Istanbul Iskembicisi is popular with Turkish families at weekends. Most dishes can be prepared as a child's portion. You might want only a child's portion of boiled brain with salad.

OPEN: Mon-Sun. **HOURS:** 5.00pm-5.00am. **CLOSED:** Christmas Day and New Year's Day. **CREDIT CARDS ACCEPTED:** All major cards. **NUMBER OF SEATS:** 80. **SERVICE:** Optional. Wheelchair access (but not lavatory). **NEAREST BR STATION:** Rectory Road

 # The Ivy

1 West Street, WC2

071-836 4751 £33

'The only place to go after the show'

London's show business restaurant par excellence – in which definition you have, of course, to include architects, weather girls, painters, authors, alternative comedians, their agents and their lawyers as well as the stars of stage and screen – The Ivy, owned and run by Jeremy King and Chris Corbin (who also own Le Caprice q.v), has a menu as long and varied in nationality as the credits of any movie. It is a clever list with constantly added twists and turns and dishes of the day to render it fresh and interesting to the many regulars (fried eggs with crispy Alsace bacon is an inspired tweaker of a jaded palate). It is possible to eat traditionally in the English manner, starting with dressed Cornish crab, moving on to Cumberland sausages with shallot gravy and mash and then lemon syllabub followed by a savoury of Scotch 'woodcock'. You could repeat the process in an American accent – Caesar salad; hamburger; rum and raisin ice cream with caramel fudge sauce – in Italian – potato gnocchi with langoustine tails; tripe Milanese; tiramisù – or on an Oriental theme – crispy pork salad; chicken masala with cardamom rice; Darjeeling tea. The surroundings are muted – save for the interesting art on the walls – which doubtless the well-known faces like to kid themselves confers a sort of anonymity. Of course tables are kept back for regulars and the famous but how else would you get the chance to sit next to Brad Pitt?

WHO NEEDS THE waffle of an extended list when most of the selections on a shorter one are well-judged and various? This is a surprisingly cosmopolitan collection, the Pulignys and Talbots balanced out by good things from Isole e Olena, Murrieta, Leeuwin and Penfolds. Multiple halves and wines by the glass satisfy the needs of temperance.

OPEN: Mon-Sun. **HOURS:** 12.00-3.00pm and 5.30pm-12.00am. **CLOSED:** Bank Holiday lunches. **CREDIT CARDS ACCEPTED:** Access, AmEx, Diner's Club, Visa. **NUMBER OF SEATS:** 100. **SERVICE:** Optional, £1.50 cover charge. **SET PRICE LUNCH:** £12.50 (weekends only). Wheelchair access (but not lavatory). Private room seats 60. **NEAREST TUBE STATION:** Leicester Square.   MAP REF: 1,E/1

Jashan

19a Turnpike Lane, N8

081-340 9880   £20

'One to note for Indian food enthusiasts'

Crossing the threshold of Jashan is like entering a decent restaurant in a chaotic Indian city. It is an oasis in a bleak and litter-strewn area. For those prepared to venture north in the quest for good Indian food, it repays the effort, if effort it is. The extra mile the kitchen is willing to go – chefs are reputed to have been chosen by catering consultants in Bombay – is signalled by rather precious sub-titles on the menu; From the Deep Sea, Lamb from the Cook's Pot, Indian Bread Basket, Basmati Rice Delights and so on. Mulugatwanni soup is a different, lighter and superior version of the English club variety; murg chaat a delicious spicy starter of chicken morsels; sukhe jhinge (stir-fried prawns) are rather swamped by tomato gravy but try instead the whole grilled, marinated pomfret. As noted last year, breads are outstanding with special mention for the Indian version of sourdough bread, masala kulcha. For a truly authentic experience finish with a dessert predicated on condensed milk and drink either lassi or thandai, a drink prepared from almond and poppyseed extract. The Cobra Good Curry Guide says that Jashan supplies curries to Harrods Food Hall.

OPEN: Tue-Sun and Bank Holiday Mons. **HOURS:** 6.00pm-12.00am. **CLOSED:** Christmas Day and Boxing Day. **CREDIT CARDS ACCEPTED:** All major cards. **NUMBER OF SEATS:** 50. **SERVICE:** Optional. Wheelchair access (but not lavatory). **NEAREST TUBE STATION:** Turnpike Lane.

Jimmy Beez

303 Portobello Road, W10

081-964 9100 LUNCH: £15; DINNER: £25

'Lively food in a lively setting'

James Breslaw who opened Jimmy Beez in Portobello Road at the end of 1993 has worked in New York at Arizona 206 and also at China Grill, modelled on LA's Chinois on Main, and in London at Smollensky's Balloon and 190 Queen's Gate. This small, funky restaurant and bar designed by architect Mick Merhemitch is his first independent venture. The menu, cooked by chef Simon Smith, is not nearly so exciting as that of the American southwestern Arizona 206 but it has some nice items; grilled fresh figs wrapped in prosciutto on a bed of rocket and mascarpone; Peking duck salad; crab and salmon fishcakes; sliced sea bass with shredded vegetables and soy and some notable side dishes, called here Accessories, in kumera potatoes, sweet Jamaican potatoes deep-fried with garlic butter, and something I described as the vegetable of the year, crisply fried spinach leaves scattered with sesame seeds. Lunch is a shorter menu than dinner. At weekends a brunch menu (try the steak sandwich) is served all day. Jimmy Beez is for the young and the young at heart, i.e. it can get noisy, sometimes with live music.

OPEN: Mon-Sun. **HOURS:** 12.00-11.00pm (11.00am-11.00pm Sat; 11.00am-10.30pm Sun). **CLOSED:** Christmas Day, Boxing Day and New Year's Day. **CREDIT CARDS ACCEPTED:** AmEx. **NUMBER OF SEATS:** 48. **SERVICE:** Optional (10% for parties of 6 or more). **SET PRICE DINNER:** £15. Tables outside seat 16. Private room seats 20. **NEAREST TUBE STATION:** Ladbroke Grove.

Jin

16 Bateman Street, W1

071-734 0908 £25

'Something different in Soho'

During the hot muggy summer of '94, this Soho restaurant provided air-conditioned respite from the pavement drinkers and boulevardiers of Frith Street. Korean food not being everybody's cup of barley tea, Jin was one of the places not swamped by people seemingly goaded into eating out by the heat. The long, narrow interior looks a little dog-eared these days as do the menus, always a discouraging sign. However, service is as friendly and gentle as ever and the strident flavours of some of the dishes make an agreeable change from ubiquitous Thai food. Pork is nicely plain; beef has been steeped in a very sweet marinade. Sugar generally now seems overly relied upon to contribute its likeability. Soups, condiments of raw vegetables including kim chee (pickled cabbage), vegetable dishes – particularly hobak chun, marrow deep-fried in a meaty batter – and rice – notably beebim bab where a fried egg and deeply savoury sauce are mixed into rice and vegetables – and noodles should predominate in the meal. Befriending owner Tony Wee can lead to ginseng cocktails being given to the chaps. Guess what, they are supposedly an aphrodisiac.

OPEN: Mon-Sat. **HOURS:** 12.00-3.00pm and 6.00-11.00pm. **CLOSED:** Easter, Christmas and New Year's Day. **CREDIT CARDS ACCEPTED:** All major cards. **NUMBER OF SEATS:** 55. **SERVICE:** 12.5%. **SET PRICE LUNCH:** £5.50 or £7.90. **SET PRICE DINNER:** £15.50 or £19.50. Wheelchair access (but not lavatory). Private room seats 24. **NEAREST TUBE STATION:** Tottenham Court Road/Leicester Square.

MAP REF: 1,E/2

Kalamaras

76-78 Inverness Mews, W2

071-727 9122/2564 £22

'The Beatles liked it in the Sixties and we still do'

In 1996 the Greek – note not Greek-Cypriot – restaurant Kalamaras will have been going for thirty years, not all of that time spent in the scruffy little mews off Queensway where now both the micro (small and unlicensed) and mega (larger and licensed) establishments flourish. I can remember from way back owner Stelios Platanos looking world-weary – his occasional smile a grudging dawn. It is a great tribute to his talents that the two restaurants continue to satisfy and sometimes delight. Some things change; the menu now has explanations in English for the dishes written in transliterated Greek thus sparing you (or denying you) a recital from the waitresses hired, says a tester, not for their looks but their sturdy efficiency and speed. Among the mezedes – first courses best shared – are some less familiar dishes such as horta, wilted wild greens with lemon juice; briam, mixed vegetables cooked with tomatoes and spring onions; rice pilafs with sauces; grilled fresh mussels and kavouropites, fresh crab in filo pastry (excellent). A main-course dish of fillets of hake and salmon, also cooked in filo, is a success as are grilled prawns and langoustines generously served. Lamb, either marinated and grilled on a skewer or oven-baked with lemon and garlic, is the obvious meat choice but for something lighter there is a fricassée of chicken and spinach with avgolemeno sauce. Best dessert is probably baklava. The low-ceilinged agreeably cluttered premises magnify noise; the best response is another bottle of Greek wine.

OPEN: Mon-Sat. **HOURS:** 6.30pm-12.00am. **CLOSED:** Bank Holidays. **CREDIT CARDS ACCEPTED:** All major cards. **NUMBER OF SEATS:** 88. **SERVICE:** 10%. **SET PRICE DINNER:** £15.50. Wheelchair access (but not lavatory). 22 seats outside. Private room seats 30. **NEAREST TUBE STATION:** Bayswater/Queensway.

Kartouche

329-331 Fulham Road, SW10

0071-823 3515

(139)

LUNCH: £15; DINNER: £20

'Don't let the noise obscure Josh Hampton's cooking'

To location, location, location, you might add contacts and who you know as important considerations when opening a restaurant. Kartouche was opened on a much strolled-along, posed-in part of Fulham Road in the hot summer of '94 by two youngish chaps with fat address books. The restaurant (with a bar and club below) was full to bursting more or less the day trading began. However, as we all know, it is the food that really counts and Kartouche is fortunate in having Josh Hampton for chef. Hampton, who has worked in London at Canal Brasserie and 192, is one of those Australian chefs who has a confident grip on that inchoate cooking style often called eclectic. He can put into a menu salmon club sandwich, bacon, salad and piccalilli; poached breast of chicken with cardamom and mint; stir-fry prawns with noodles in a Malay curry; bluegrass pie with chocolate chip ice cream and with the requisite expertise make it happily coherent. The meal kicks off with an unusually well-textured powerful version of hummus and a head of roasted garlic – the cloves soft enough to be squeezed from their skins – served with breads and olives (£1.50). Hampton can put together a great picnic under the guise of 'antipasto with savouries', get the balance of spices and the elastic texture right in Thai fishcakes and bring off a mean roast belly of pork with state-of-the-art crackling. I cannot comment on his talent as a patissier as the evening noise of shrieking voices and loud music bouncing off unforgiving hard surfaces drove us from the restaurant before the dessert stage was reached. Unless you like that sort of thing, use Kartouche for lunch (when bookings are taken).

OPEN: Mon-Fri. **HOURS:** 12.30-3.00pm (12.00-3.30pm Sat-Sun) and 6.00pm-12.00am (6.00-11.00pm Sun). **CLOSED:** Christmas and New Year. **CREDIT CARDS ACCEPTED:** AmEx, Mastercard, Visa. **NUMBER OF SEATS:** 80. **SERVICE:** Optional. Wheelchair access. **NEAREST TUBE STATION:** South Kensington/Gloucester Road.

MAP REF: 2,B/3

Kastoori

188 Upper Tooting Road, SW17

081-767 7027

(140)

LUNCH: £8; DINNER: £13

'Delicately executed vegetarian and vegan dishes from India out of Africa'

Don't be put off by the utilitarian appearance of this square, brightly lit high-street restaurant. The charm of the waiters, the benignity of the generously proportioned goddesses whose plaster bas-reliefs line the walls, and the variety and intrigue which its vegetarian (and vegan) food provides soon dissipates any lingering sense that you may have wandered into an Indian Wimpy Bar. It's family-run, and there is a welcome homeliness and lack of guile about the way that explanations are offered and cautions against ordering too much are given. Incense trickles into the room from somewhere or other, and a journey to the (exemplarily clean) lavatories may take you past a meditating grandmother. Vegetarians will hardly need convincing as to the merit of the enterprise, but non-vegetarians risk having their prejudices dislocated by the variety of dishes on offer: ten starters, for example, including mashed kachori (lentils) served with a small splash of different sauces, herbs and fine noodles. The vegetable curries are also varied by dint of subtle saucing, and the main dishes and specials (a range of six, one of which is available each day) are more elaborate in construction and call more on exotic ingredients, such as green banana (the Thanki family spent a spell in Africa before coming to Britain), the artichoke-like drumstick vegetable, and karela bharela. A range of breads includes Kastoori bhatura, flavoured with herbs alone. Desserts are less interesting, while the wine list is short but sensible: Riverside Farm Zinfandel at £8.50 is soft and full enough to cope with most dishes. Timing your visit for Sunday is worthwhile: a number of dishes are only available then, and the Sunday Special Thali, at £6, is perhaps best value of all in a remarkably inexpensive restaurant.

OPEN: LUNCH: Wed-Sun. DINNER: Mon-Sun. 12.30-2.30pm and 6.00-11.00pm. **CLOSED:** 1 week mid-January. **CREDIT CARDS ACCEPTED:** Access,Visa. **NUMBER OF SEATS:** 82. **SERVICE:** Optional. Wheelchair access. **NEAREST TUBE STATION:** Tooting Bec/Tooting Broadway.

Kenny's

2A Pond Place, SW3

(141)

071-225 2916   LUNCH: £10; DINNER: £16

'Cajun food and gospel singing'

Kenny Miller, English but an Honorary Senator of Louisiana and Honorary Citizen of New Orleans, is for the moment serving food inspired by the bayou and the Big Easy only in this brick-lined South Kensington cellar. The (original) Hampstead restaurant is no longer but plans are afoot for a City bar and a Louisiana-style fish restaurant. Reports on the food are good. The over-richness described in last year's guide seems to have given way gracefully to lightness and sensitivity. French-fried eggplant is cooked in a thin, conceivably buttermilk, batter with breadcrumbs and served with a rémoulade of grain mustard, mayo, blackening spices and horseradish. Crab cakes, miraculously free of any starchy padding, are served with a roasted red pepper sauce. Jambalaya, a rice assembly of shrimp, sausage, chicken and tomatoes, is delicious although slightly tame in the spicing. On most evenings the rock music is turned off and four black guys, the Channels, sing *a capella* gospel and soul, as they do every Sunday brunchtime. Even with the advent of Chapel Lafayette (q.v.) there is nothing quite like Kenny's. It helps if you find amusing notices like 'Work is for those who don't know how to fish' or think diverting the sight of a stuffed alligator.

OPEN: Mon-Sun. **HOURS:** 12.00pm-12.00am (11.30am-10.30pm Sun). **CLOSED:** Christmas Day and Boxing Day. **CREDIT CARDS ACCEPTED:** AmEx, Mastercard,Visa. **NUMBER OF SEATS:** 80. **SERVICE:** Optional. **NEAREST TUBE STATION:** South Kensington.   MAP REF: 2,C/3

Kensington Place

201-207 Kensington Church Street, W8   142

071-727 3184   £27

'A phenomenally good restaurant'

'. . . and Kensington Place, apart from the noise'. So concludes many people's list of favourite restaurants in London when I ask them, as frequently, predictably, boringly, I do, to name where they like to go to eat. I have figured out a solution to this problem which if adopted by everyone will soon cease to be one. Go early, say at 12.30pm for lunch or 7.30pm for dinner, having booked a table on the periphery of the room. Start talking and as the noise builds up you either won't notice it or you will subconsciously adjust your own volume. You might imagine that the racket results in a clientele composed entirely of young, brash people but one of the many nice things about Kensington Place is that it attracts all sorts and all ages and the sheer size (seating 130) also confers a sense of egalitarianism rare in London's successful restaurants.

Rowley Leigh's menu is a tempting list of dishes and he has the sense not to jettison what he knows is liked – e.g. carrot soup with risotto and dill, griddled scallops with pea purée, griddled foie gras with sweetcorn pancake, couscous with rabbit and merguez sausages and baked tamarillos with vanilla ice cream – for self-indulgent flights of fancy. I overheard one woman urging her friend to try another tried and true first course, chicken and goat's cheese mousse with olives, and her friend sighing 'I wish I could cook like this.' Dishes of the day, a menu patch where regulars tend to graze, are offered as a set price menu (£13.50) at lunchtime or à la carte in the evenings. They invariably include a fish dish, sometimes luxurious as in blanquette of turbot and scallops with mousserons or robust, as in an almost lacquer-coated roast wing of skate in red wine sauce. The hand-written section will also include items such as sweetbreads (perhaps served with a spiced dip) that are not to everyone's appetite. Some desserts still reflect the public-school educated ownership (chef included) e.g. steamed chocolate pudding with custard. Others tend to home in on soft fruits. Bunter would choose the Grand Selection at £9.50. Constant business and bustle pays tribute to the consistently sound standards at Kensington Place and to the fair pricing. The stretch of window that gives the impression of a department store that sells people eating remains a pleasure both inside and out.

THIS IS AN uncommunicative wine list: no organization other than price order, no descriptive help of any sort. Pity: there are some good wines on it (Rioja from Campillo, Mascarello's Nebbiolo, Chardonnay from Leeuwin and St Hallett's, the Douro red from Quinta de la Rosa – here rendered as Quinta de la Rosso) hidden among less interesting options.

Open: Mon-Sun. **Hours:** 12.00-3.00pm (12.00-3.30pm Sat-Sun) and 6.30-11.45pm (6.30-10.15pm Sun). **Closed:** Christmas Eve, Christmas Day, Boxing Day and New Year's Day. **Credit cards accepted:** Access, Visa. **Number of seats:** 140. **Service:** Optional. **Set price lunch:** £13.50 (3 courses). Wheelchair access. **Nearest tube station:** Notting Hill Gate. MAP REF: 4,C/1

Kleftiko

163-165 Chiswick High Road, W4

081-994 0305   LUNCH: £10; DINNER: £18

'For a rollicking Greek time'

Corfu comes to Chiswick describes this popular taverna on Friday and Saturday nights in summer when the pavement tables are packed with Britons getting in the mood for their hols. There are two reasons to recommend Kleftiko: first, as Conran on a more sophisticated level has proved with Quaglino's, people love a really busy restaurant; second, the food here has a wholesome, homemade flavour. Dishes such as hummus, taramasalata and dolmades – some of the constituent part of a mezedes – which so often taste as if prepared by the same central source that supplies supermarkets, here have more character. The only dull first course sampled was deep-fried squid rings. Main courses include generous kebabs of mixed fish, decent meatballs and the commendable eponymous kleftiko, a succulent, slow-cooked knuckle of lamb. On slower, cooler evenings, the owner likes to stop and chat.

Open: Mon-Sun. **Hours:** 12.00pm-12.00am. **Closed:** Christmas Day and Boxing Day. **Credit cards accepted:** AmEx, Diners Club, Mastercard, Visa. **Number of seats:** 65. **Service:** 12.5% (included in prices). **Set price lunch:** £7.95. No-smoking area. Wheelchair access (but not lavatory). Tables outside seat 40. Private room seats 20. **Nearest tube station:** Turnham Green.

Lahore Kebab House

2 Umberston Street, E1

071-481 9737   £9 (Bring your own wine)

'Simple caff, great Indian food'

The cooking at this unprepossessing establishment – definitely a caff, not a restaurant – continues to delight and impress. Spicy-hot, juicy chicken tikka has been described as 'the best I have ever eaten' and similar praise showered on lamb tikka, lamb chop curry and the mixed vegetables. There is no menu as such – you can look at the list on the waiter's pad – but at these prices (£3 for meat curries, a bit more for chicken and prawn) it is tempting just to ask for one of everything. Be aware too that there are daily specials such as brain masala and quails. Roti which is replenished throughout the meal unasked is first rate. A disadvantage, or maybe an advantage, is the speed of service. A friend driving from Hampstead said he spent longer getting there than eating there. His visit was on the eve of a Test match when a group of overgrown schoolboys in MCC ties caused him to dwell on the curious relationship of Indian food to male bonding: overgrown schoolboy loudly to male companion 'Why would your friend Melissa most like this restaurant?' Answer; 'Because it is called La Whore Kebab House.' This sally was apparently greeted with gales of hearty male laughter. Be prepared to queue and to share a table.

OPEN: Mon-Sun. **HOURS:** 12.00pm-12.00am. **CREDIT CARDS ACCEPTED:** None. **NUMBER OF SEATS:** 60. **SERVICE:** Optional. 2 tables outside. **NEAREST TUBE STATION:** Whitechapel/Aldgate East.

The Lansdowne Public House

90 Gloucester Avenue, NW1   145

071-483 0409   **£17**

'Not your average boozer'

Chefs Amanda Pritchett and Simon Green continue to please *le tout NW1* with their mainly Italian food at this large haphazardly furnished pub. A typical menu, changing in part between lunch and dinner, includes a soup such as chilled chive and watercress, a well-thought-through assembly along the lines of Parma ham, rocket, pears, roasted fennel and Parmesan, a tart, say aubergine, feta and oregano served with a mint and cucumber salad, a pasta dish, for example linguini with melted onion and thyme sauce, a main-course salad and a grill. Italian sausages are popular. It is a formula comparable to that at the Eagle and the Peasant (see entries). Would that more pubs be converted in a similar manner taking some of the pressure off this one. Customers and noise can overwhelm.

OPEN: LUNCH: Tues-Sun. DINNER: Mon-Sun. **HOURS:** 11.00am-11.00pm. (6.00-11.00pm Mon, 11.00am-10.30pm Sun). **CLOSED:** Christmas Day and New Year's Eve. **CREDIT CARDS ACCEPTED:** None. **NUMBER OF SEATS:** 70. **SERVICE:** Optional. Wheelchair access (but not lavatory). 36 seats outside. **NEAREST TUBE STATION:** Chalk Farm.   MAP REF: 5,B/2

Launceston Place

1a Launceston Place, W8   146

071-937 6912   **£30**

'As fine an institution as its Sunday lunch'

In an industry in which consistency and quality are paramount, Launceston Place (sober sister of Kensington Place q.v.) offers a reassuring example of a restaurant whose patrons can rely not only on the charm and intimacy of its surroundings but also the integrity of its cooking and pricing. Anglo-Mediterranean might be one way of describing the varied menu. It can veer from the homey – hot sauté potatoes with soft-boiled eggs, crisp bacon and mustard dressing – to the sophisticated – griddled foie gras with a shallot tart – via the mildly exotic – griddled baby squid in a black bean sauce. And that is in the first course. Main courses are well thought through, demonstrating considerable flair and imagination on the part of the chef: roast noisettes of hake with red wine sauce and celeriac mash; whole roast coquelet with capers, artichokes and tarragon jus. The star of the desserts tried was scented geranium pudding with wild strawberries. Wines are ranged by price rather than nationality or grape variety. There are some interesting bottles among what must be to the steady drinker a crowd of familiar faces.

OPEN: LUNCH: Sun-Fri. DINNER: Mon-Sat. HOURS: 12.30-2.30pm (12.30-3.00pm Sun) and 7.00-11.30pm. CLOSED: 5 days at Christmas. CREDIT CARDS ACCEPTED: Access, AmEx, Visa. NUMBER OF SEATS: 80. SERVICE: Optional. SET PRICE LUNCH AND DINNER: £13.50 and £16.50. No-smoking area. Wheelchair access (but not lavatory). Private rooms seat 14 and 30. NEAREST TUBE STATION: Gloucester Road.

Laurent Restaurant

428 Finchley Road, NW2

(147)

071-794 3603   £13

'Simply terrific couscous'

This simple, unpretentious place with red and white checked vinyl tablecloths and North African posters on the white walls pleases as soon as you walk in. Laurent has the air of a friendly neighbourhood establishment which knows exactly what it can do; in this case couscous. Couscous comes five ways, chicken couscous and fish couscous being new additions to the menu. There is also vegetarian (chick-peas, courgettes, root vegetables); complet (like an exotic lightly spiced version of Irish stew plus merguez sausages); and royal (as before with a mixed grill on the side, only for the very hungry). You can start with an egg fried in filo pastry and end with sorbet or ice creams but the couscous is what counts. The proprietor, who with his family provides the charming service, is a beaming enthusiast who makes you feel loved without embarrassing you. His recommendation of an appropriate wine is a dry Moroccan rosé named Boulaouane.

OPEN: Mon-Sat. HOURS: 12.00-2.00pm and 6.00-11.00pm. CLOSED: Bank Holidays and first 3 weeks in August. CREDIT CARDS ACCEPTED: Access, AmEx, Visa. NUMBER OF SEATS: 36. SERVICE: Optional. Wheelchair access (but not lavatory). NEAREST TUBE STATION: Golders Green.

Leith's

92 Kensington Park Road, W11

071-229 4481   £50

'After twenty-five years the hors d'oeuvre trolley is still rolling'

Leith's did not make an appearance in last year's edition of the guide, an omission that Leith's manager Nick Tarayan was quick to point out was quite unjustifiable. I duly revisited Leith's, once for dinner and on another occasion for a lunch to celebrate the launch of *The Michelin Guide 1994* and the fact that Leith's had been awarded one star. The cooking of young chef Alex Floyd is indeed commendable. Prices which I have described as punishing have been ameliorated somewhat and are now just mettlesome but the 15% 'optional' service charge grates. Now quarter of a century old, certain culinary traditions of Leith's are maintained; the dish of Leith's duckling served for two and the hors d'oeuvres trolley. The price of choosing the latter (£11.75 per person) tends to make customers select too many items resulting in a muddled plateful. But even when you restrain yourself sensibly, do include the artichoke and olive pie. There are seasonal à la carte menus, a vegetarian menu (something that Leith's could be said to have pioneered) and Alex Floyd's two-course, set price menu of the week (£25 + 15%). Here we found some of the best cooking; ravioli of braised lamb's tongue with turnips and wild mushrooms followed by salmon poached in olive oil with spinach and beetroot. On another day the choice could have been charlotte of cod and aubergine with roasted scallop and tapenade, gazpacho sauce followed by pot-roasted loin of pork topped with black pudding, cream of celery sauce. It is an inventive, skilled performance. The excellence of caramelized plum tart trimmed with blackcurrants and served with damson ice cream bodes well for all desserts. The services of Virgile and Stone have lightened up the look of Leith's. I wonder if there is a comparable company that could goose the service.

RATHER GUSHING NOTES, and prices which quickly romp over the £20 barrier (there is little under £20 if you opt to acquiesce in the 15% service charge), yet this is a list which has been compiled with enthusiasm and curiosity, and offers some very good drinking – sparkling wines, for example, including a larger-than-usual range of Cavas. Clarets and burgundies are founded on value alternatives to the big names (d'Angludet, Cantemerle or de Fieuzal, for example, with good village burgundies from Lignier, Clair, Boillot and others). There are plenty of halves, and some of the flashier classics are in large bottles (including an impériale – eight bottles in one – of Lafite '66 for £1,695).

OPEN: Mon-Sun. **HOURS:** 7.30-11.30pm. **CLOSED:** August Bank Holiday, 4 days at Christmas. **CREDIT CARDS ACCEPTED:** AmEx, Diner's Club, Mastercard, Switch, Visa . **NUMBER OF SEATS:** 80. **SERVICE:** Optional. **SET PRICE DINNER:** £25 or £22.50 vegetarian. Private room seats 4-40. Wheelchair access (but not lavatory). **NEAREST TUBE STATION:** Notting Hill Gate/Paddington.   MAP REF: 4,B/1

Lemonia

89 Regents Park Road, NW1

071-586 7454

(149)

£17

*'Good food, good value and good service turn out to be
the secrets of success'*

This large, friendly Greek/Cypriot restaurant sited in a light, bright pub-
to-taverna conversion is a longstanding favourite with North Londoners
and indeed with others happy to travel to enjoy the carefully cooked,
reasonably priced food. (Don't even think of coming without booking
except perhaps at lunchtimes). The family who run it manage to be
genuinely welcoming to everyone, but especially their many regulars, and
will take real trouble over special occasions like birthday parties for which
the upstairs private room is ideal. There are few surprises on the menu
but the familar litany – hummus, tarama, aubergine salad, tabbouleh
(heavy with parsley), dolmades, kleftiko, keftedes, calamari – is definitely
a cut above the Charlotte Street and Camden Town equivalents. More
interesting dishes tend be listed on the daily menu of specials; fresh
artichokes and broad beans is beautifully, painstakingly prepared, grilled
sea bass is a bargain compared with prices charged elsewhere and seasonal
vegetable dishes are lively. Service is almost overwhelmingly amiable.
Unless you enjoy shouting your head off go early or late or at lunchtime
or go opposite. The original Lemonia premises on three floors of a terrace
house have reopened as Limani and are just as good.

OPEN: LUNCH: Sun-Fri. DINNER: Mon-Sat. **HOURS:** 12.00-3.00pm and 6.00-
11.30pm. **CLOSED:** Christmas Day and Boxing Day. **CREDIT CARDS ACCEPTED:**
Access, Mastercard, Visa. **NUMBER OF SEATS:** 140. **SERVICE:** Optional. **SET PRICE
LUNCH:** £7.95. **SET PRICE DINNER:** £9.50. Wheelchair access. Private room seats
40. **NEAREST TUBE STATION:** Chalk Farm.

The Lexington

45 Lexington Street, W1

071-434 3401

(150)

£23

'A cool place, reasonably priced'

Martin Saxon, who was once known for popping up as waiter or manager
at almost every fashionable place that opened, has stayed put at The
Lexington (which he opened) for what might be a record two years. It is
amazing how stabilizing a bit of investment can be. Chef Mark Holmes
who has worked at The Square, which started with Saxon as manager, and
the Ivy has got into his stride and is now producing excellent, relatively
simple food. A cost-effective way of trying it is via the £10 set price menu
for two courses and coffee served every evening from 6pm to 11pm. From
the à la carte a salad of Jerusalem and globe artichokes was a nice conceit
concerning two actually unrelated species and beetroot crisps and garlic
mash were splendid accompaniments to roast pheasant breast. The

Lexington paysanne (see review of Chester's for details) is a constant on the daily-changing menu. Desserts are fine, particularly nougat glacé with apricot coulis. The wines are an interesting motley crowd with the widest band of selections between £10 and £19. The unencumbered look of the place is pleasing; dark green banquettes, bare tables, linen napkins, Bruce McLean enamel prints on a wall newly painted a warm orange are all details. The rooms upstairs – lit only by candles – in this pretty Georgian house are terrific for romantic private parties. I know because I have been to one.

OPEN: LUNCH: Mon-Fri. DINNER: Mon-Sat. **HOURS:** 12.00-3.00pm and 6.00-11.30pm. **CLOSED:** From Christmas to New Year and Bank Holidays. **CREDIT CARDS ACCEPTED:** Access, AmEx, Diner's Club, Visa. **NUMBER OF SEATS:** 45. **SERVICE:** Optional. **SET PRICE DINNER:** £10. No-smoking area by request. Wheelchair access (but not lavatory). 2 private rooms each seat 20. **NEAREST TUBE STATION:** Oxford Circus/Piccadilly Circus/Tottenham Court Road.

MAP REF: 1,D/2

The Lobster Pot

3 Kennington Lane, SE11

071-582 5556 £23-£35

'A meal on the ocean waves'

'Welcome Aboard' says the doormat and as you enter this ship's cabin of a restaurant the sound of seagulls is heard overhead. You are welcomed by Natalie Lim (wife of the chef/patron), a beauty from Mauritius shipshape in navy blue with gold braid. In case you haven't got the point that this is a fish restaurant, portholes with fish swimming past, coiled ropes and nets, a portrait of a pipe-smoking old tar and waiters kitted out as Breton fisherfolk give you a few more clues. Hervé Regent's menu is disconcertingly long for such a small, cramped place with seventeen choices on the three-course gastronomic menu alone (£18.50 plus supplements). The mainly fishy à la carte also has a section with quite a wide choice of meat dishes including ox tongue, guinea fowl and calves kidneys. However, it would seem perverse in the circumstances to choose anything but fish. House fish soup served with rouille makes the most of the variety of fish to hand, as does la bouillabaisse Bretonne, le plateau de fruits de mer, the selection of grilled fish entitled la selection de la mer à l'ail, and le couscous de poisson à la Hervé. Quality is good. The dessert of coffee ice cream was excellent but there are fancier options such as tarte Tatin and les profiteroles au chocolat. The clientele has been described as dividing up between wide boys and their girlfriends from Elephant and Castle and suits from Kennington. The wide boys have more fun. The wine list could use some of the prolixity of the menu.

OPEN: Tues-Sat. **HOURS:** 12.00-2.30pm and 7.00-11.00pm. **CREDIT CARDS ACCEPTED:** Access, AmEx, Connect, Diner's Club, Mastercard, Switch, Visa. **NUMBER OF SEATS:** 24. **SERVICE:** 12.5%. **SET PRICE LUNCH:** £12.50. **SET PRICE DINNER:** £18.50. Wheelchair access (but not lavatory). **NEAREST TUBE STATION:** Kennington.

London Istanbul OrientExpress

62 Streatham High Road, SW16

081 677 5100 £14

'From Turkey with tenderness'

There are more people than you might credit wandering up and down Streatham High Road of an evening, looking for somewhere to eat, and those guided by a lucky star, or possibly solicited by a beaming waiter, end up here, gazing at the absurdly appealing ceiling lamps and listening to the improbably soothing synthesized live Turkish music. (On Friday and Saturday nights you may get an undulating belly thrown in.) The dishes are drawn from the usual Turkish repertoire, but are prepared and served with unusual care and delicacy. The pink tablecloths and corporate wood-panelled walls give a clean and tidy feel, while the mosque-like blue-and-gold ceiling lends a note of prettiness; the waiters are gentle and kind, and lower dishes onto the table with slow, deliberate, unstressed gestures. Female diners leave clutching ingenuously offered flowers.

OPEN: Mon-Sun. **HOURS:** 12.00-3.00pm and 6.00pm-12.00am. **CREDIT CARDS ACCEPTED:** All major cards. **NUMBER OF SEATS:** 60. **SERVICE:** Optional. **SET PRICE LUNCH:** £6.95. **SET PRICE DINNER:** £10.90. No-smoking area. Wheelchair access. Private room seats 40. **NEAREST BR STATION:** Streatham Hill.

Lou Pescadou

241 Old Brompton Road, SW5

071-370 1057 £23

'A snatch of the Marseillaise'

You'd have to be spectacularly impercipient to fail to log the message that maritime prints, lobster pots, hurricane lamps, boating caps, scallop-shell ash trays, ceiling-mounted helm wheel and fishy plates convey. Oysters, clams, mussels, squid, John Dory, turbot, cod: the variety is good, freshness fair, cooking uncomplicated. And very French: sauces, for example, rarely contain balancing acid notes, the assumption being that that's what your glass of wine is for. Fish soup is grittily good, and ladlefuls of it spill over into other dishes, like prawn-head-strewn assiette du pàcheur. Other Provençale specialities are worth pursuing; pancake-thin apple tart is Calvados-sodden, then ignited in front of you. Good bread, good butter, good coffee: it all comes together, which may be one reason why most of the customers, as well as the staff, seem to be French. The waiters can be sweetness itself on occasion, and are always professional enough to come near to meriting the generous service charge. The wine list is spare, but contains good Chablis and good Pouilly-Fumé; and late opening is much appreciated in this insomnious and often lurid corner of town.

OPEN: Mon-Sun. HOURS: 12.00-3.00pm and 7.00pm-12.00am. CLOSED: 10 days at Christmas. CREDIT CARDS ACCEPTED: All major cards. NUMBER OF SEATS: 55. SERVICE: 15% optional. Wheelchair access (but not lavatory). 20 seats outside. Private room seats 40. NEAREST TUBE STATION: Earls Court.

Ma Goa

244 Upper Richmond Road,
Putney, SW15

081-780 1767 £15

'A sweet little place with unusual Indian dishes'

An Indian winter holiday with some of the time spent in Goa confirmed my suspicion that there is little that is gastronomically authentically Goan here but so what? The menu is quite different from the usual lists and for that we must give heartfelt thanks. Family-run by the Kapoors (Mr Kapoor was formerly manager of Shezan) the service in this small, usually crowded place is charming. Share a variety of first courses; low prices and, indeed, the modest content, makes it almost immaterial if they are not all a resounding success. Chick chick wings and shrimp balcao, a dry curry served with something resembling mini-pitta bread, was liked at a test meal. Achar gosht, incorporating pickle, is a piquant rather than spicy lamb dish. Hundee dishes cooked in sealed terracotta pots have resonant results. Fernandez salad, a salsa-like cold concoction of chopped tomatoes, cucumbers and onions, offsets curries well. There are items with names like Strip Steak Sizzler and Goan Beach Party Barbecue but I would hate to think that these are the reasons for Ma Goa's popularity in Putney. Note the good-value set price lunch.

OPEN: Tue-Sun. HOURS: 12.30-2.30pm (1.00-9.30pm Sun) and 7.00-11.00pm. CLOSED: Christmas Day, Boxing Day and New Year's Day. CREDIT CARDS ACCEPTED: Access, AmEx, Mastercard, Visa. NUMBER OF SEATS: 50. SERVICE: 10%. SET PRICE LUNCH: £6.95. Wheelchair access (but not lavatory). 10 seats outside. NEAREST TUBE STATION: East Putney. MAP REF: 3,A/1

Malabar

27 Uxbridge Street, W8

071-727 8800 LUNCH: £15; DINNER: £18

'Indian food in the atmosphere of an Italian restaurant'

The name of the restaurant can be taken as a reference to the spices grown on that fertile South Indian coast, not to the cooking of Kerala or even South India generally. Spices and also herbs are used quite distinctively here and in some instances integrated with relatively uncommon ingredients (for mainstream Indian restaurants) such as chicken livers, venison, bananas and pumpkin. First courses always have the advantage of undimmed appetites but, even bearing that in mind, first courses at Malabar seem more vivid and are certainly served with greater generosity than the dishes that come later. Try hiran, marinated venison with the singular, slightly sour flavour of tamarind; the charcoal-grilled, well-seasoned mixture of ground lamb called keema kebab; prawn philouries, prawns deep-fried in potato flour. Main courses of long chicken (with cloves and ginger) and the red-dyed prawns masala had me looking longingly at the vegetarian thali (£11.75) on the next door table. It is possible that better choices would have been the lemon zesty lamb dish nimbu gosht or cumin flavoured jeera chicken. Began bhaji, barbecued aubergine, is good. Part-English ownership contributes, I think, to the *comprehensibility* of Malabar and its consequent success.

OPEN: Mon-Sun. HOURS: 12.00-3.00pm and 6.00-11.00pm. CLOSED: Last week in August, 4 days at Christmas. CREDIT CARDS ACCEPTED: Access, Switch, Visa. NUMBER OF SEATS: 56. SERVICE: 12.5% (included in prices). SET PRICE LUNCH AND DINNER: £15. Private room seats 20. NEAREST TUBE STATION: Notting Hill Gate.

MAP REF: 4,C/1

Mamta

692 Fulham Road, SW6

156

071-736 5914 or 071-371 5971   **£15**

'Can make converts of ardent carnivores'

Indian vegetarian is one of my favourite ways of eating so I deliberately sent a true blue British meat-loving man miles across London to see what he would make of Mamta, in my view a particularly good Indian vegetarian restaurant in the far reaches of Fulham Road. He was not impressed by the minimalist interior done out in virtually unrelieved light brown but loved the food and thought it particularly well-defined and fresh-tasting. Pani puri, light pastry shells into which you pour a sweet and sour sauce and masala dosa, a 'glorious, light-as-gossamar' pancake stuffed with potato and onion and served with coconut chutney were revelations; 'Our spirits soared.' Other dishes chosen were Chef's Specials called Aubergine Sparkle and Shimla Green, predicated on fresh spinach. Vegetable curries can be served dry or without spices (why would anyone want that?). Breads and dals (lentil assemblies) are good as are, in my experience, uttapam, a savoury spicy sort of crumpet, and panir matter, a green pea curry. My inspector makes the points that thalis – set meals – are the sensible way of ordering for newcomers to the cuisine and that stainless steel plates, however authentic, are uncongenial.

OPEN: Mon-Sun. HOURS: 12.30-3.00pm and 6.00-11.00pm. CLOSED: Christmas Day, Boxing Day and New Year's Eve. CREDIT CARDS ACCEPTED: All major cards. NUMBER OF SEATS: 42. SERVICE: Optional. SET PRICE LUNCH: £4.95. SET PRICE DINNER: £7.25-£11.50. No-smoking area. Wheelchair access (but not lavatory). NEAREST TUBE STATION: Parsons Green.

THE LITTLE PEPPER UPPER.

Burberrys

OF LONDON

For details of featured merchandise contact:
The Wholesale Showroom, 165 Regent Street, London W1R 8AS.
Telephone: 071–734 5929.

Mandarin Kitchen

14-16 Queensway, W2

071-727 9012/9468 £15

'Go for shellfish reasons'

In West London's Chinatown – Queensway – support for the restaurants must be sought outside an indigenous Chinese population. At Mandarin Kitchen the management takes menu space to assure its customers that lobsters are live, wild and Scottish, that crabs come live from the south or south-west coast and that different kinds of king prawn have been carefully chosen just for them. A meal in this cavernous, crowded space should certainly include either baked lobster or crab with garlic and chilli (or ginger and spring onion) with extra-soft noodles to soak up the juices or pot of crab with bean noodle and dry shrimps in chilli sauce, a sensationally good dish, enough for two shameless people or four fairly polite ones. The range of fish served is wider than at most other restaurants. Eels are good. Try the fillets in black bean and chilli sauce on a sizzling plate. Before these centrepiece dishes, look to the chef's special recommendation starters for the crunchy roast baby squid, soft shell crabs, steamed scallops and the subtle, slippery crab meat sauce on fried king prawns. Meat dishes are more commonplace but the black pepper veal chop provides a pungent contrast to delicate fish dishes. Noodle assemblies are good and it is possible to order just one seasonal vegetable in ginger and garlic rather than the unsatisfactory mix usually supplied. Set menus are for saps or those 'out for a Chinese' who made a mistake in coming to such a good place. Service is brisk and efficient but smiles can be coaxed from the stern waitresses by a show of enthusiasm, by which I mean greed.

OPEN: Mon-Sun. HOURS: 12.00-11.30pm. CLOSED: Christmas Day and Boxing Day. CREDIT CARDS ACCEPTED: AmEx, Diner's Club, JCB, Mastercard, Visa. NUMBER OF SEATS: 110. SERVICE: Optional. SET PRICE LUNCH AND DINNER: £8.90. Wheelchair access (but not lavatory). NEAREST TUBE STATION: Queensway/Bayswater.

Mandeer

21 Hanway Place, W1

071-323 0660 £15

'Hippy-dippy healthy food'

The Mandeer restaurant opened in 1967. George Harrison and Ravi Shankar were there. A sweet air of gram flour-power idealism still adheres to the premises and you reach the basement dining room decorated with faded Indian artefacts down a corridor papered with astrology leaflets, offers of yoga breakfasts and teach-yourself-Urdu books. The menu is described as Ayurvedic but dishes are much the same as those you find at other Gujerati or Southern Indian vegetarian restaurants. Five thalis, including a vegan option and one suitable for Jains, are offered in addition to the long list of dishes based on vegetables, pulses, nuts, yogurt, grains and unleavened breads. 'For your well being . . . dishes carefully balance the elements of fire, earth, water and (naturally) wind.' So says a promotional leaflet. The drinks list includes organic wines and beer and furthermore all the food is kosher. The Mandeer is a timewarp haven in an unsalubrious area.

OPEN: Mon-Sat. **HOURS:** 12.00-3.00pm and 5.30-10.00pm. **CLOSED:** Bank Holidays. **CREDIT CARDS ACCEPTED:** AmEx, Diner's Club, Mastercard, Switch, Visa. **NUMBER OF SEATS:** 60. **SERVICE:** 10% optional. **SET PRICE LUNCH:** From £2.90. **SET PRICE DINNER:** £7.25. No-smoking area. Private room seats 30. **NEAREST TUBE STATION:** Tottenham Court Road.   MAP REF: 1,E/2

Mantanah Thai Cuisine

2 Orton Buildings,
Portland Road, SE25

081-771 1148   **£20**

'A Thai restaurant worth a detour'

Philip Harris, owner of Bahn Thai in Soho (q.v.) wrote nobly to point out the existence of this Thai restaurant in South Norwood where he enjoyed, he said, a meal comparable in quality and authenticity to one he had had at the house of a Thai friend in Bangkok. The finesse of the food seems to depend somewhat on who is cooking but the standard is certainly above average. To shape into an order some of the 123 dishes offered, it helps either to be vegetarian – there is a commendable vegetarian menu – or to favour the chilli-hot assemblies and singular charcuterie of north and north-east Thailand. The set menus are useful as a guide to the structure of a meal but building it from the à la carte is more rewarding gastronomically. The gentleness and sweetness of service at the small, simply decorated Mantanah is, equally, authentically Thai.

OPEN: Tues-Sun. **HOURS:** 6.30-11.00pm. **CREDIT CARDS ACCEPTED:** AmEx, Mastercard, Visa. **NUMBER OF SEATS:** 40. **SERVICE:** Optional. **SET PRICE DINNER:** £12.95 and £16.00. Wheelchair access (but not lavatory). **NEAREST BR STATION:** Norwood Junction

Manzi's

1-2 Leicester Street, WC2

071-734 0224   **£28**

'A Soho hotel fish restaurant'

Established in 1928 and with a plaque commemorating the fact that Johann Strauss the elder stayed there – the building is also an hotel –

Manzi's traditional fish restaurant holds out against encroaching Chinatown. A loyal clientele keeps it busy and they know that the best dishes are the simpler ones; oysters or fresh whitebait perhaps, followed by Dover sole or 'irreproachably fresh' grilled halibut or turbot. At a test meal a bold man essayed the quenells (sic) and defended his decision on the grounds that the English spelling explained the bready texture and the tomato and fish-flavoured sauce studded with sliced button mushrooms. Fried potatoes are in fact chips and they tend to find more favour than some of the other vegetables. The waiter did not encourage an order of Continental ice cream (homemade Swiss recipe). He could well have extended his lack of enthusiasm to the tiramisù which seemed to have emerged from a catering pack. The ground-floor dining room decorated with cheeky ceiling paintings of can-can dancers, seafood charts decorated mirrors and huge ancient chollahs – perhaps originally spurned by Johann Strauss – is in my view preferable to the first-floor Cabin Room with its fancier menu, except perhaps if you were later heading up to a room . . .A dockland's branch of Manzi's is at Glengall Bridge, Turnberry Quay, Cross Harbour, E14 (071-538 9615).

OPEN: LUNCH: Mon-Sat. DINNER: Mon-Sun. **HOURS:** 12.00-2.40pm and 5.30-11.40pm. **CLOSED:** Christmas Day and Boxing Day. **CREDIT CARDS ACCEPTED:** All major cards. **NUMBER OF SEATS:** 120. **SERVICE:** 10% optional. **SET PRICE LUNCH AND DINNER:** £12 (pre- and post-theatre). Wheelchair access (but not lavatory). Private room seats 30-50. **NEAREST TUBE STATION:** Leicester Square.

MAP REF: 1,E/1

Maroush

21 Edgeware Road, W2　　　　　　　　　　　　　　　**161**

071-723 0773　　　　　　　　　　LUNCH: £19; DINNER: £48

'Highly-rated Lebanese'

Maroush has been at the forefront of the burgeoning London Lebanese restaurant scene, so successfully that it has opened a further three branches (two of which, curiously, are less than 500 yards from the original). The menu lists the usual array of Middle Eastern delights, some familiar some not supplied by your average supermarket – basturma, batata harra – and some possibly intimidating – fresh raw lamb's liver (reassuringly delivered daily) and salat nikhaat, blanched fresh brains with special dressing. Pastries are excellent; light, buttery and aromatic with rosewater, cardamom and pistachio. Within glossy marble and brass surroundings, the service is as immaculate as it is attentive. With belly dancing provided most nights, you can a get a taste of uptown Beirut in downtown Edgware Road.

OPEN: Mon-Sun. **HOURS:** 12.00pm-2.00am. **CLOSED:** Christmas Day. **CREDIT CARDS ACCEPTED:** All major cards. **NUMBER OF SEATS:** 110. **SERVICE:** Optional. Wheelchair access (but not lavatory). **NEAREST TUBE STATION:** Marble Arch.

MAP REF: 1,A/3

McClements Bistro

2 Whitton Road, Twickenham

162

081-744 9610   **£18**

'Offal nice'

Creating a bistro version of your fancy restaurant, as John McClements did here near the Twickenham rugby stadium, is accepted chef practice. But then to turn your original fancy restaurant into a Petit Bistro (McClements Petit Bistro q.v.) seems to be scoring an own goal. The good news at both establishments is that the menus, far from being mechanistic or predictable, are muscular, quirky, enticing lists particularly bewitching to those who like offal. Such folk – and it is a gang of which I am a member – will think a meal kicked off to a flying start with the pâté of gizzard that accompanies the offer of homemade bread. To continue studying entrails move on to stuffed lamb's heart, lamb's tongue and a baked potato with tripe Provençal. This back to basics is not of course compulsory. Another meal could start with sea scallops roasted with caramelized chicory and move on to four cut of beef; fillet, rump, sirloin, skirt served with a green pepper sauce or salmon, scallops and brill roasted with garlic and ginger. Prices are fair with, at time of writing, first courses starting at £3.50 for chilled gazpacho and croûtons and main courses at £8 for roast pigeon with liver dumplings and sauté cabbage. Vegetables, which are not always strictly necessary, are also reasonable. Note chips (good ones) at £1. The flair in execution of all these bright ideas varies somewhat and items irritatingly described as crispy (crisp would do) can disappoint in their flaccidity but as a bistro it is entirely devoid of culinary cliché. Penny-pinching in the operation seems confined to decor. The room painted the colour of mushroom soup is decorated with a few art gallery posters blu-tacked to the walls plus inept Toulouse-Lautreckish murals. Tables are close to one another and I would imagine the time not to go is after a match has finished.

OPEN: Mon-Sun. HOURS: 12.00-2.30pm and 7.00-10.30pm. CREDIT CARDS ACCEPTED: Access, Visa. NUMBER OF SEATS: 45. SET PRICE LUNCH: £12.50. SET PRICE DINNER: £18. No-smoking area. Wheelchair access. Private room seats 10. NEAREST BR STATION: Twickenham.

McClements Petit Bistro

12 The Green, Twickenham

163

081-755 0176   **£20**

'A little house of big food'

In a review that appeared in the *Evening Standard* in May '94, I described the premises of McClements Petit Bistro as a dolls' house owned by dolls with negative equity. Not a great lure I admit, but the restaurant's new name is not (I think) so much a reference to the small size of the premises but the fresh approach to the menu. In bringing prices down and embracing less convoluted but no less interesting cooking, chef/proprietor John McClements has brought his original eponymous restaurant more or less in line with his bistro operation. If you are planning a jaunt to Twickenham in order to eat in a bistro owned by John McClements you might ask yourself, 'Which one do I choose?' It is difficult to advise. Both have their gastronomic lures, invested to some extent in the creative cooking of offal, and both have their drawbacks in terms of restaurant interiors. Because the Petit Bistro was previously a more expensive restaurant, it wins in terms of comfort and certain dishes tried there have the edge in sophistication and subtle saucing. Examples are cassoulet of Dublin Bay prawns with gizzard (a gifted assembly with a potent shellfish sauce); wild mushroom charlotte baked in a pancake; grilled breast of duck with caramelized apple and chicory; stuffed pig's trotter served with slice of crispy cooked cod. A dish not tried because unavailable on that day but much wanted was fish nobs (skate cheeks) pan-fried with lemon butter sauce. Desserts are authentically bistro simple with the exception of hot soufflé with Calvados sauce, worth ordering at the start of your meal. The New World wines tend to offer the value consistent with the menu pricing. Note the admirably fair price of £1.50 for a selection of fresh vegetables.

OPEN: Tues-Sat. HOURS: 12.00-2.30pm and 7.00-10.30pm. CREDIT CARDS ACCEPTED: Access, Visa. NUMBER OF SEATS: 35. SERVICE: 10%. SET PRICE LUNCH: £15. SET PRICE DINNER: £18. No-smoking area. Wheelchair access (but not lavatory). Private room seats 15. NEAREST BR STATION: Twickenham.

Le Meridien – The Oak Room

21 Piccadilly, W1

071-465 1640   LUNCH £25; DINNER £55

'Brings into question the supposed superiority of French chefs'

Chef David Chambers has moved from the Meridien in Piccadilly to the London Hilton on Park Lane. He has been replaced by Alain Marechal who was previously executive chef of L'Habit Blanc of the Meridien in Nice. Michel Lorain from the three-star Michelin La Côte Saint-Jacques in Burgundy stays as consultant chef. A test lunch with Marechal at the stove was a disappointment, proving something I have suspected to be the case which is that a certain sort of fancy French cooking will nowadays strike Londoners who eat out a lot in their own town as old hat. Seeing little dabs of intricate garnish arranged round a plate like numerals on a clock face, noting a hideous reliance on lollo rosso, receiving meat denatured into unidentifiable (by looking) cylinders, tasting a wildly oversweetened compote of kumquats served with rabbit but belonging on toast at breakfast, sighing over the prissiness and dullness of the dessert trolley made me suggest to Jean Quero, the restaurant manager, that he take Marechal to see what, for example, Gordon Ramsay of Aubergine, Simon Hopkinson of Bibendum and Philip Howard of The Square are doing. However, that was early days in Marechal's stint. The Oak Room is a beautiful, comfortable dining room, the service is superb, and the wines, well, see below. I shall be trying again.

TRADITIONAL FRENCH drinking is what's expected in such surroundings, and that's what's delivered. What distinguishes the Oak Room is that there is a higher percentage of outstanding winemaking talent in its cellars than in most, with burgundy (Lafarge, de Montille, Sauzet, Leflaive, Vincent, Domaine de l'Arlot, Méo-Camuzet, Tollot-Beaut . . .) particularly glittering. Loire (Marionnet, Mellot, Dagueneau), Alsace (Hugel, Trimbach and Zind-Humbrecht) and the Rhîne (Chapoutier, Guigal and Colombo) are not far behind, and clarets are sound (the better '85s, like Lascombes and Fieuzal, are drinking well now). The opportunity to drink Dom Pérignon by the glass is one worth taking.

OPEN: LUNCH: Mon-Fri. DINNER: Mon-Sat. **HOURS:** 12.00-2.30pm and 7.00-10.30pm. **CLOSED:** Bank Holidays (open for lunch on Christmas Day). **CREDIT CARDS ACCEPTED:** All major cards. **NUMBER OF SEATS:** 45. **SERVICE:** Optional. **SET PRICE LUNCH:** £24.50. Wheelchair access. **NEAREST TUBE STATION:** Piccadilly Circus. MAP REF: 1,D/1

Le Metro

28 Basil Street, SW3

071-589 6286 £15

'Where it's a waste not to eat'

Le Metro's facelift sees it bidding adieu to French prettiness and hallo to the space-station look: hard surfaces, cold light, bold lines, Spock ears. Food and drink remains prime motive for boldly going down its basement stairs. A pressed terrine of sole interleaved with leek and mint served on simple tomatoes dressed with pungent olive oil typified the clean, clear restraint of a menu which manages to be both contemporary and sensible. Duck confit on a sweet claret sauce with crunchy baby turnips matched visual interest with perfect flavour and texture contrasts. Black pudding and blackened salmon steak are more martial still; flakes of steamed cod and broccoli sautéed with lobster butter divert the temperamentally Venusian. Desserts are as sure-handed. The wine list's distinction is a choice of 50 by the glass – and *good* ones, too, like Schloss Johannesburg's irresistibly delicate 1992 QbA, Mount Langi Ghiran's cindery 1992 Shiraz, or Weinert's extraordinarily deep and accomplished 1989 Argentinian Merlot. What a great idea this is; what a shame it's not more widely imitated. What a tragedy, too, that many of the clientele simply pile in here to smoke Silk Cut, shriek, and drink unaccompanied bottles of the cheapest and the worst wine on the list: white Vin de Levin. Not the way to preserve your looks, girls: eat up, do!

OPEN: Mon-Sat. **HOURS:** 8.00am-11.00pm. **CLOSED:** Christmas Day and Easter Monday. **CREDIT CARDS ACCEPTED:** All major cards. **NUMBER OF SEATS:** 50. **SERVICE:** Optional. 4 seats outside. **NEAREST TUBE STATION:** Knightsbridge.

MAP REF: 2,F/4

Mijanou

143 Ebury Street, SW1

071-730 4099   Lunch: £25; Dinner: £41

'Stimulation on all fronts'

Few restaurants contrive to combine the excellent and the suspect so seamlessly as this one. Under 'excellent', you'd have to file the flower-filled window boxes and plants outside, the selection and scope of Neville Blech's wine list (see below), the eager-to-please waiters, the broadly tasteful decor, and the furious energy of Sonia Blech's cooking. Sautéed calves' liver and kidney, muddy and dull, arrive on a wild rice and chanterelle risotto with baby vegetables dancing at their edge and cabbage laboriously and oozingly stuffed with celeriac and carrot purées – much of which one would have foregone to taste better liver and kidney to start with. Arachnophobes may feel threatened by the towers of ingredients, from which leg-like vegetables wave and writhe. Yet underneath the baroque excess there are sound technical skills, evinced by a fricassée of fish and scallops in a delicious seafood sauce, a melting mixture of grilled summer vegetables, or a splendid though gross strawberry pancake soufflé. Having to ring the doorbell before anyone will let you in is a bore, the tables are overtightly packed, and the lurid medievalism of the wall paintings and illuminated ceiling downstairs is mildly disconcerting. And, good though the wine list is, it should never have been allowed to acquire as many holes (especially in halves, of which the winematch scheme needs a profusion) as it had during an early July visit, nor should the waiters have served corked wine by the glass without checking it themselves first.

It's easy to poke fun at Neville Blech's elaborate 'winematch' scheme (dishes on the menu come keyed with appropriate sections on the wine list), but no customer is obliged to use it, and it does have the virtue of providing clear indications of each wine's style. Add to this the well-informed descriptions of most of the wines; the fact that they have been selected by a restaurateur who cares passionately for individual, unusual flavours in wine, who doesn't mark up to the same extent as many of his flashier rivals, and who provides a choice of over a dozen wines by the glass and ample halves – and what do you have? A wine list to revel in. Particularly rewarding are wines from Kistler, Stag's Leap, Petaluma and Penley. Ask for guidance on the burgundies.

Open: Mon-Fri. **Hours:** 12.00-2.00pm and 7.00-10.00pm. **Closed:** 10 days at Easter, 2 weeks at Christmas and last 3 weeks in August. **Credit cards accepted:** Access, AmEx, Visa. **Number of seats:** 30. **Service:** Optional. **Set price lunch:** £13.50 (2 courses) or £16.50 (3 courses). **Set price dinner:** £35 (5 courses). No-smoking area. Wheelchair access (but not lavatory). Tables outside seat 16. Private room seats 25. **Nearest tube station:** Victoria/Sloane Square.

MAP REF: 2,F/2

Milestone Hotel – Cheneston's

1 Kensington Court, W8

167

071-917 1200   **£35**

'There's a small hotel . . .'

One of the nicer things people think about restaurant critics is that they keep to themselves the addresses of groovy little restaurants so that they and their friends alone can enjoy them. In fact, I am so thrilled when I find some place I can recommend that I do so as quickly and vociferously as possible. I have written about Cheneston's several times in the *Evening Standard* and an entry appeared in last year's guide, but it is still, somehow, a sort of secret place and one the casual observer would be unlikely to discover even if wandering past the high Victoriana façade of the Milestone Hotel. Cheneston's could hardly be described as groovy. The food has been toned down since the opening days when it balanced on the Pacific Rim and the front parlour decor, is the perfect setting for a Daphne du Maurier story. But the modern English menu now offered is carefully constructed and interesting and the service punctilious. The set price table d'hôte menus are reasonable. They have provided a great soup in cream of fennel and saffron with prawn fritters and notable meat dishes of medallions of beef with leeks, black olives and a Pommery mustard sauce and best end of lamb served sliced and fanned on rosti and infant vegetables. Desserts are less assured. Also useful to know about in this rather dowdy part of town is the hotel's Park Lounge where salads and small dishes are served all day.

OPEN: Mon-Sun. **HOURS:** 7.00-10.30am (7.30-11.00am Sun), 12.30-2.30pm and 7.30-11.00pm (7.30-10.30pm Sun). **CREDIT CARDS ACCEPTED:** All major cards. **NUMBER OF SEATS:** 30. **SET PRICE LUNCH:** £13. Private room seats 6. **NEAREST TUBE STATION:** High Street Kensington.

Ming

35-36 Greek Street, W1

168

071-734 2721   **£20**

*'The only Chinese restaurant to advertise
in the Spectator'*

Being situated since 1986 on the north side of Shaftesbury Avenue (the other side to Chinatown proper) is not the only distinguishing feature of Ming. The restaurant belongs to a woman, Christine Lau, who goes to considerable effort to do things a bit differently including offering a list of quite inventive specials capitalizing on what is fresh in the market. Two of these that are light and delicious are steamed plaice with a julienne of salted turnip and crabmeat foo yung. Lau has also devised The Ming Bowl Menu with its self-contained rice- and noodle-based meals and, most interestingly, assemblies made with the Northern Chinese white flour bread called mantou served steamed or wok-grilled. Try it steamed, when it is almost creamy in texture, contrasted with the sharpness of shredded duck, winter greens and chilli. The main menu is basically Northern Chinese, long on fish and shellfish and with some lamb, beef and pork dishes particular to Ming and worth trying. The breadth of the menu means that there are some disappointments but the effort made with the wine list should help you over those. A signed photograph of Jeffrey Bernard looking distinctly unwell hangs like a doleful icon on one wall of the blue painted interior.

Open: Mon-Sat. **Hours:** 12.00-11.45pm. **Credit cards accepted:** Access, AmEx, Diner's Club, JCB, Visa. **Number of seats:** 70. **Service:** Optional. **Set price lunch:** £10. **Set price dinner:** £12-£19.50. No-smoking area. 10 seats outside. Private room seats 40. **Nearest tube station:** Leicester Square/ Piccadilly Circus. MAP REF: 1,E/2

Mr Kong

21 Lisle Street, WC2

071-437 7341 £20

'One of the reliable fixtures in Chinatown'

Mr Kong, long-established in Chinatown, is, as far as I can make out, the only restaurant of that area named after its chef. This should bode well and on the whole it does. That more than knee-jerk cooking is going on is demonstrated by details such as sesame prawn toast presented not as the usual prawn paste, but butterflied whole prawns perched on croûtons; the superiority of the chilli spare ribs cooked en papillotte and the high quality of the baked Mediterranean prawns with chilli. The long menu is chiefly Cantonese with some of Peking's and Szechuan's greatest hits added in for good measure. To deal with its daunting length go for the chef's specials but unless it has some peculiar appeal for you, I would avoid the liasons of meat and fish with mango and pineapple. The service in the usually crowded rooms seems brisker and brusquer than is these days the norm. On a Saturday evening no one appeared to understand anything inconvenient such as Perrier or Napkin, but Bill Please soon got through.

Open: Mon-Sun. **Hours:** 12.00pm-1.45am. **Closed:** 3 days at Christmas. **Credit cards accepted:** Access, AmEx, Diner's Club, JCB, Visa. **Number of seats:** 140. **Service:** 10%. **Set price lunch and dinner:** £8.60-£21. Private room seats 30. **Nearest tube station:** Leicester Square. MAP REF: 1,E/1

Mon Petit Plaisir

33c Holland Street, W8

071-937 3224 £25-£28

'Voulez-vous diner avec moi ce soir?'

This five-year-old branch of Mon Plaisir (q.v.) continues to deliver little pleasures such as a tartelette fine de crevettes à l'anis, with good prawns, a delicate sauce and homemade pastry shell, and bigger ones too, such as filet de boeuf aux morilles. Another person at this same meal was less thrilled with profiterole de tomate et thon and tagliatelle surprise where the most surprising element was that the cheesy sauce included slivers of turnip among the vegetables. However, this small restaurant, in summer opening onto a charming Kensington street, fleshes out well the notion of a romantic French bistro. In this aim it is loyally backed up by the decor; sheet-music covers and flea market finds all do their bit for the cause. Simple, directed lighting works well. Wines are French domaine-bottled.

OPEN: LUNCH: Mon-Fri. DINNER: Mon-Sat. **HOURS:** 12.00-2.30pm and 6.30-10.30pm. **CLOSED:** Bank Holidays, Easter and 1 week at Christmas. **CREDIT CARDS ACCEPTED:** All major cards. **NUMBER OF SEATS:** 27. **SERVICE:** 12.5%. **SET PRICE LUNCH:** £13.95. 7 tables outside. **NEAREST TUBE STATION:** High Street Kensington. MAP REF: 4,D/1

Mon Plaisir

21 Monmouth Street, WC2

071-836 7243 £32

'Perennial gingham in a bulging bistro'

This is the corner of our foreign metropolis that is forever Montmartre. Little chance you'll forget it, either: from the initial 'Bonjour' to the final 'Bonsoir', every detail (with the exception of the Peter Mayle *Toujours Provence* poster) genuinely succeeds in suggesting a bustling restaurant du coin. The dishes share the assurance and confidence of that world, though prices are stiffer in exile. Tradition and regionalism are more successful here than innovation and sometimes even tradition can be a little mechanical, as when an over-large Chavignol goat's cheese is entombed in filo pastry for a galumphing first course. Yet the successes are carried off stylishly: a delicate prawn tartlet, for example, flavoured with aniseed and fennel; seared calves' liver served with a tarragon-infused reduction and unusually flavoursome leaf spinach. Desserts are more routine: marbré de Croatie, heavily sold by the waiter who had made it, was a straightforward gâteau. Cheese is the better bet. Service, especially for those seated near the service lift, entertains with frenzied Dickensian scenes somehow in keeping with the Chocolat Revillon clock and prehistoric soda siphons. The wine list is short, yet the selection is generally good: fresh, lean Chablis (Domaine Malante); softly spicy Châteauneuf (Vieux Télégraphe); Goundrey's Langton Chardonnay. Yes, a pair of Australians have elbowed their way onto the list, but don't be fooled: still the accordion plays, still Piaf trills.

OPEN: LUNCH: Mon-Fri. DINNER: Mon-Sat. **HOURS:** 12.00-2.15pm and 5.30-11.15pm. **CLOSED:** Bank Holidays. **CREDIT CARDS ACCEPTED:** All major cards. NUMBER OF SEATS 90. SERVICE 12.5%. SET PRICE LUNCH AND DINNER: £13.95. Wheelchair access (but not lavatory). Private room seats 28. **NEAREST TUBE STATION:** Covent Garden/Leicester Square. MAP REF: 1,E/1

Monkeys

1 Cale Street, SW3

071-352 4711 **£35**

'A civilized place for Homo sapiens'

According to a visitor to this Chelsea neighbourhood restaurant owned by (chef) Tom Binham and his French wife (manageress) Brigitte, Hoorays are still in evidence among the clientele but they are segregated, confined to the front room. He advises that anyone over 35 wishing for peace should specify a table in the sheltered back part of the restaurant. Monkeys – reference to the name is in pictures and prints – is a reassuringly well-dressed restaurant with impeccable napery, cutlery, glassware, flowers and so forth. What is conveyed is the idea of the importance of a good meal and a glance below to the details of closures shows that the proprietors must generally attach importance to leading a civilized life. The menu remains mercifully unadventurous. When something succeeds it tends to be a fixture. Foie gras in some guise usually features. Other luxurious ingredients, including game in season, are confidently handled. In true French style vegetables are underplayed. In the dessert course the English idea of a reward for eating up your greens (here only a small bundle of beans) is exemplified in items such as a rich crème brûlée and hot treacle tart. Note the relative good value in the set price lunches.

OPEN: Mon-Fri. **HOURS:** 12.30-2.30pm and 7.30-11.00pm. **CLOSED:** 2 weeks at Easter, 3 weeks in August. **CREDIT CARDS ACCEPTED:** Access, Visa. **NUMBER OF SEATS:** 35. **SERVICE:** Optional. **SET PRICE LUNCH:** £12.50. **SET PRICE DINNER:** £22.50. Private room seats 10. **NEAREST TUBE STATION:** South Kensington/Sloane Square. MAP REF: 2,D/2

Le Muscadet

25 Paddington Street, W1

071-935 2883 £30

'French without airs'

Before designers insinuated their way into restaurants, as well as into every other area of public life, the simple, classical cooking offered by Le Muscadet would have been considered authentic and appealing. To the credit of proprietor François Bessonard he continues to provide simple, fulfilling food of the kind that any provincial French restaurant would be happy to serve. The petit bourgeois surroundings, complete with fruitwood chairs and arcadian tapestries, are an appropriate accompaniment to a variety of equally orthodox dishes, cream-based sauces and unpretentious desserts. First courses have included a surprisingly hearty crème de laitue, young asparagus with hollandaise (a sauce much favoured by the young chef) and warm escalope de foie gras with caramelized pears. Main courses will be in the styles of sole de Douvre, sauce à l'oseille; delice de canard aux baies roses; medaillon de veau à la crème de foie gras. Gâteau de chocolat truffe avec crème Anglaise is light but intense in flavour. The full menu is solemnly recited to diners in its entirety by the indisputably French maître d'hotel. The short, rather expensive French wine list is embellished by more moderate wines of the day.

OPEN: LUNCH: Mon-Fri. DINNER: Mon-Sat. **HOURS:** 12.30-2.30pm and 7.30-10.45pm (7.30-10.00pm Sat). **CREDIT CARDS ACCEPTED:** Access, Visa. **NUMBER OF SEATS:** 35. **SERVICE:** 12.5%. **SET PRICE LUNCH:** £17.00. Wheelchair access (but not lavatory). **NEAREST TUBE STATION:** Baker Street. MAP REF: 1,B/4

Museum Street Café

47 Museum Street, WC1

071-405 3211 LUNCH £21; DINNER £35

'Grown larger and, to some extent, grown up'

Some of the observations made about the Museum Street Café in last year's guide have been made otiose by the expansion and redecoration of the premises. The Café, now more of a restaurant, is licensed and credit cards are taken. It remains closed at weekends and proscribes smoking – on the dinner menu with the maddeningly sententious phrase 'This is a no-smoking restaurant'; on the lunch menu there is the chummier 'No smoking please'. The new look is stylishly frugal placing the kitchen, quite rightly, at the centre of the action. Menus are short – slightly more choice at lunchtime than in the evening – with heavy dependence on the ramifications of baking (Gail Koerber's skill) and chargrilling (Mark Nathan's talent). Soups much enjoyed have been chilled cucumber with tomato relish and Jerusalem artichoke with double-blanched garlic. Chargrilled fish and meat is lightly sauced, mostly with flavoured oils or salsas. Vegetable accompaniments have been known to be identical whatever the starting point of the main dish, which seems a bit feeble. Desserts, cakes and tarts are usually brilliant. Long waits can be experienced, adding to the impression that the owners here take it all a bit too seriously. It's only a meal.

ONLY TWO DOZEN wines, but every one is worth trying (including good Mâcon from Merlin and Chianti from Selvapiana). The notes are helpfully explanatory, and the prices a model of restraint. Corkage of £4 on your own bottles of Latour and Mouton complete the appeal.

OPEN: Mon-Fri. HOURS: 12.00-11.00pm. CLOSED: Bank Holidays. CREDIT CARDS ACCEPTED: Access, Mastercard, Switch, Visa. NUMBER OF SEATS: 34. SERVICE: Optional. SET PRICE LUNCH: £12 (2 courses) or £15 (3 courses). SET PRICE DINNER: £17 (2 courses) or £21 (3 courses). No smoking area. Wheelchair access. NEAREST TUBE STATION: Tottenham Court Road/Holborn.   MAP REF: 1,F/2

Mustard's Smithfield Brasserie

60 Long Lane, EC1

071-796 4920   **£30**

'A French corner of London's Les Halles'

Fortunately for Londoners – but perhaps not for those who own businesses in the area – the projected yuppification of Smithfield coincided with the recession and, despite the ongoing revamp of the actual meat market, the area remains pleasantly untidy and unstreamlined. In the evenings Mustard's Brasserie and its next-door Bistro à Vin is one of the few pockets of light and noise, something known to visitors, staff and performers of the Barbican Centre nearby. Sally Kimbell and François de Kerbrech (responsible for the above-average wine and drinks list) own what amounts to three operations; a wine bar and restaurant, established in 1988, and the Bistro à Vin which opened in early 1994. The little red and cream restaurant has an authentic French feel which extends to the cooking. A most satisfactory lunch one day was crab cakes with a sea spice sauce and a salad of Bayonne ham, smoked chicken, roast pepper, artichoke and chicory followed by monkfish with leeks in a soothing creamy sauce and robustly seasoned rabbit served on a sauté of potatoes, tomatoes and mushrooms. Service is French. The napkins are white linen.

At the next door **Bistro à Vin** (tel 071-600 1111) the look is archetypal cod-Parisian Victoriana but with some out-of-synch modern prints. There is that quite rare find these days, a chariot of charcuterie and hors d'oeuvres (served as a first or main course) and what must be the cheapest assiette de fruits der mer in London ((£13.75 for two). Main courses enjoyed have been grilled boudin blanc served with a bland potato purée and grilled chicken breast which had been marinated in a forceful mixture of coriander, lime and chilli. Apple mousse tart with apple and raisin compote was rich and delicious. There are various fixed-price deals (at all three establishments) and also here a bar menu of 'casse croûtes'. The whole operation has been well thought through for the pleasure of the customer.

Open: Mon-Fri. **Hours:** 9.00am-11.00pm. **Closed:** Bank Holidays, Christmas and New Year. **Credit cards accepted:** Access, AmEx, Diner's Club, Visa. **Number of seats:** 30. **Service:** 12.5% optional. **Set price lunch:** £15.95 (3 courses). **Set price dinner:** £10 (dinner). Wheelchair access. **Nearest tube station:** Barbican.

Namaste Indian Restaurant

30 Alie Street, E1

071-488 9242 or 071-702 1504 £18

'Ever had curried goose?'

Chef Cyrus R. Todiwala has weathered changes of ownership at this plain-in-appearance City Indian restaurant and continues to offer unusual Indian regional dishes including several from Goa where he worked for The Taj hotel, Fort Aguada. The printed menu is interesting in its own right with its Goan, South Indian and Parsi sections but the typed list of chef's specialities often reveals ground-breaking cooking in the sense of the ingredients utilized; smoked duck Goan style, pheasant mussalum, goose tikka cafreal, tandoori red snapper, fried oysters, lobster à la Sinquerim, kohlrabi mixed with yellow moon beans and spinach. Details such as chutneys are not spared Todiwala's creativity and they are better by far than the mass-produced stuff usually served. The wine list has also been carefully considered. Wines of the month are selected from one particular country. When you try Namaste do not omit from the order lasania naan, stuffed with chopped garlic. You will be waved quickly past the police patrols as you leave the City.

Open: **Lunch:** Mon-Fri. **Dinner:** Mon-Sat. **Hours:** 12.00-3.00pm and 6.00-11.00pm (7.00-10.00pm Sat). **Closed:** Bank Holidays and 1 week at Christmas. **Credit cards accepted:** All major cards. **Number of seats:** 70. **Service:** Optional. Tables outside seat 12. Private room seats 35. **Nearest tube stations:** Aldgate/Aldgate East.

The Neal Street Restaurant

26 Neal Street, WC2

071-836 8368 £45-£50

'High prices take the fun out of fungi'

The Neal Street Restaurant is owned by Antonio Carluccio, wild mushroom bounty-hunter and star of printed page and TV screen. For lovers of fungi there is a mushroom and bacon salad, a wild mushroom soup, a sauté of fungi of the day, pappardelle with fungi, turbot with honey fungus and Judas ears, medallions of beef with cep sauce, ragu of sweetbreads and morels and parcel of duck and fungi. These and other mushroom-free dishes command bravura prices plus 15% service. And they are not always as well executed as one would hope. The Neal Street is a stylish and welcoming environment but the prudent and foresighted might prefer to shop at Carluccio's admirable delicatessen next door and rustle up the dishes quickly at home.

LOGICALLY ENOUGH, an intelligent selection of Italian wines dominates this mid-length list, with Jermann, Borgo Conventi (Puiatti's second label), Allegrini and Clerico providing some of the highlights. The four house wines (at £12.50 per bottle or £8 per half) are cleverly plucked from each end of Italy, providing variety and contrast. France and the New World are present in smaller selections; a good flush of dessert wines includes the curious Picolit and the splendid Moscato di Pantelleria. No bargains, though.

OPEN: Mon-Sat. **HOURS:** 12.30-2.30pm and 7.30-11.00pm. **CLOSED:** Bank Holidays and 1 week at Christmasand New Year. **CREDIT CARDS ACCEPTED:** Access, AmEx, Diner's Club, Mastercard, Visa. **NUMBER OF SEATS:** 60. **SERVICE:** 15%. Wheelchair access (but not lavatory). Private room seats 24. **NEAREST TUBE STATION:** Covent Garden. MAP REF: 1,F/1

The Nosh Brothers

773 Fulham Road, SW6

071-736 7311 £25

'Mess with the big boys'

Dinner at Mick and Nick Nosh's is a bit like eating at a club of which you are not a member; enjoyment of the evening is to some extent dependent on whether you like the other members and the loud music. Nick Nosh's background as film-maker/chef has attracted a band of regulars, all of whom look as if they are 'something in TV or the music biz'. The menu is simply laid out and, in the modern manner, enticing. It changes daily but you can infer the style from this (much-liked) meal: plate of savouries which included prawns, chorizo, tapenade, couscous and more. The one flat note was insipid chopped steak on a garlic croûton overwhelmed by blue cheese. By the time you are thinking of dessert, the genial host tends to be dispensing bonhomie to his friends with a largesse that verges on the alarming and you may be left to your own devices, but reports indicate that you will not be missing much if you never manage to order any. The wine list is short and savvy.

OPEN: Mon-Sat. **HOURS:** 7.30pm-12.00am. **CLOSED:** Christmas and Easter. **CREDIT CARDS ACCEPTED:** Access, AmEx, Visa. **NUMBER OF SEATS:** 80. **SERVICE:** 12.5%. Private room seats 60. **NEAREST TUBE STATION:** Parsons Green.

Nusa Dua

11 Dean Street, W1

071-437 3559 £8

'The friendly place to discover Indonesian food'

This gentle, family-run Indonesian and Singaporean restaurant just off Soho Square continues to serve food that, to my mind, is considerably more interestingly alien than the offerings of the several Thai restaurants of the area. There are rijsttafel – set meals of many dishes – at two prices, the more expensive one at £15 a head including a bottle of house wine, dessert and coffee. And if you eat before 8.30pm there is a short set price meal at £3.95. However, for best results comb through the long menu. Here are some of my finds: in the first course, sate kedelai, skewers of grilled marinated beancurd served with a potent peanut-based sauce; lumpia, exceptionally good spring rolls with chicken, shrimps and vegetables. Of the noodle dishes, of which you should order at least one, ke tiaw laksa is a big bowl of broad rice noodles in a spicy coconut broth with prawns, fish cakes and beansprouts. Itik panggang is an eerily good dish of grilled duck topped with a spicy yellow sauce. Each time I go I cannot resist ordering tahu telor, a beancurd omelette with a crisp crust covered in a glancingly sweet sauce. However, this is a very small sample of the 155 savoury options; you will make many discoveries of your own. The wine list is eminently reasonable. Good jazz tapes are played.

OPEN: LUNCH: Mon-Fri. DINNER: Mon-Sat. **HOURS:** 12.00-2.30pm and 6.00-11.30pm (4.30pm-10.30am Sat-Sun). **CREDIT CARDS ACCEPTED:** Access, AmEx, Visa. **NUMBER OF SEATS:** 60. **SERVICE:** 10% for parties of 5 or more. **SET PRICE LUNCH:** £4.95 (three courses). Private room seats 14. **NEAREST TUBE STATION:** Tottenham Court Road. MAP REF: 1,E/2

Odette's

130 Regents Park Road, NW1

071-586 5486/8766 £30

'One of the attractions of urban village life'

Romantic is a word often used to describe this long-established restaurant in one of London's more charming shopping streets (where parking is far from charming). In warm weather the doors fold back and tables move onto the wide pavement; in bright or, indeed, in glum weather the conservatory is an agreeable place to be but the heart of the restaurant is the gilt-framed mirror lined, dark green front room where well-groomed white-clothed tables and relatively formal service convey a special event, a romantic one if you like. Owner Simone Green runs the establishment with commendable professionalism. Chef Paul Holmes produces a menu with never a dull moment and many an under-exploited ingredient but ocasionally the wish to be inventive outstrips the kitchen's ability or results in a mix of metaphors – as happened with a Japanesey plate of fish savouries. However, there are successes and should you want to eat relatively plainly plenty of scope; creamed salsify and wilted sorrel soup (soups generally use interesting seasonal ingredients); pan-fried calves liver, Savoy cabbage and bacon; fillet of beef, sprouting broccoli and roasted shallots; home-made macaroni with wild mushrooms. Desserts, a course that many modern chefs cop out on, this kitchen produces particularly well. There is also always a plate of Spanish cheese with quince jelly. The notion of romance need not imply careless spending; the no-choice set lunch restaurant menu is only £10 for three courses. In addition the front part of the basement of Odette's houses a wine bar with better than average food.

A WELL-MIXED LIST, stylistically organized, making it easy to avoid flavour collisions. Highlights include the elegant burgundies of Henri Prudhon and more forceful realizations from Ghislaine Barthod, Bonny Doon's smouldering Cigare Volant, and Iosetta Saffirio's expressive Dolcetto. There are plenty of half bottles. The descriptive notes allow effusive enthusiasm to cloud objectivity.

OPEN: LUNCH: Mon-Fri. DINNER: Mon-Sat. **HOURS:** 12.30-2.30pm and 7.00-11.00pm. **CLOSED:** 1 week at Christmas and Bank Holidays. **CREDIT CARDS ACCEPTED:** Access, AmEx, Diner's Club, Visa. **NUMBER OF SEATS:** 60. **SERVICE:** Optional. **SET PRICE LUNCH:** £10. 12 seats outside. Private rooms seat 8 and 30. **NEAREST TUBE STATION:** Chalk Farm. MAP REF: 5,A/1

Ognisko Polskie

55 Exhibition Road, SW7

071-589 4635 £20

'Central European refuge from bruschetta and basil'

Once you've shaken off the conviction that you're walking into the Ruritanian embassy, and ignored the mild and senseless intimidation of the Members Only notices, there is much to enjoy here. The elegant drawing room, divided into two (restaurant and bar) by a palm and weeping figs; the priests and promenaders dining alone, intensely; the Polish cooking of careful authenticity. Beetroot soup, dill-strewn and served with kolduny dumplings, has all the intensity of flavour its colour promises: when good, this is a great beginning to a meal. Main-course dumplings are stuffed with minced pork, though the dressing of chopped, part-rendered belly fat may be a little too generous; the bigos, too – Poland's national dish, made of stewed pickled cabbage with sausages and dried mushrooms – is fat-prodigal, though deliciously smoky, served with potatoes good enough to change one's nationality for. Wimps are catered for by catch of the day in vermouth sauce, breast of duck in Cointreau sauce, and suchlike; hare and venison feature regularly, too. Dessert stuffed pancakes are crisply refried in the Polish way, bringing the meal to a fecklessly high-calorie close. The wine list is short and largely uninspired, though prices are appealing; the 1988 Berberana Rioja Carta de Oro, at £5.60 per half, was proactive with all that belly fat. Or throw everything to the wind with the flavoured vodkas. Service is fresh-faced and old-world: if you're lucky, you may get your hand kissed.

OPEN: Mon-Sun. **HOURS:** 12.30-3.00pm and 6.30-11.00pm. **CLOSED:** Easter Sunday and Monday, Christmas Day and Boxing Day. **CREDIT CARDS ACCEPTED:** AmEx, Diner's Club, Mastercard, Visa. **NUMBER OF SEATS:** 70. **SERVICE:** Optional. **SET PRICE LUNCH:** £7.50. 30 seats outside. Private rooms seat 35 and 120. **NEAREST TUBE STATION:** South Kensington. MAP REF: 2,D/4

O'Keefe's

19 Dering Street, W1

071-495 0878 £21

'Stylish sustenance for an undernourished area'

A recent revamp of the decor, the removal of a deli counter and the installation of a long bar have taken O'Keefe's even further away from its sandwich bar antecedents. The creation of Romano Crolla and art dealer Thomas Dane, this simply styled café/restaurant serves the (under-nourished) area well. Those who have to get into a size 8 go for items like ceviche; sweet-cured herrings with celeriac rémoulade; grill-seared swordfish served on salad leaves with chilli, garlic and lemon grass dressing; rocket, mozzarella, avocado and plum tomato salad. Those who don't enjoy items such as devilled field mushrooms on garlic toast; salmon fishcakes with dill mayonnaise; Tuscan rabbit served on chargrilled polenta; bread and butter pudding (sometimes made with almond croissants); crème caramel. My sister Beth Coventry is chef which of course predisposes me hugely to like O'Keefe's but I have heard people who are not even blood relatives praise the food to the skies. Craig Brown (writer and restaurant reviewer) said the treacle tart was by far the best he had ever tasted. (Beth was the original chef at the quintessentially English Green's q.v.). O'Keefe's is licensed with a simple wine list.

OPEN: **LUNCH:** Mon-Sat, **DINNER:** Mon-Fri. **HOURS:** 8.00am-10.00pm (10.00am-5.00pm Sat). **CREDIT CARDS ACCEPTED:** None. **NUMBER OF SEATS:** 38. **SERVICE:** 12.5% evenings. Wheelchair access (but not lavatory). Tables outside seat 8. **NEAREST TUBE STATION:** Bond Street. MAP REF: 1,C/1

Old Delhi Restaurant

48 Kendal Street, W2

071-723 3335 £20-£25

'An unusual combination of Indian and Iranian'

Extended Iranian families make up a significant part of the clientele at this hybrid restaurant in Iranian family ownership. The welcome is warm and explanations of the dishes readily given if you wish to stray from familiar Indian dishes into specialities of the house or the dish of the day, a temptation not to be overcome. Persian first courses are either ash, a soup made with beans and fresh herbs, or kashke-bademjun, thin slices of grilled aubergine topped with yogurt, mint sauce and plenty of crisply fried onion. You might pair this last with the particularly well prepared prawn puri, or chicken chat or perhaps a kebab cooked in the tandoor. Good-quality poultry and meat also distinguish the curries but since curries are easily found and dishes such as fesenjune (chicken in a sweet/sour pomegranate sauce) and gaimeh (lamb pieces cooked with split peas, mixed spices and the sharp, almost vinegary flavour of dry limes) are not, I tend to go for those or the sultani, a combination of grilled slender lamb slices and grilled minced lamb with Iranian spicing including a sprinkling of sumac. The fesenjune is a potent, mushy mixture best strafed through a large heap of the beautifully cooked fragrant basmati rice, some of it yellowed with turmeric. Breads are also notably good. For dessert, a Persian water ice flavoured with rose water or Indian mango kulfi is not too rich, nor are fresh exotic fruits when available. The wine list serves mainly to inflate what will anyway be a biggish bill for 'going out for an Indian' but in visiting the Old Delhi that is not really what you have done. Booking is advisable.

OPEN: Mon-Sun. **HOURS:** 12.00-3.30pm and 6.00-11.30pm. **CREDIT CARDS ACCEPTED:** Access, AmEx, Diner's Club, Visa. **NUMBER OF SEATS:** 56. **SERVICE:** 15%, optional. Wheelchair access (but not lavatory). Tables outside seat 20. **NEAREST TUBE STATION:** Marble Arch.   **MAP REF:** 1,A/4

Olivo

21 Eccleston Street, SW1

071-730 2505   £30

'Sunny walls and a sunny menu'

Jollier decor is there none: the just-baked walls in bright blue and yellow, the earthenware eggs on threads from which light cascades, a few flowers, the wholesomely stripped wood. The Franco-Italian staff seem to enjoy being there, and customers pick up the mood. The menu is as simple as can be: just four main courses for the set price lunch, for example, with a dish of the day; choice is greater in the evenings, though the informing imagination remains uncomplicated. The name comes good from the moment you sit down, welcomed by a dish of seasoned olive oil. Garganelli with an artichoke sauce comes prettily served with a lily of artichoke leaves; buffalo mozzarella with grilled aubergine; marinated swordfish with a dribble of green sauce on perfectly dressed salad. Baked main-course John Dory (head and all), artlessly strewn with potatoes and a single olive, proved firm-fleshed and sweetly fresh; three slabs of chargrilled ox tongue, its salsa verde borrowed from bollito misto, were juicily tender. Fresh strawberry tart was thoughtfully cooked, the custard sparse enough to keep the pastry crisps and the fruit fruity. Expresso is so strong it hurts, while the Italian wine list tries assiduously to stray off beaten paths and, not surprisingly, succeeds better with reds (Conterno's Grignolino, Sella e Mosca's Tanca Farra) than whites. Most wines, though, are under £20, encouraging experiment.

OPEN: LUNCH: Mon-Fri. DINNER: Mon-Sat. **HOURS:** 12.00-2.30pm and 7.00-11.00pm. **CLOSED:** Bank Holidays, 1 week at Christmas and first 3 weeks of August. **CREDIT CARDS ACCEPTED:** Access, AmEx, Visa. **NUMBER OF SEATS:** 45. **SERVICE:** Optional. **SET PRICE LUNCH:** £13.50 (2 courses) and £15.50 (3 courses). Wheelchair access. **NEAREST TUBE STATION:** Victoria.

192

192 Kensington Park Road, W11

071-229 0482   **£25**

'Still trendy after all these years'

The modern menu at this popular Notting Hill restaurant where expansion has not, as so often happens, skewed its impact or its success, nowadays seems commonplace. This is not surprising when you think of the alumnae of 192 who have gone forth and worked elsewhere – Alastair Little, Rowley Leigh, Adam Robinson, Rose Gray, Sebastian Snow, Maddalena Bonino, Margot Clayton, Dan Evans, Josh Hampton to name some that you will find scattered through this guide. Chef at time of writing is Albert Clarke, son of Celia Birtwell and Ossie Clarke, who has put what must be a genetic talent for fashioning things into food. A test meal is emblematic of the daily-changing list: luscious bruschetta with grilled aubergine; rocket, Jerusalem and sun-dried tomato salad embellished with exotic touches; scallops with guacamole; a simple grilled veal chop. All tasted as good as it looked. Lemon tart was smooth, light and sharp like most of the customers.

OPEN: Mon-Sun. **HOURS:** 12.30-3.00pm and 5.30pm-11.30am. **CLOSED:** Christmas Day, Boxing Day, New Year's Day and Bank Holidays. **CREDIT CARDS ACCEPTED:** Access, AmEx, Diner's Club, Switch, Visa. **NUMBER OF SEATS:** 108. **SERVICE:** Optional. **SET PRICE LUNCH:** £8.50. No-smoking area. Wheelchair access (but not lavatory). Tables outside seat 12. **NEAREST TUBE STATION:** Ladbroke Grove.   MAP REF: 4,A/1

Oporto Grill-Restaurant

67 Wornington Road, W10

081-960 9669   **LUNCH: £6; DINNER: £13**

'Brilliant Brazilian barbecue'

A feature of this restaurant, bar, tapas bar and pool hall is a Brazilian churrasco – about a metre of glowing coals sited in the basement entrance yard where fish and meat are barbecued by a practised churrasco chef, wise in the ways of living fire. Their stated speciality is chicken but I would also put in a word for the spare ribs – the best I have had in a restaurant. There is lamb, pork and beef. What was originally a very simple formula – to start; olives, cheese and bread, wine; red or white – has become more ambitious and there is now a wide range of Portuguese specialities and a longer wine list on offer. Whilst I can understand the allure of tripe stew, feijoada, rabbit chasseur, calf's foot stew with chick-peas, eel stew and various ways with salt cod, it would be difficult to forego the particular pleasure of well-handled barbecue. The answer would be to go often. The restaurant welcomes private parties - a good thought.

OPEN: Tues-Sun. **HOURS:** 11.30am-12.00am. **CREDIT CARDS ACCEPTED:** All major cards. **NUMBER OF SEATS:** 75. **SERVICE:** Optional. **SET PRICE LUNCH:** £8.50. Tables outside seat 40. Private room seats 40. **NEAREST TUBE STATION:** Ladbroke Grove.

Orsino

119 Portland Road, W11

071 221 3299 £30

'The paperback version'

Orso in New York and Covent Garden and now Holland Park specializes in putting itself in the right place for a captive audience. Residents of Holland Park/Notting Hill or staff at the BBC might be forgiven for feeling slightly insulted by this seemingly calculated bid for their presumed tastes. In the way of all Orsos the entrance is extremely discreet; when you get in there is an arrestingly shaped peninsula of a room which looks out through wooden flaps onto Portland and Clarendon Roads. From noon to 6.30pm a set price menu is offered in addition to the à la carte. From this a pizza with courgettes, red peppers, cheese and tomatoes proved soggy and dull, quite unlike the thin crisp crust you find at Orso or the liveliness of the toppings at any Pizza Express. Grilled chicken was a different story; juicy and zippy served with spinach tinged with garlic. From the main menu steamed mussels had a good broth fortified by white wine and cream but the mussels themselves seemed to have died giving up all their flavour to it. Espresso coffee gave more of a kick than did the piece of angel cake with a chocolate topping. Orso has always been somewhat inconsistent in cooking standards. Orsino comes across as the paperback version but without the appropriate price drop. Waiting staff endure with fortitude the ritual anger of customers who cannot believe the stupidity of a management which refuses credit cards (but with no consequent amelioration of prices).

OPEN: Mon-Sun. **HOURS:** 12.00pm-12.00am. **CLOSED:** Christmas Eve and Christmas Day. **CREDIT CARDS ACCEPTED:** None. **NUMBER OF SEATS:** 90. **SERVICE:** Optional. **SET PRICE LUNCH:** £11.50 or £13.50. Private room seats 30. **NEAREST TUBE STATION:** Holland Park.

Orso

27 Wellington Street, WC2

071-240 5269 £30

'The restaurant of the novel'

Eating at Orso takes on new potential if you have read Karen Moline's novel *Lunch*. That the heroine, a portrait painter, is picked up in this basement Italian restaurant by a sadistic Hollywood heart-throb seems plausible enough. Despite the fact that many of Orso's 'innovations' – grilled vegetables, paper-thin pizzas, vegetables served at room temperature, rustic pottery plates – are now all over the place, it hangs on to a glitzy crowd. The staff know how to deal with a celebrity or a high-rolling regular but it has been noted this year that even ordinary people like you and me get a smile and a 'thank you' from time to time. This may be a response to more competition in Covent Garden. Certainly the reasonable set price menus offered at weekends between noon and 5pm must be designed as a lure and a draw. The quality of ingredients is high, extremely important when they are often simply assembled – e.g. thinly sliced raw wild salmon with arugula, olive oil and lemon – or grilled – e.g. rabbit with spinach, balsamic vinegar and new potatoes. There are also braised dishes including of course lamb shank – the chicken Kiev of the Nineties. Pizzas are still popular. Desserts are simple and just as good a way to end a meal is with pecorino and pear or vin santo with cantucci biscuits. The next step forward that Orso could take in the name of user-friendliness would be to take credit cards.

RIGOROUSLY ITALIAN, unannotated and fairly short, this is nevertheless a well-chosen list of wines, with Maculan, Colle Gaio, Masi, Tedeschi and Lodovico Antinori among the better producers. The price structure is reasonable, though those wanting less than a bottle will have no choice other than the anonymous house wines.

Open: Mon-Sun. **Hours:** 12.00pm-11.45am. **Closed:** Christmas Eve and Christmas Day. **Credit cards accepted:** None. **Number of seats:** 100. **Service:** Optional. No-smoking area. **Nearest tube station:** Covent Garden.

MAP REF: 1,F/1

Osteria Antica Bologna

23 Northcote Road, SW11

071-978 4771 £17

'La cucina antica with elbow-rubbing'

It would be impossible to pack another table into this long, thin, bipartite restaurant, and the press of humanity by 10.00pm provides the human version of Hyde Park Corner during a rainy rush-hour. Conversations are of necessity shared, and it's just as well that tables and floors are wooden to absorb the copious quantities of candle wax and food that are liable to be spilled on them. Old Bologna was doubtless ever thus. The menu is genuinely interesting, sometimes more so than the food itself. Among the assaggi (starters or tapas, depending on how you want to structure your meal), the historical capunata antica, combining over-cooked spinach, cauliflower and chicory under a drizzle of seasoned breadcrumbs, scarcely merits reviving, though mussels with a sauce of almonds, tomato, basil and garlic are pungently good. You'll need a pastapaedia to help choose between strozzapreti, strangoli, farfalle and tortellacci; the sauces dress the shapes with genuine Italian restraint. The house speciality of goat has an antique chewiness despite its evident long cooking, and many of the other main- course alternatives are partnered with those complex confections of herbs, vegetables, nuts, lemon, tomato and olive oil which soothingly suggest former ages. The tiramisó is as generous as anyone's, while the pouting waitresses are liable to say things to you in Italian first with English translation afterwards, which helps in getting you mentally Bologna-bound.

Open: Mon-Sun. **Hours:** 12.00-3.00pm and 6.00-11pm Mon-Thur; 12.00-3.00pm and 6.00-11.30pm Fri; 12.00-11.30pm Sat; 12.30-10.30pm Sun. **Closed:** 10 days at Christmas. **Credit cards accepted:** Access, AmEx, Switch, Visa. **Number of seats:** 75. **Service:** 10% optional on large groups, 60p cover charge. **Set price lunch:** £7.50. Wheelchair access (but not lavatory). 15 seats outside. **Nearest BR station:** Clapham Junction.

Osteria Basilico

29 Kensington Park Road, W11

071-727 9957/9372   **£20**

'Traditional dishes served with country candour'

The bare, scrubbed tables and unbreakable glass tumblers here add a rural, whole-earth touch to the increasingly familiar burnt-ochre-and-burnt-bread formula of the post-trattoria Italian restaurant. This one, at the increasingly Mediterranean bottom end of the Kensington Park Road, is on two floors. The basement is definitely second choice. The food, is insouciant about appearance: basil-dressed diced tomato was unceremoniously but tastily heaped on bruschetta; spinach salad had pink strips of ham and fistful of pine kernels dumped on it with canteen artistry. Risotto of the day was pea and radicchio – uninspired as a flavouring, though the dish was executed with appealing unction. Ricotta and spinach ravioli was well up to grandmother standard. Pizzas (good dough, served in squares as complimentary bread) are an alternative, and can be taken away; desserts are routine; service please-yourself. The wine list on the menu is terse and full of knee-jerk names, yet for some reason there is a second one, with eight described (though vintage-less) among them the fine Salice Salentino Reserva (1988 on this occasion).

OPEN: Mon-Sun. HOURS: 12.30-3.00pm and 6.30-11.00pm (12.30-4.30pm and 6.30-11.00pm Sat; 12.30-3.15pm and 6.30-10.30pm Sun). CLOSED: Christmas Day, New Year's Day and Bank Holidays. CREDIT CARDS ACCEPTED: None. NUMBER OF SEATS: 85. SERVICE: Optional. Wheelchair access (but not lavatory). NEAREST TUBE STATION: Notting Hill Gate/Ladbroke Grove.

MAP REF: 4,A/1

Le P'tit Normand

185 Merton Road, SW18

081-871 0233   **£25**

'A corner of Northern France in Southfields'

This modest establishment brimming with French bistro clichés – red-checked tablecloths, a blackboard menu of daily specials, native waiting staff who decline to speak English – is a pleasant and fairly inexpensive surprise in Southfields. The menu is a history of French favourites – soupes à l'oignon et de poisson, carré d'agneau, magret de canard, a reputable entrecôte with excellent chips, crème brûlée, mousse au chocolat – but each is well executed. There are daily fish specialities on the board. Half a loaf of baguette could be used to mop up the heady juices of shrimps with Calvados or the delicious outpourings of the mussels. There is also an excellent cheese board. House aperitifs are pushed with an enthusiasm from the waiters that tends to wane as the meal progresses. All the more reason perhaps to kick off with a kir (with peach is a discovery) or a muroise (cider with blackberry spirit). House wines are acceptable and only £7.95.

Open: Lunch: Sun-Fri. **Dinner:** Mon-Sun. **Hours:** 12.00-2.00pm and 7.00-10.30pm. **Credit cards accepted:** Access, AmEx, Diner's Club, Mastercard, Visa. **Number of seats:** 35. **Service:** 12.5%, optional. **Set price lunch:** £9.95. Wheelchair access (but not lavatory). Private room seats 40. **Nearest tube station:** Southfields.

Le Palais du Jardin

136 Long Acre, WC2

071-379 5353   **£23**

'A people's palace for eating'

Do not be misled by the name. What is in fact a brasserie open all day is neither dauntingly palatial, nor is there a garden, unless you include in the definition the balmy efficiency of the air-conditioning. The modest street-café façade belies the varied vast space within. First comes an oyster and seafood café, then at a slightly higher level a rhomboid-shaped bar and beyond this the restaurant proper, a space at once both stimulating and restful. The sight of waiters scuttling about with great trays of lobsters (temptingly reasonably priced), whether pink, perky and nubile or supine wrecks of empty shells, lifts the spirits. The menu is fundamentally French with some modern flourishes. There are grills (including whole grilled lobster at £9.95 at time of writing), fish and meat specialities and a section called Cuisine Grand'mère, a woman who, unlike my granny or doubtless yours, has a rather odd repertoire; fish cakes, bangers and mash and coq au vin. Desserts come in a wide range and as an assiette gourmandise at £3.50. Generally the prices give you that rare frisson of looking at your bill and wondering; how can they do it for the price? Le Palais du Jardin is one that, if I were Queen and to please Mo Mowlam, I would consider moving into.

Open: Mon-Sun. **Hours:** 12.00pm-12am. **Closed:** Christmas Day and Boxing Day. **Credit cards accepted:** All major cards. **Number of seats:** 220. **Service:** 12.5%. No-smoking area. Wheelchair access. 15 seats outside. Private room seats 22. **Nearest tube station:** Covent Garden/Leicester Square.

MAP REF: 1,E/1

Pearl

22 Brompton Road, SW1

071-225 3888   Lunch: £26; Dinner: £46

'Surprisingly authentic Cantonese cooking in SW1'

Whilst not quite the lustrous treasure the name suggests, this Cantonese restaurant offers authentic dishes carefully cooked. The signs are there that at least part of the target audience are the Chinese themselves; dishes described in Chinese characters, expensive specialities based around shark's fin and abalone and whole suckling pig Kwantung style, set menus that do not play safe and fruit integrated into fish and meat dishes. Another noticeable part of the clientele are tourists or visitors from abroad who presumably are pleased and relieved to find a Chinese restaurant on the outskirts of Harrods. The anonymous decor – apart from strange-looking but comfortable chairs designed by Charles Rennie Mackintosh's Chinese penpal – might also be a consolation; Pearl could be a restaurant anywhere in the world. A Western fondness for a structured three courses is pandered to by the long list of hot, cold and vegetarian appetizers. Steamed dumplings with whole shrimp filling, drunken chicken and sliced pork knuckle and minced mixed vegetables wrapped with iceberg lettuce are three to be getting on with. Lobster and duck are natural centrepiece dishes but so is sea bass braised in fragrant herbal and garlic sauce where the garlic cloves come confit. At £15 a pound, a pound-size fish is plenty for two. Asparagus poached in consommé is a vegetable dish that is more a course than an accompaniment; very good. To ring the changes on rice or noodles there is rice dumpling, steamed or deep-fried. The wine list is better than most Chinese restaurants aspire to with some New World bottles that tolerate a cacophany of flavours.

OPEN: Mon-Sun. **HOURS:** 12.00-3.00pm and 6.00-11.00pm (12.00-11.30pm Sat; 12.00-11.00pm Sun). **CLOSED:** Christmas Day and Boxing Day. **CREDIT CARDS ACCEPTED:** Access, AmEx, Diner's Club, Visa. **NUMBER OF SEATS:** 130. **SERVICE:** Optional, £2 cover charge. **SET PRICE LUNCH:** £8.50, £11, £12.50. **SET PRICE DINNER:** £25, £35, £45, £55. Private room seats 40. **NEAREST TUBE STATION:** Knightsbridge. **MAP REF:** 2,F/4

The Peasant

240 St John Street, EC1

071-336 7726 **£20**

'Only chic peas served here'

The Peasant is the transformation of a Finsbury pub called the George & Dragon into an enterprise not dissimilar from the Eagle and the Lansdowne (see entries). The new look makes use of some of the handsome original features such as an Italianate mosaic floor and the moulded ceiling. Bare tables are spaced around the original central bar but the drinking trade seems to have gone elsewhere – well, they've taken out the telly. Reports have been mixed of late on the finesse of the cooking of the dishes devised by Carla Tomasi and an ascent into luxury ingredients that seems at odds with the name and the aim has been noticed; happy the churl who sat down to lobster or sea bass with garlic and saffron mayonnaise. There is a certain amount of repetition of the words tomato and mozzarella but parmigiana of chicken involving those two ingredients harked back to the heyday of the London trattoria. Better items have been rocket, chic (sic) pea and mushroom salad with chorizo; potato coriander and chilli fritters with tomato jam (the latter too apt a description); a noble minestrone made without tomato and served with pesto. Despite Tomasi's proficiency with pasta, pasta seems infrequently offered but interesting Italian desserts such as cenci (Tuscan fried pastries) and Neapolitan ricotta are. The recently introduced longer opening hours reflect interest from visitors to the Barbican Centre, Sadler's Wells and other theatres of the area.

OPEN: LUNCH: Mon-Fri. DINNER: Mon-Sat. **HOURS:** 12.30-2.30pm and 6.30-10.30pm. **CLOSED:** Bank holidays, 23th Dec–5th Jan. **CREDIT CARDS ACCEPTED:** Access, Mastercard, Switch, Visa. **NUMBER OF SEATS:** 80. **SERVICE:** 10%. Wheelchair access. **NEAREST TUBE STATION:** Angel/Farringdon.   MAP REF: 8,C/1

Le Petit Max

97a High Street, Vicarage Road,
Hampton Wick

081-977 0236 £28 (Corkage £2)

'Caff to cuisine bourgeois'

When Le Petit Max opened in the teeth of the recession, run by Max and Marc Renzland, restaurant-goers hailed it as a small miracle of gastronomic achievement. Its dual identity – by day it functions as a caff called Bonzo's – coupled with the location appealed to their sense of adventure. Success here led to the twins – who bear a disarming resemblance to Tweedledum and Tweedledee – to also open Chez Max in Fulham (q.v.). At time of writing chef Matthew Jones, who was left behind to run this Hampton Wick establishment, has departed and Essex-born Max and Marc are back in the evenings, front of house and in the kitchen, calling to each other in Ted-Heath French, as is their wont, and addressing the customers as messieursdames. The menu, £23.50 for three courses, has been somewhat shortened and altered in presentation. However the same passion for French bourgeois food is evident and Marc's pleasure in cooking first-rate ingredients, such as chargilled peppered Aberdeen Angus côte de boeuf (served for two with gratin Dauphinois, sauce béarnaise and haricots verts); guinea fowl (sautéed until crisp served with a creamy cep and white truffle-flavoured sauce plus vegetables) is still palpable. First courses might be a typically French assembly of rillettes, celeriac rémoulade, red onions and tomatoes and in summer those same ripe tomatoes made into a Provençal soup flavoured with olive oil and extraordinarily potent basil grown by the local greengrocer from Tuscan seeds sent over by a relative. Star of the desserts, to my mind, is tarte à la crème made from Normandy cream reduced until almost toffee-like. The premises remain cramped and unlicensed but there is a not very brilliant off-licence next door; better to bring your own wine (corkage £2). Making a booking can be a pain; having to leave messages, needing to field the replies, and you can be asked to eat earlier or later than you would perhaps like, but it is usually worth it.

OPEN: LUNCH: Sun. DINNER: Tue-Sun. **HOURS:** 12.30-3.45pm and 8.00-11.00pm. **CLOSED:** Easter, Christmas and Bank Holiday Mondays. **CREDIT CARDS ACCEPTED:** Access, Visa. **NUMBER OF SEATS:** 34. **SERVICE:** 12.5%. **SET PRICE LUNCH AND DINNER:** £23.50. Wheelchair access (but not lavatory). **NEAREST BR STATION:** Hampton Wick.

Pied-à-Terre

34 Charlotte Street, W1

196

071-636 1178

LUNCH £25; DINNER £57

'Coming into its own as a main residence'

This is a serious restaurant, business-like about the subject of intricate eating and good drinking and carrying little else by way of baggage such as a place to see or be seen or a showcase for a media-star chef. Since last year's guide prices have come down a fraction, the look of the restaurant has softened, warmer colours have been introduced and the wine list, the province of Bruno Asselin, formerly sommelier at Le Manoir aux Quat'Saisons, considerably expanded. Pied-à-Terre has one Michelin star and the attendant, apparently requisite little ceremonies. But the quelque chose you are given before the meal and the petits fours with coffee are here not just gestures; they are further involved conceits and confections for the kitchen to cope with. Neat turns his back on the dictum, make it simple. Sometimes the results are over-elaborate – particularly for a lunchtime appetite – but the efforts can also pay off magnificently. Snails with morilles, girolles, asparagus and garlic purée is a dish where preparation as labyrinthine as embroidery – for example the snails are poached in a coating of chicken mousse – results in a delicious whole and a particularly successful sauce. What seems like a whole rabbit goes into the dish of saddle of rabbit which also features the kidney, the liver and strips of deep-fried skin. Neat's passion for offal is – in a summer menu anyway – more contained then before but deep-fried lambs' brains crept into a set lunch first course of white bean casserole with confit as did a slice of foie gras. Prices which are fairly unflinching – £33 for first and main course à la carte – are at least fully inclusive and the lunch menu at £16.50 for two courses comes across as something of a snip. Complexity is not abandoned in the desserts; try coconut crème and mango with pineapple sorbet, the coconut mixture served in a hollow brandy snap ball. Among the petits fours go straight for the apple dumpling and the nougat. Service can be a bit tight-lipped. I don't get the feeling that staff share a lot of jokes.

MOST OF THE WINES on this mid-length list are French, and well-selected (explore, in particular, the flurry of craftsmanlike Burgundy growers, among them Sauzet, Coche-Dury, Raveneau, Lafarge and Domaine de l'Arlot). New World wines are short but equally choice. It would be nice to see the 'regional French' section bolstered, giving greater choice under £20 without any loss of cultural definition.

OPEN: LUNCH: Mon-Fri. DINNER: Mon-Sat. HOURS: 12.15-2.00pm and 7.00-10.00pm. CLOSED: 2 weeks at Christmas and last 2 weeks of August. CREDIT CARDS ACCEPTED: Access, AmEx, Connect, Diner's Club, JCB, Switch, Visa. NUMBER OF SEATS: 40. SERVICE: Inclusive. SET PRICE LUNCH: £19.50. SET PRICE DINNER: £38. Wheelchair access (but not lavatory). Private room seats 10. NEAREST TUBE STATION: Goodge Street. MAP REF: 1,E/3

Pizza on the Park

11 Knightsbridge, SW1

197

071-235 5273 £18

'Pizzas and all that jazz'

Pizza on the Park – perhaps a more accurate name would be Pizza on the dual-carriageway – along with Kettners in Soho remains in the ownership of Peter Boizot, founder of the Pizza Express chain. It has all the strong points of a Pizza Express – consistently good pizzas with properly kneaded, yeast-raised dough, high-quality traditional Italian toppings – no sweetcorn or pineapple here – friendly, efficient service, good music (plus live jazz most evenings in the basement) and design by Enzo Apicella. The large high room with its geometrical wood panelling is one of the few London restaurants of significant size where you can comfortably converse and this despite its popularity with familes and parties. Pizzas are great; the dishes that go towards demonstrating that this is more than a pizza restaurant are considerably less successful. Stick with what they know which to some extent includes the salads and big sandwiches. Breakfast and afternoon tea are also served.

OPEN: Mon-Sun. **HOURS:** 8.15am-12.00am. (9.30am-12.00am Sat-Sun). **CLOSED:** Christmas Day. **CREDIT CARDS ACCEPTED:** Access, AmEx, Diner's Club, Switch, Visa. **NUMBER OF SEATS:** 200. **SERVICE:** 12.5% optional on parties of 10 and over. No-smoking area. Wheelchair access. 40 seats outside. Private room seats 100. **NEAREST TUBE STATION:** Hyde Park Corner (exit 4).

Poissonerie de l'Avenue

82 Sloane Avenue, SW3

198

071-589 2457 £33

'Back to piscatorial basics'

Leaded windows and dark wood panelling give La Poissonnerie a resemblance to Ye Olde Tudor Rose restaurant as found in many county towns; something of a relief in this relentlessly fashionable area. For the core of rather stately patrons the ground-floor dining room is definitely the place to sit. The capable staff can engender an old-fashioned sense of being well looked after, but the restaurant of the fishmonger next door is not the period piece it may first appear to be. The list of fish dishes is long; more than 30 on the standard menu plus dishes of the day. The quality of ingredient is impressive and it is good to find un-enobled fish such as deep-fried fresh anchovies and pan-fried mackerel on the list of specials. However, it is the likes of turbot, sole, salmon and shellfish that are the backbone of the menu. Those not fished out might finish a meal with angels on horseback or herring roe Mephisto. Otherwise there are French desserts or cheeses. The wine list is mainly French with few suprises. Surprise might come with the bill where separately priced vegetables and an automatic 15% service charge take their toll.

Open: Mon-Sat. Hours: 12.00-3.00pm and 7.00-11.45pm. Closed: Bank Holidays, Easter and Christmas. Credit cards accepted: All major cards. Number of seats: 90. Service: 15%. Set price Lunch: £16.50. Wheelchair access (but not lavatory). Tables outside seat 18. Private room seats 22. Nearest tube station: South Kensington.

Le Pont de la Tour

Butlers Wharf Building, 36 Shad Thames, SE1

071-403 8403   £45-£55; Bar & Grill £22

'Great views'

In the preparation of food there is a point at which admirable simplicity can slide into being simplistic. When a lot of money is charged, as it is here, you have to stare very hard indeed at the Thames and the view of Tower Bridge or the artistic detailing of the restaurant's design to make it begin to seem worthwhile forking out quite so much for, say, some Bayonne ham with bland celeriac rémoulade followed by a grilled veal chop with a creamy shallot sauce. Obviously there are many other options but chef David Burke, who was Simon Hopkinson's sous-chef at Bibendum, has perhaps to put up with too great a pressure of numbers to come near his mentor's standards of precise cooking. Dishes of the day seem to engage him – and his kitchen – more, and they are conceivably the ones to choose. Alternatively, to lessen the outlay, eat at lunchtime or early, from 6–6.45pm or late, from 10.30pm to midnight, and take advantage of the set price menus. Or eat at the Bar and Grill. The 15% service charge which Sir Terence says removes from the staff the temptation of 'wriggling around the law' when dealing with the taxman, also seems to remove from them the need to be charming either with customers or with one another. In this now-extended world trade fair pavilion that includes an Italian restaurant, Cantina del Ponte, and a British restaurant, the Butler's Wharf Chop House, reports and my own experiences conclude that, since the setting alone is worth a detour, there is a certain cynicism attached to putting such a premium on form over content.

THIS IS, BY VIRTUE of the wine merchant facility next door, one of London's most extensive lists: you could eat here daily for a year, bank balance and liver allowing, and still not drink the same wine twice. The list begins, sensibly, with three diners' digest versions – one up to £20, one up to £40 and one up to £55 (before, that is, they've hit you with the 15% service surcharge). These are annotated, mostly usefully. The rest of the list is good for Alsace, Rhine and Loire as well as the expected burgundy and claret. Italy (Vernaculum and Cepparello and the New World (try Coppola's apocalyptic Cabernet Franc) are well-represented, though the price structure means that there are no bargains.

Open: Restaurant: Lunch: Sun-Fri. Dinner: Mon-Sun. Bar and Grill: Mon-Sun. Hours: 12.00-3.00pm and 6.00pm-12.00am (6.00-11.00pm Sun.) Bar and Grill open 12.00-11pm, cold food only 3.00-6.00pm. Closed: Christmas. Credit cards accepted: Access, AmEx, Diner's Club, Visa. Number of seats: 105 in Restaurant, 70 in Bar and Grill. Service: 15% included in price. Set price lunch: £25. Wheelchair access. Restaurant seats 65 outside; Grill seats 35 outside. Private room seats 20. Nearest tube station: London Bridge/Tower Hill.

Poons

4 Leicester Street, WC2

071-437 1528   £15

'Where food is not sun-dried but wind-blown'

The time when in Chinese restaurants you had to choose between the food and and the surroundings is now long past. Further proof is the stylish reworking of the decor at the Cantonese restaurant Poons in Leicester Street – and indeed the new paint job at the original café-like Poons in Lisle Street. The unique selling point of this family business is wind-dried food, a curing process applied to duck, pork and, most interestingly, pork sausages with their singular anise flavour. The best effect from wind-dried food is its emanation into a hot pot of rice but another way to savour one variety is in boneless chicken sandwiched with wind-dried pork. Noodle assemblies and rice dishes – ideal for a one-plate lunch – are keenly priced. Some Western chefs are great fans of the casseroles, particularly eel and roast pork belly casserole. The last time I tried, it lacked the quantity of garlic necessary to cut the unctuousness, but any suspicion that a chic look – greater in impact on the ground floor – has resulted in cooking being adapted for the presumed preferences of round eyes was not borne out by the rest of the meal. Service, if not effusively friendly, is civil and efficient.

OPEN: Mon-Sun. **HOURS:** 12.00-11.30pm. **CLOSED:** 4/5 days at Christmas. **CREDIT CARDS ACCEPTED:** None. **NUMBER OF SEATS:** 130. **SERVICE:** Optional. **SET PRICE LUNCH AND DINNER:** £7-£19. Private room seats 30. **NEAREST TUBE STATION:** Leicester Square/Piccadilly.   MAP REF: 1,E/1

Quaglino's

16 Bury Street, SW1

071-930 6767   £35

'Still the talk of the town'

The buzz of excitement that attended the opening of Quaglino's on Valentine's Day in 1993 has not diminished. The popularity of the closest thing London has to compare with the big Paris brasseries means that it is still a struggle to get a table but the management now claims that at least the bookings system has been streamlined. As a glorious piece of design and a celebration of art and technology on a magnificent scale it continues to impress but what impresses this restaurant reviewer most is the high standard of cooking maintained when feeding the numbers – over 400 at a sitting. The strongest section of the kitchen seems to be the rotisserie and grill (visible from the main dining room) from where, with spot-on timing, despite a disclaimer that rotisserie items cannot be cooked to order, come items like rare peppered rib of beef served with horseradish; flavourful shoulder of pork with crackling and apple sauce. If you start such a meal with oysters or something else from the crustacea bar you have reduced the margin for error to almost nothing. But other first courses recently successfully tried were potato pancake with seared salmon and the house antipasti, a selection of marinated and grilled vegetables marred only by a slab of cold polenta. Deep-fried lemon sole and chips pleases aficionados of fish and chips. The list of desserts is immediately likeable – not always the case – and two seductive ones have been pavlova with berries and Stilton in a custard with Armagnac prunes. Service does its best. It seems ironic that the name of one of the restaurant world's great hosts – Giovanni Quaglino – has been utilized when there is such a palpable absence of anyone charismatic at the helm. If you are averse to noisy restaurants, you will not like Quaglino's but you might consider eating early evening (it opens from 5.30pm).

GOOD SHORT WINE lists are actually more difficult to compile than long ones, since there is no room for idlers. Quag's has a good short wine list, roughly organised by variety, with a sound balance between different contributing nations (only Spain and Chile need feel aggrieved). Zind-Humbrecht, Jermann, Tim Adams, Verget and Coldstream Hills are among those worth spending money on, with a glass or a half-bottle of Niepoort's fine 1987 vintage to finish. The fine wine list is expensive – dangerously so, by the time the rapacious service charge has been added (so, for example, a bottle of Hermitage La Chapelle '85 will cost £79.93 here, compared with £39.50 Downstairs at One-Ninety). Best to use it for its adventurous collection of digestifs by the glass.

OPEN: Mon-Sun. **HOURS:** 12.00-3.00pm and 5.30pm-12.00am. (5.30pm-12.30am Fri-Sat; 5.30-11.00pm Sun.) **CLOSED:** Christmas. **CREDIT CARDS ACCEPTED:** Access, AmEx, Diner's Club, Visa. **NUMBER OF SEATS:** 400. **SERVICE:** 15%. **SET PRICE LUNCH:** £12.95 (Sat and Sun). Wheelchair access. Private room seats 40. **NEAREST TUBE STATION:** Green Park. MAP REF: 1,C/1

The Quality Chop House

94 Farringdon Road, EC1

071-837 5093 **£22**

'A period piece with up-to-date food'

It may be in my imagination but since Terence Conran opened Butler's Wharf Chop House as part of his Epcot-style gastronomic village south of the river, the Dickensian production values of Charles Fontaine's Quality Chop House in Farringdon seem to have been stepped up. Seeing it in the evening no one – unless already aware of the treats in store – but a true optimist would push open the door in the drab façade that reveals just a glimmer of light from within. The interior with its uncomfortable wooden pews, painted anaglypta and sauce bottles keeps up the momentum. The menu, although printed daily, remains fairly similar. It is left to the dishes of the day to break away from the pleasing amalgam of traditional and modern: eggs, bacon and chips; sausages (Toulouse), mash and onion gravy; French black pudding with apple compote; confit of duck. Some of the most popular dishes such as salmon fish cake with sorrel sauce and corned beef hash with fried egg straddle the divide. Many first courses refer back to Charles Fontaine's stint at Le Caprice where he learned to please most of the people most of the time with dishes like warm asparagus with pecorino; Caesar salad; bang bang chicken and roast snails with garlic butter. The drinks list suits the food and in an egalitarian sort of way offers beers and ciders as well as wines and champagne. One of the ways that Fontaine's achievement can be measured is the genuine mix of clientele attracted. Sharing tables – a necessity – encourages cross-fertilization.

OPEN: LUNCH: Sun-Fri. DINNER: Mon-Sun. **HOURS:** 12.00-3.00pm (12.00-4.00pm Sun) and 6.30pm-11.30pm (7.00pm-11.30pm Sun). **CLOSED:** Christmas Day to New Year's Day and Bank Holiday lunches. **CREDIT CARDS ACCEPTED:** None. **NUMBER OF SEATS:** 48. **SERVICE:** Optional. **NEAREST TUBE STATION:** Farringdon.   MAP REF: 8,C/1

Quincy's

675 Finchley Road, NW2   ⓴⓪③

071-794 8499   £27

'We're going to David's for dinner'

There is an air of the middle-class English dinner party attached to eating at this long-running North London neighbourhood restaurant. Fostering it are the many regulars who are on first-name terms with proprietor David Wardle, the caring, sharing service, the plethora of vegetables, the importance attached to the pudding course and the monthly-changing set price three-course menus written in a rather childish hand. However, chef David Philpott cooks the basically British menu – with five choices in each course – with definite professionalism and a dedication to prime ingredients. A notably good olive oil perfumed both a cold fish terrine, its aspic flecked with saffron and its blandness offset by a pungent tapenade, and a melting charlotte of aubergine (one of the several vegetarian options). Fresh fish (including fine sea bream) may be betrayed by vague saucing; the reduction accompanying excellent paupiettes of veal and slightly leathery calves' kidneys, by contrast, can be dark and intense. Other successes have been a soup of the day that was a version of garbure and rabbit cooked with cannellini beans, parsley and mustard. Vegetables are cooked al denture rather than al dente. Desserts such as a biscuit-leaved tower of chocolate and apricot fool are constructed along the lines that bring forth an Oooh, I shouldn't from the ladies who then invariably do. The wine list is good and reasonably priced.

OPEN: Tue-Sat. **HOURS:** 7.00-11.00pm. **CLOSED:** Christmas Day and Boxing Day. **CREDIT CARDS ACCEPTED:** Access, AmEx, Visa. **NUMBER OF SEATS:** 30. **SERVICE:** Optional. No-smoking area. Wheelchair access. Private room seats 12. **NEAREST TUBE STATION:** Golders Green/Finchley Road.

EC2

COOPER BISHOPSGATE

SERVICE ON A PLATE

At Cooper Bishopsgate, the BMW dealership for the City, service and choice are the specialities of the house.

We offer a full selection of tempting new BMW cars, all covered by our 3 - year, 60,000 mile dealer warranty; together with over 40 BMW Approved Used cars (not to mention access to hundreds more through our most extensive dealer network).

We also serve a wide menu of finance options. And, every customer who orders a BMW from us will enjoy the many aftersales privileges of the Cooper Bishopsgate Premier Club.

Of course, first class service is always the order of the day. For instance, when it comes to servicing, we will collect and deliver the car - anywhere in the City.

With Cooper Bishopsgate, you're guaranteed service on a plate. So if we've whetted your appetite and you'd like to book a test drive, the number to call is 071 377 8811.

Cooper Bishopsgate

THE BEST SPOT IN THE SQUARE MILE FOR BMW

20 Paul Street, London EC2A 4JH.
Tel: Sales 071 377 8811 Service & Parts 071 375 1301 (24 hours)

HOLIDAY CAR HIRE FOR UP TO 70% LESS.

(EVEN CAR HIRE CAN BE MOUTHWATERING).

At Holiday Autos we guarantee the lowest prices, often up to 70% less than others. If you find a lower deal we'll beat it. See your local travel agent or phone: **071-491 1111.**

NOBODY BEATS OUR PRICES.

Ragam

57 Cleveland Street, W1

071-636 9098 £15

'Somewhere in the West End to do the sambar'

Leafing through this guide you might think there are a disproportionate number of Indian vegetarian restaurants included. I have actually tried to restrain myself this year but I do believe that Southern Indian and Gujerati vegetarian food delivers some of the most subtle, delicious and cheap eating in London. This little place is in the same family ownership as Sree Krishna (q.v.). The menu is by no means all vegetarian and even the first page of Southern Indian specialities includes what I suppose to be the heretical (but terrific) idea of filling a dosa – the large, crisp pancake made of rice and lentil batter – with meat. (Chutney Mary q.v. do it to even better effect with prawns). Try also uthappam, an onion, tomato and chilli-covered sort of crumpet, and the Keralan kaalan, a nicely bland yogurt and coconut curry that, as the menu says, goes well with rice. Fish curries go better with this food than meat and king prawn fry, an 'exotic starter', has been praised for its 'gooey chilliness'. Service can be lackadaisical but the 10% you pay for it is usually of a very modest bill.

OPEN: Mon-Sun. **HOURS:** 12.00-3.00pm and 6.00-11.30pm. **CLOSED:** Christmas Day and Boxing Day. **CREDIT CARDS ACCEPTED:** Access, AmEx, Diner's Club, Mastercard, Visa. **NUMBER OF SEATS:** 34. **SERVICE:** 10%. Wheelchair access. Private room seats 20. **NEAREST TUBE STATION:** Warren Street/Goodge Street/Tottenham Court Road/Great Portland Street. **MAP REF**: 1,E/3

Rani

7 Long Lane, N3

081-349 4386/2636 £20

'Entrepreneurial Indian vegetarian'

Adding to the crowd who appreciate this ten-year-old North London family-run restaurant for its estimable Indian vegetarian food (tendency Gujerati) might be those on the fashionable new diets which proscribe certain foodstuffs. Here there is guidance on the menu as to which dishes are free of sugar, wheat, dairy products, nuts, onions or garlic. Start with bhel-poori, dhai vada, the well-made bhajias or the daily choice, for example Saturday's stuffed green chilli, medium in size and heat, stuffed with spiced vegetables and perfectly fried in gram flour paste; a sort of Indian chilli rellenos. Follow with vegetable curries, some also served according to the day of the week, and accompany them with the notably good breads such as methi bhatoora, the dough fashioned from flour, yogurt and fenugreek deep-fried to a soft, puffy consistency. Freshly made chutneys can also be a revelation. If you have developed a liking for slightly childish Indian desserts they are here. The Pattni family are true entrepreneurs. They will organize delivery by cab; there is a frequent-eater discount card; a Monday and lunchtime buffet; a children's menu including tomato ketchup and ice cream; a Saturday no-smoking rule and no-smoking areas other days of the week; gift vouchers and a menu in braille. It is all laudable – particularly 'gratuities not accepted' – and also delicious.

OPEN: LUNCH: Tue-Fri, Sun. DINNER: Mon-Sun. **HOURS:** 12.15-4.00pm and 6.00pm-12.00am. **CLOSED:** Christmas Day. **CREDIT CARDS ACCEPTED:** Access, Amex, Delta, Switch, Visa. **NUMBER OF SEATS:** 90. **SERVICE:** Gratuities not accepted. **SET PRICE LUNCH:** £8. **SET PRICE DINNER:** £18.70. No-smoking area. Wheelchair access (but not lavatory). Private room seats 23. **NEAREST TUBE STATION:** Finchley Central

Ransome's Dock Restaurant

35-37 Parkgate Road, SW11   **206**

071-223 1611 or 071 924 2462   **£35**

'The ransom for a good meal is eminently reasonable'

'About the highest ratio of flair to cost that you can hope to find,' said Justin de Blank about Martin Lam's Ransome's Dock restaurant. Lam, whose previous job was chef of L'Escargot, has settled on a sound, popular formula offering relatively simple food that capitalizes on cleverly sourced ingredients. These days that is not an unusual approach but what Lam has managed well is the pitch of the place; how casual it seems balanced against fairly professional service; how items such as breads and wines (see below) are well thought out; the extent to which he is prepared to cultivate a clientele who for the most part are spending their own money, imposing no minimum charge and offering set price lunches, weekend brunches (extremely popular with families) and children's smaller portions. Fish dishes, which Lam particularly likes to cook, make up the daily specials. Some meat dishes from a typical menu (menus change monthly) are sauté of guinea fowl with mushrooms, smoked paprika, piquillo peppers & rice; Scottish sirloin steak with Roquefort butter, chips and watercress salad (something of a fixture). Innes goats' cheese and Morecambe Bay potted shrimps are well-bought ingredients that figure in two of the first courses. The patisserie section of the kitchen is strong and, again, buying in – as in Rocombe Farm ice cream – is done knowledgeably. The blue and green rooms with the kitchen visible at their heart are decorated with an eclectic selection of pictures and well-chosen jazz.

THIS IS A MODEL wine list in many ways: well-organized, by style and grape variety; inexpensive (£20 will give you plenty of choice); and full of unexpectedness and originality. Italy (good wines from Mascarello and Vajra) and Australia (Moss Wood, Wirra Wirra, Charlie Melton) chip in with just as much as France. Wines by the glass change continually, sensibly; there are a dozen halves; and this is a restaurant where the value of chilling light reds and decanting big ones is acted on. Clever work all round.

OPEN: LUNCH: Mon-Sun. DINNER: Mon-Sat. **HOURS:** 11.00am-11.00pm (12.00pm-12.00am Sat; 12.00-3.30pm Sun). **CLOSED:** Christmas. **CREDIT CARDS ACCEPTED:** Access, Amex, Delta, Diner's Club, Switch, Visa. **NUMBER OF SEATS:** 65. **SERVICE:** Optional. **SET PRICE LUNCH:** £11.50. No-smoking area. Wheelchair access. 20 seats outside. **NEAREST TUBE STATION:** Sloane Square.

Rebato's

169 South Lambeth Road, SW8

071-735 6388 or £071-582 8089 £20

'Two for one: a finger-clicking tapas bar and a well-run neighbourhood restaurant'

This drab end of Lambeth has long been a Little Iberia, and the original purpose of this tapas bar and restaurant was to service the needs of local Carmens and Joses – from whence its authenticity. Now everyone's in there with consequent bustle and concessions to Britishness, most noticeable in the clotted-cream-panelled restaurant to the rear. Mixed grill of fish brought overcooked huss, skate wings, salmon and trout into conference with one serious gamba; mint sauce is offered as an alternative to the delicious garlic mahonesa with lamb; and sole dieppoise, salmon trout bretonne and supreme of chicken Devon slug it out with decent paella and sauté of kidneys al Jerez. The dessert trolley (tinned figs aside) could have trundled out of a thousand hotel kitchens. The tapas bar to the front (hermetically sealed, thank goodness, from the South Lambeth Road) is more thoroughgoingly Spanish, with surging flamenco music, dark and wilful waiters, fino sherry in copitas (Osborne's Quinta), and tapas ranging from sardines, fresh anchovies in vinegar and octopus to Spanish omelette, chorizo and salchichas. Portions are generous enough to dine on with ease. It's worth asking for the wine list, which (in addition to everything from Torres and Marqués de Cáceres) has some good Riojas and the fine 1990 Felix Callejo Ribeira del Duero at only £10.25. Treat time for Spanish brandy aficionados, too.

OPEN: LUNCH: Mon-Fri. DINNER: Mon-Sat. **HOURS:** 12.00-2.30pm and 7.00-11.00pm. **CLOSED:** Bank Holidays. **CREDIT CARDS ACCEPTED:** Access, AmEx, Diner's Club, Visa. **NUMBER OF SEATS:** 65. **SERVICE:** Optional. **SET PRICE LUNCH AND DINNER:** £13.95. **NEAREST TUBE STATION:** Stockwell.

The Red Fort

77 Dean Street, W1

071-437 2115 £30

'For modern moguls'

The Red Fort makes a certain amount of visible effort to signal the fact that the aim is serious Indian food – there is a beribboned bronze-edged menu printed on heavy card inserted into a padded silk cover with handles you might otherwise expect to find on the Ark of the Covenant; there is, of course, an award-winning chef hired as consultant; there are occasional regional festivals (a Rajasthani one at the time of this guide's publication) and there is something called the Parliamentary Privilege Club – but the confident prices charged only work as proof if the food lives up to the promise. It does not always, in part because, particularly with Indian first courses, an alluring description such as that for hara kebab – a patty of spinach, gram flour and lentils stuffed with cottage cheese and raisins, coated with poppy seeds and pan-grilled with butter –

delivers a drab-looking little brown patty. However, the various flavours are discernible. Tandoori pomfret is worth ordering as are the lamb dishes including a conscientiously prepared, delicious Hyderabadi biryani where the bone left in the meat adds depth of flavour. Relatively high prices for vegetable dishes, breads and condiments can inflate a bill. It is left to the ambitious wine list and assortment of cocktails rather than the surroundings – which dwindle into dullness in the dining rooms – to remind you that this is an upmarket establishment. The lunchtime buffet – when scents of the dishes arranged beside the front window hook you in from Dean Street – is popular with those who work in Soho.

OPEN: Mon-Sun. **HOURS:** 12.00-3.00pm and 6.00-11.30pm. **CREDIT CARDS ACCEPTED:** All major cards. **NUMBER OF SEATS:** 130. **SERVICE:** Optional. **SET PRICE LUNCH:** Buffet £12.50. No-smoking area. Wheelchair access. Private room seats 70. **NEAREST TUBE STATION:** Tottenham Court Road/Leicester Square.

MAP REF: 1,D/2

Rhapsody

25 Richmond Way, W14   **209**

071-602 6778   **LUNCH: £16; DINNER: £25**

'An Argentinian restaurant that goes beyond steak'

Perhaps if the then Mrs Thatcher had met musician and chef Alberto Portugheis, one-time organizer of a British Food Festival in Buenos Aires, conflict with the Argentinians could have been side-stepped and settled over a plate of matambre – the name translates literally as 'kill hunger'. Or perhaps not. Rhapsody in the Shepherd's Bush premises of what was Chinon (q.v.) was, in any case, only opened in the summer of '93, one of a flourish of Argentinian establishments that have been emboldened to open recently, but one with a more profound grasp on the cuisine than just offering a choice of rump, sirloin or fillet. The original set price menus have given way to an à la carte and a wider range of dishes. Try the matambre, a dish of meat wrapped around hard-boiled egg, worthy of a better description than the waiter's 'sort of Scotch egg'. A lighter start would be escabeche or ceviche, different methods of marinating fish, the first of cooked, the second of raw, or coxinha, another dish traduced by its description, chicken croquettes. Authentic and interesting are bacalhau (salt cod) in chilli and almond sauce, rabbit in peanut sauce and of course the grilled meats including spicy chorizos. With them come various hot sauces. There are a couple of vegetarian options, perhaps necessary in these days of beef fright, but nevertheless an odd thing to choose in an Argentinian restaurant where, were it the old days, steak would arrive as a matter of course, rather the way bread does in a French establishment. It's hard to beat dulce de leche, a take on condensed milk, as a dessert. Argentinian – and Chilean – wines are the sensible choice for drinking.

OPEN: LUNCH: Mon-Fri. DINNER: Mon-Sat. **HOURS:** 12.00-3.00pm and 7.00-12.00pm. **CLOSED:** Bank Holidays. **CREDIT CARDS ACCEPTED:** Access, AmEx, Diner's Club, Transmedia, Visa. **NUMBER OF SEATS:** 26. **SERVICE:** Optional. Tables outside seat 8. Wheelchair access (but not lavatory). **NEAREST TUBE STATION:** Shepherds Bush/Olympia. **MAP REF:** 7,C/1

The Ritz Restaurant

Ritz Hotel,
Piccadilly, W1

071-493 8181   LUNCH £40; DINNER £50

'An exquisite setting for a set-price meal'

You could make out a case – someone has – that as the Ritz dining room is quite simply the most beautiful restaurant in the entire world, and to dine there on a summer evening as the dusk fades from the garden terrace and the golden garlands begin to gleam against their painted sky is an experience so haunting, that it would be almost churlish to notice what you are eating. But this is a guide to eating out, not just the world of interiors and the enchantment of 'Edwardian luxe et volupté' so I would suggest that the sensible approach is to choose the set price menu. At dinner the inclusive price is for four courses and coffee – you want to spin this occasion out. Perfect parma ham is served with spiced pear, lightly cooked strips of fennel and a tuile made savoury with pecorino cheese. An airy quenelle of turbot and lobster with asparagus and champagne sauce follows on seamlessly. Beef has been like 'pink satin' and served with roasted veal kidneys on baby leaf spinach. Desserts echo the choice on the à la carte; in general you are not taking the bargain basement route by eating table d'hôte, and David Nicholls is a chef of considerable skill. The cheaper three-course lunch menu has daily, mainly British specialities such as braised oxtail (Thursday) and chicken, leek and onion pie with bacon and eggs (Friday) as well as a daily roast from the trolley. Reports of service this year are much better. This almost extinct brand of glamour can be yours for about £50 a head, which makes you think.

EVEN BY GRAND HOTEL standards this is a conservative list, filled with page after page of the usual distinguished French names at the usual haughty prices. For those who know what they like and can afford it, there are plenty of treats: the Ritz's cellar stretches back in time as well as space, and pre-1980s claret is plentiful; burgundy from Rousseau, Trapet, Dujac, Tollot-Beaut and Pousse d'Or should all prove ritzy; and you can't go wrong, other than financially, with Krug '82. Those seeking a reasonable bottle for £25 or under will have a harder time of it: Trimbach's Pinot Blanc, Muscadet from Sauvion, the Savennières of Baumard and Penfold's brilliant Bin 28 would be my recommendations.

OPEN: Mon-Sun. **HOURS:** 12.30-2.30pm and 6.00-11.30pm. **CREDIT CARDS ACCEPTED:** All major cards. **NUMBER OF SEATS:** 100. **SERVICE:** Inclusive. **SET PRICE LUNCH:** £26. **SET PRICE DINNER:** £39.50 (£43.50 Fri and Sat). Wheelchair access. 20 seats outside. Private room seats 14. **NEAREST TUBE STATION:** Green Park.   MAP REF: 1,C/1

Riva

169 Church Road, SW13

(211)

081-748 0434   **£25**

'Northern Italian, south of the river'

After four consistently busy years since opening, the confidence that a comitted customer base can bring spurs Andrea Riva and his chef Francesco Zanchetta to produce an increasingly interesting and authentic Northern Italian menu. Riva comes from Lombardy, his chef has worked most formatively in Venice and evidence is in the dishes and particularly the daily specials. To sample as much as possible it is tempting (and wise) to choose a first course that serves an array, some of them designed to satisfy two people. Sapore di mare is a plate of home-smoked scallops served in the shells with brown lentils, asparagus spears onto which crab meat has been baked, small steaks of fresh tuna and a wonderful cream of salt cod (baccala) with grilled polenta. Stuzzichini comprises a crêpe with robbiola and watercress, endive with tomino (small fresh cheese) and smoked salmon, fonduta (melted fontina cheese and eggs) with fried polenta chips and perch fillet with a tuna sauce. Pastas are served at two prices for first and main course sizes. Farfalle is sauced with a new and diverting ingredient, buffalo ricotta, a much tastier version of the more usual cow's milk ricotta, plus pine kenels and basil.

In the main course sturgeon fillet is steamed wrapped in cabbage and served with saffron sauce and new potatoes. Another speciality, reflecting the traditional diet of Lombardy, is roast best end of lamb with pecorino and herbs served with barley pancakes. It is a wonderful dish. Riva sports an unusually creative list of desserts. If you try only one (foolish) make it sbrisolona, a maize and almond crumble soaked in vin santo and served with a mound of mascarpone. The entirely Italian wine list is interesting but it is worth asking Andrea Riva (who is almost always around; he is a natural restaurateur) what else he happens to have. His mark-ups are modest. New or infrequent diners may resent the camaraderie of the regulars in this cramped, simply decorated room but my response to this is, become a regular. Service has become noticeably more cheerful and is as professional as you would find in Italy.

THIS SHORT, ALL-ITALIAN wine list is largely well-selected, with good wines from Lageder, Negri, Jermann, Capezzana and Allegrini, most of them under £20. The majority have a story to tell, and it would be nice to see them given a chance to tell it via a little annotation. The `vast selection' of grappe defeats the list's compiler, but is there for the sampling.

OPEN: LUNCH: Sun-Fri. DINNER: Mon-Sun. **HOURS:** 12.00-2.30pm and 7.00-11.00pm (7.00-11.30pm Sat; 7.00-9.30pm Sun). **CLOSED:** Christmas, Easter and Bank Holidays. **CREDIT CARDS ACCEPTED:** Access, Visa, Mastercard. **NUMBER OF SEATS:** 50. **SERVICE:** 10%. Wheelchair access (but not lavatory). 8 seats outside. **NEAREST BR STATION:** Barnes.

The River Café

Thames Wharf,
Rainville Road, W6

212

071-381 8824   **£35**

'Much copied but still the best'

The transformation of the interior of the River Café, which took place quite suddenly in the summer of 1994, brings the appearance and atmosphere more in line with its unique, sparsely luxurious approach to Italian food. Deceptive simplicity was always the underpinning of the menu and now it also applies to the cleverly lit, cobalt-blue carpeted space. By the time you read this, a wood-fired oven should have been successfully installed, producing not just superior breads and pies but slow-cooked food and magnificent roasts. In other respects the strengths of the menu remain as before; beautifully balanced vegetable soups created with an eye to colour as well as to texture and flavour; grilled vegetables and the ever-popular charcoal-grilled squid with fresh chilli and rucola; delicate home-made pastas; salt-baked sea-bass, grilled meats and a slow-cooked dish. The impact of the cooking is invariably mainly lodged in the quality of the ingredients and the use of spices and abundant fresh herbs. Desserts are not the usual winding down of the Italian meal but an important course in their own right – maybe thanks to the influence of American co-owner and chef Ruthie Rogers. Typical examples (on a menu that changes in part twice a day) are pannacotta with grappa and tayberries; chocolate nemesis (as rich as you would suppose); apricot and almond tart. The revamping of what was originally designed to be the canteen for the complex of offices and studios that house Richard Rogers Partnership and its much-improved relationship with the gardens and river beyond answers to some extent the complaints about the cost of a meal here. The fact that prices seem not to have increased since last year also helps. The local strictures on opening times do not increase the likelihood of tables being turned over – and thus profits improving, prices falling – but they do lead to a car jockey in the evenings who will park your car.

YOU REALLY NEED half an hour in the corner with this list. It's all Italian, and it's an education in itself – not only because the selections (from the exemplary Winecellars portfolio) are so nimbly on the ball, but also because they're justified with notes which convey flavours and philosophies with uncommon intelligence (and not an exclamation mark in sight). To know Italy, drink here.

OPEN: LUNCH: Mon-Sun. DINNER: Mon-Sat. **HOURS:** 12.30-3.00pm (1.00-3.00pm Sun) and 7.30-11.00pm. **CLOSED:** Christmas and Bank Holidays. **CREDIT CARDS ACCEPTED:** Access, Mastercard, Switch, Visa. **NUMBER OF SEATS:** 100. **SERVICE:** 12.5%. Wheelchair access. Tables outside seat 48. **NEAREST TUBE STATION:** Hammersmith.

Royal China Restaurant

13 Queensway, W2

071-221 2535

£27

'Maybe where Chris Patten will eat in 1997'

Queensway is lined with Chinese restaurants; Royal China at the Bayswater Road end comes closest to feeling like a direct import from Hong-Kong. The decor is dark and glossy. Hokusai waves spar with art deco curves lacquered on the black blockboard panelling – so reminiscent of maritime conditions in the South China sea. Service can be pushy and one visitor was made to wait 15 minutes for his table before being seated in a more or less empty restaurant. However, the long menu can deliver interesting and authentic Cantonese cooking particularly if you think yourself into a Hong Kong frame of mind and order items such as shark's fin soup, fresh abalone and lobster. On the whole the restaurant is strongest on fish dishes although I like their idea of combining veal with black bean sauce and honey. For those who might be inclined to start a meal with something like sliced beef shin marinated in spices with jellyfish, there is a list called Chiefs (presumably Chef's) Favourites that has some mildly arcane dishes including an interestingly fatty steamed minced pork with salted egg. Dim sum is well thought of here and on Sundays is a big draw.

The (original) Putney branch of Royal China has reopened after refurbishment – the imposing door like something that slams shut at the end of a Kurosawa film remains – making this little corner of Putney next to a bus garage another slice of Hong Kong. The exotic fish tank in the corner hints at seafood being the sage order and a wide variety of ingredients garner imaginative treatments; for example, soft shell crab fried and served with shredded vegetables and chilli; a carefully seasoned seafood mixture served in rice baskets and garnished with pine kernels. Some sauces sink into over-sweet mundaneness and complication of presentation can get the better of sense. The wine list is more ambitious than usual. The staff are sinuous and smiley.

OPEN: Mon-Sun. **HOURS:** 12.00-11.15pm (12.00-10.30pm Sun). **CLOSED:** Christmas Eve and Christmas Day. **CREDIT CARDS ACCEPTED:** Access, AmEx, Diner's Club, Mastercard. **NUMBER OF SEATS:** 100. **SERVICE:** 12.5%. **SET PRICE DINNER:** £20-£26. Wheelchair access (but not lavatory). Private room seats 10-15. **NEAREST TUBE STATION:** Queensway/Bayswater.

RSJ Restaurant and Brasserie

13a Coin Street, SE1

071-928 4554

£26

'Reinforces a love of Loire wines '

Despite its somewhat butch name, RSJ offers its clientele a prettified English interior and a modern British menu. The restaurant is arranged over three levels with the basement styled as brasserie but, as is so often the case, not keeping brasserie hours. At the time of going to press the chef is changing, making comment on dishes recently tried not to the point. It is to be hoped that in a culinary sense the new regime will stand proudly alongside the exceptional wine list and attract comment more wholehearted than useful in an area (behind the National Theatre) that has a dearth of attractive alternatives.

RSJ'n wɪɴᴇ ʟɪsᴛ is in a class of its own, beating all comers (wine merchants included) with the thoroughness with which it explores the wines of one of France's less fashionable regions – the Loire valley. Nigel Wilkinson's knowledge of his growers makes this a more forgiving list than most in which to explore the unknown. Especially worthwhile are the white Savennières and red Chinon selections, with Anjou-Villages providing some of the best value for money. The annotations are useful, particularly as the complexities of the list are sometimes beyond the waiting staff in Wilkinson's absence. Prices, given this quality, are fair. The only real disappointment is that there aren't more dessert wines in half-bottles. Depardieu fans can drink the old rogue's wine, the next best thing to kissing him.

OPEN: **LUNCH:** Mon-Fri. **DINNER:** Mon-Sat. **HOURS:** 12.00-2.00pm and 6.00-11.00pm. **CLOSED:** Bank Holidays. **CREDIT CARDS ACCEPTED:** Access, AmEx, Visa. **NUMBER OF SEATS:** 75. **SERVICE:** 10%. No-smoking area. Wheelchair access (but not lavatory). Private room seats 20. **NEAREST TUBE STATION:** Waterloo.

Rules

35 Maiden Lane, WC2

071-836 5314 £27

'Rules are made for the good of the people'

The rooms at Rules, their plush-banquetted, illuminated-pictured, mock-chaotic cosiness have not noticeably changed since anyone can remember, probably not in the soon-to-be-two-hundred years since it was opened by Thomas Rule at a time when Napoleon's strict views on the EC put the kybosh on the coach-set bowling off to Paris for a decent meal. The kitchens, we are told, have been modernized and recently propelled into the 21st century. Rules, as its name might imply, runs a tight and traditional ship. Its Pennine estate provides game and fresh-water fish, its own smoke-house the smoked grouse and pheasant, Ireland its oysters, Morecambe Bay its potted shrimp, Seagrams its gin. Cooking has improved of late but it is still prudent – and in keeping with the ethos – to stick to the simpler dishes which require little intervention. There are some good deals in the weekend lunches (note the accommodating opening hours) and the pre-theatre special. Wines, including champagne, are well priced. Some come from the New World as do many of the staff.

OPEN: Mon-Sun. **HOURS:** 12.00pm-12.00am. **CLOSED:** 5 days at Christmas. **CREDIT CARDS ACCEPTED:** Access, AmEx, Delta, Mastercard, Switch, Visa. **NUMBER OF SEATS:** 140. **SERVICE:** 12.5% parties of 7 and over. **SET PRICE DINNER:** £12.95. Wheelchair access (but not lavatory). Private rooms seat 18, 20 and 48. **NEAREST TUBE STATION:** Charing Cross/Covent Garden.   MAP REF: 1,F/1

Sabai Sabai

270/272 King Street, W6

081-748 7363 £19

'Relax Relax is the translation from the Thai'

This stretch of King Street in Hammersmith is taking on a new restaurant identity with the arrival of Wild World (q.v.) and the sweet, unlicensed Robbie's. All to the good if this highlights Sabai Sabai, a notable Thai restaurant with a strong local following. It attracts a cosmopolitan crowd. Few people eating there, noted a tester with relief, would have passed the Norman Tebbit patriotism test. Decor in the two light rooms is of the Thai grotto school with suitable reliance on fairy lights and pastel hangings. Soups are excellent but in choosing, say, hot and sour chicken or 'fish trap' soup served in a clay pot do not miss out on the pork and prawn dim sum; hotter, lighter and spicier than a Chinese version. For some reason noodle dishes are not the pleasure they usually are and too much sugar can occasionally creep in as it also did to the (allegedly) steamed spare ribs. Sabai means relax which is easy to do in what seems like a genuinely happy place.

OPEN: Mon-Sun. **HOURS:** 11.00am-2.30pm and 6.00-11.30pm (6.00-10.30pm Sun). **CLOSED:** Christmas Day and Boxing Day. **CREDIT CARDS ACCEPTED:** All major cards except Diner's Club. **NUMBER OF SEATS:** 70. **SERVICE:** 10%. **SET PRICE LUNCH:** £6.95. **SET PRICE DINNER:** £15.00. Wheelchair access (but not lavatory). **NEAREST TUBE STATION:** Ravenscourt Park.

Sabras

263 Willesden High Road, NW10

081-459 0340 LUNCH: £8; DINNER: £12

'Homemade Indian vegetarian food in twinkling surroundings'

The Indian vegetarian Sabras, now in its 21st year and no stranger to accolades – *thrice*, they say on the menu, best of the year award winner – in '94 was much praised in the Gault Millau guide to London. The French, I think, were wanting to show how on the ball they can be gastronomically. In the same year the restaurant was reviewed in the *Independent on Sunday* but Daisy Waugh, the reviewer, found the whole business of getting to Willesden just simply too frightful. Sabras does indeed serve exceedingly good, homemade (by co-owner Mrs Nalinee Desai) vegetarian and vegan food at very attractive prices. Start with some Gujerati savouries served with fresh chutneys. Steamed khamans made from chick-pea flour and garnished with fried mustard seeds, coconut and coriander leaves are unusual and particularly good. Try one of the Southern Indian dishes such as the dramatic masala dosa (Mysore and Madras style is hot with chilli); the potato cake topped with a yellow pea purée, tamarind, onion and lemon called ragada patish; a familiar vegetable dish, say mutter-paneer, and some perhaps unfamiliar seasonal Indian vegetables such as the delectable govar (cluster beans), a dal (udad is good) and breads. The meal will be paced by the kitchen and not arrive all at once. There are reasonably priced wines and all kinds of schemes and offers to study; you could join the Tycoons Beer & Wine Club; pay £125 up front for 25 dinners at £5 each which must be eaten within a period of 30 days; plan a party with the Desais as your caterer or simply give them all your money to invest in their M.I.P.P. programme (more interest per pound). Lunch at Sabras – called Mysore Café, the name for South Indian vegetarian restaurants all over India – is even cheaper.

OPEN: Tue-Sun. **HOURS:** 12.00-3.00pm and 6.30-10.30pm. **CREDIT CARDS ACCEPTED:** None. **NUMBER OF SEATS:** 32. **SERVICE:** Optional. **SET PRICE LUNCH:** £5.95- £7.55. **SET PRICE DINNER:** £8-£12. No-smoking area. Wheelchair access (but not lavatory). **NEAREST TUBE STATION:** Dollis Hill/Willesden Green.

Saigon

45 Frith Street, W1

071-437 7109/1672 £22

'A wide choice of Vietnamese dishes'

Get hold of the video of *The Scent of Green Papaya*, watch it and then, with your appetite aroused as it will be by the touching scenes of cooking, go to Saigon in Soho. Unlike most 'Vietnamese' establishments that offer a few specialities backed up by Chinese dishes, the menu here offers a wide, completely Vietnamese choice; 39 dishes in all. To start there is a green papaya salad but try also mixed wind-dried duck sausage with bamboo shoot and water chestnut; cold spiced chicken with pickled vegetables; squid balls served with herbs, vegetables and lettuce as the wrapping. Wrapping is an activity much encouraged and under the heading of Specialities are two to try using rice paper for the parcel; barbecued beef with herbs and raw vegetables and aromatic duck the same way. Vegetables and noodles can be accomplished in one by ordering bun tau rau tuoi, a pot of vegetables and vermicelli. Portions tend to explain the slender size of the waitresses, some of whom, at a lunch anyway, seemed to have seen the film and learned the lesson about the rewards of obedient service.

OPEN: Mon-Sat. **HOURS:** 12.00-11.30pm. **CLOSED:** Bank Holidays. **CREDIT CARDS ACCEPTED:** Access, AmEx, Diner's Club, Visa. **NUMBER OF SEATS:** 80. **SERVICE:** 10%. **SET PRICE LUNCH AND DINNER:** £14.40. Private room seats 40. **NEAREST TUBE STATION:** Piccadilly Circus/ Tottenham Court Road. **MAP REF:** 1,E/2

St James's Court Hotel – Auberge de Provence

41 Buckingham Gate, SW1

219

071-821 1899
LUNCH: £25; DINNER: £40

'The closest bit of Provence to the Palace'

The idea that a room, any room, in what was originally an Edwardian mansion block could summon up the herb-scented Alpilles in the South of France is, by any measure, absurd. L'Auberge de Provence, the French restaurant of the Taj-owned St James's Court Hotel, down the road from Buckingham Palace, is supposed to evoke its parent restaurant L'Oustau de Baumanière in the village of Les Baux, one of the prettiest settings of any restaurant in the world. Happily, to some extent, it manages to do this through some of the dishes and wines of the region. Filet de loup de mer au basilic is so noble a fish, so judiciously steamed and flavoured with olive oil that has been infused with tomatoes and basil, that it does almost transport you to a place where lavender blooms and cicadas shudder. Roasted lamb fillet with rosemary gravy and a mousse of fennel compresses a year in Provence into a meal. Outstanding among the desserts – a course you tend to take when having paid for it as part of the £30 three-course Menu Provencal – is crêpes soufflés flavoured with Grand Marnier. Vegetarian dishes, an interest of consultant chef Jean-Andre Charial of Baumanière, are interesting. Charial is well served in London by chef Bernard Brique. Service, too, does its best to drag the world of Marcel Pagnol practically to the steps of New Scotland Yard.

OPEN: LUNCH: Mon-Fri. **DINNER:** Mon-Sat. **HOURS:** 12.30-2.30pm and 7.30-11.00pm. **CLOSED:** 1 week January, 2 weeks August. **CREDIT CARDS ACCEPTED:** All major cards. **NUMBER OF SEATS:** 65. **SERVICE:** Optional. **SET PRICE LUNCH:** £23.50. **SET PRICE DINNER:** £30. No-smoking area. Private room seats 30. Wheelchair access (but not lavatory). **NEAREST TUBE STATION:** St James Park.

St Quentin

243 Brompton Road, SW3

220

071-589 8005
£30

'The patron saint is Quentin Crewe, also patron saint of restaurant writing'

This restaurant sits well in the outpost of France that is South Kensington. The French, homesick for the clichés of their cuisine, use it and it has style. Some of this is located in the look of the ground-floor room – once the Brompton Grill – with its long dark bar, brass trimmings, etched mirrors, twinkling columns and closely packed well-dressed tables. Chef Nigel Davies who has also worked at The Ivy and Sud-Ouest has, as you might have guessed, an interest in the food of South-West France. This is just about apparent in the menu in dishes such as rillettes d'oie; jambon de Bayonne et celeri-rémoulade; confit de canard aux petits pois; cassoulet de Toulouse; mousse aux pruneaux et à l'Armagnac. My favourite way of eating here is to start with a salade St Quentin and then share a poulet des Landes rôti or otherwise have that quintessentially French, rather tough cut of steak, bavette, with frites. The French wine list is not over-priced. I'm sure some frightfully interesting study on the effects of passive smoking could be carried out here.

The nearby **Grill St Quentin** (3 Yeoman's Row, SW3, 071-581 8377) is a splendid space – almost La Coupole in a basement – but here stylishness has been lost to an imprecise kitchen and unco-ordinated, unmarshalled young staff whose uniform of blue denim shirts and dark skirts or trousers are reminiscent of an episode of *Cell Block H*. These surroundings call out for black outfits with floor-length white aprons. Dressed thus, waiters might not leave dirty plates on the table displaying cheese and desserts and other such infelicities. Oysters are, unforgiveably, sometimes not available. Chips are not good; looking, feeling and tasting like frozen oven chips. However, start with rillettes – nicely presented in a large bowl with a jar of cornichons – have some charcoal-grilled red meat or the rognons à la moutarde and a bottle of red wine and enjoy the spaciousness and matter-of-factness of the surroundings.

OPEN: Mon-Sun. **HOURS:** 12.00-11.30pm. **CREDIT CARDS ACCEPTED:** All major cards. **NUMBER OF SEATS:** BRASSERIE: 80; GRILL: 140. **SERVICE:** 12.5%. **SET PRICE LUNCH:** £8. Wheelchair access to Brasserie (but not lavatory). Private room at Brasserie seats 25. **NEAREST TUBE STATION:** South Kensington. **MAP REF:** 2,D/4

Salloos

62-64 Kinnerton Street, SW1

071-235 4444 **£27**

'Near perfection in Pakistani food – at a price'

Willingness to pay what is required to eat here will depend on your enthusiasm for Indian, or more accurately Pakistani, food. The premises are not especially inviting and the service has the effect of the more it tries, the more it grates, but the cooking is exceptional. Prime ingredients are used - only halal meats – and unusually for this cuisine, many dishes are only cooked after the order has been taken. Such items are marked with an asterisk on the menu. Of course, marination has been taking place and it is this process that informs the chicken, quails, lamb kebabs and prawns that are cooked in the tandoori and – as the restaurant puts it – the reknowned tandoori chops, which are indeed delicious; fat-free and flavourful. These plus one of the breads such as nan or aloo paratha make a splendid first course. One of my favourite main courses is gurda masala, lamb's kidneys, cooked to a recipe Salloos claims as its own. It is uniquely good in texture as well as taste. If you are not wary of things deep-fried then chicken taimuri cooked in a spiced batter is interesting, as is the unorthodox-sounding chicken in cheese. Pulao Jehangiri promotes the interesting concept of cooking the basmati rice in lamb stock before garnishing it with chicken, almonds and raisins. It is worth ordering a biryani to see how this dish should be made. Vegetables are so expensive (£7.50 each dish) that is tempting to forego them. I won't tell your mother. If you drink wine that will send your bill spiralling ever higher, as will the cover charge of £1.50 and the 15% service charge. Salloos is nevertheless worth it, just to see how good Pakistani food can be.

OPEN: Mon-Sat. **HOURS:** 12.00-3.00pm and 6.30pm-12.00am. **CREDIT CARDS ACCEPTED:** Access, AmEx, Diner's Club, Visa. **NUMBER OF SEATS:** 65. **SERVICE:** 15%, £1.50 cover charge. **SET PRICE LUNCH:** £16. **SET PRICE DINNER:** £25. **NEAREST TUBE STATION:** Knightsbridge/Hyde Park Corner.   MAP REF: 2,F/4

San Lorenzo Fuoriporta

Worple Mews, Wimbledon, SW19

081-946 8463/8976   **£30**

'The Wimbledon Berni inn'

While Momma and Poppa Berni have become mini-celebrities in their own right as they cosset their glitzy regulars in Beauchamp Place, the pace at this branch of San Lorenzo in Wimbledon is more relaxed. The Bernis' son Ghigo and his wife Angela apply the same sort of mwah mwah kisses, teeth and smiles and bonhomie (even the dog, Floyd, named after the Pink Floyd, is a professional schmoozer) but it somehow seems more sincere in the suburbs. They obviously like children, an attitude that translates into balloons, crayons and paper and extra attention for the under-tens. Habitués of Beauchamp Place will recognize many dishes and the format is similar; pizzas and pastas are strong, there is much grilled meat and fish and prices are not backward in coming forward (no antipasti less than 650p, as they express it) and there is a cover charge of £2 per person. To start try polenta with gorgonzola; tuna carpaccio; Parma ham with paw-paw. In wild mushroom season, the risotto involving them is lovely. Pizzas are thin and crisp and the toppings traditional. In the main course poached sea bass and grilled wild boar cutlets with beans, olive oil and rosemary are a bit different. For dessert, try the homemade ice creams, Angela Berni's special province.

OPEN: LUNCH: Mon-Sun. DINNER: Mon-Sat. **HOURS:** 12.00-3.00pm and 7.00-11.00pm (12.30-3.30pm Sun). **CLOSED:** Bank Holidays, Christmas and Easter. **CREDIT CARDS ACCEPTED:** All major cards. **NUMBER OF SEATS:** 120. **SERVICE:** Optional. Wheelchair access (but not lavatory). Tables outside seat 60. Private room seats 30. **NEAREST TUBE STATION:** Wimbledon.

Santini

29 Ebury Street, SW1

071-730 4094   LUNCH: £25; DINNER: £45

'A meal that may exceed the cost of flying to Milan'

This was the first of Gino Santini's upmarket restaurants (c.f. L'Incontro) and conceivably the first London Italian restaurant to adopt a cool, chic look. To anyone aware of the quality and price of Italian food now to be found in many parts of London, the menu has a certain cool cheek of its own. As a first course, mozzarella and tomato salad is priced at £11.50. Fish dishes exceed £20. Santini suits customers with a taste for conspicuous consumption and preferably Italian-speaking. It is admirable that young European waiters come here to practise English but perhaps it should not be on the indigenous public at this price. The price also makes harder to bear faults such as the oversalting of an artichoke sauce for pasta, and the intrusive flavour of orange in an osso bucco served innocent of a gremolada but needing more of the good risotto Milanese as accompaniment. There are good dishes; juicy lobster is divided neatly, almost heraldically; the dessert of almond cake is exquisite. A hefty cover charge and a 'servizio' charge included on the bill but not acknowledged by the waiter only makes things more expensive.

OPEN: LUNCH: Mon-Fri. DINNER: Mon-Sun. **HOURS:** 12.30-2.30pm and 7.00-11.30pm (7.00-10.30pm Sun). **CLOSED:** Christmas Day and Boxing Day. **CREDIT CARDS ACCEPTED:** All major cards except JCB. **NUMBER OF SEATS:** 55. **SERVICE:** 12%. No-smoking area. Wheelchair access (but not lavatory). **NEAREST TUBE STATION:** Victoria. MAP REF 2,F/2

 ## Les Saveurs
37a Curzon Street, W1

071-491 8919 LUNCH £27; DINNER £35

'Now getting the following it deserves'

The new French kid on the block is very definitely Joël Antunès at Les Saveurs. Last year's guide lamented a slow start and lack of following for this blandly luxurious Mayfair basement restaurant; now, quite rightly, you must book ahead, particularly at lunchtime when the set price menu at £21 for three courses offers stunning value. Antunès has a style of his own that is lively and creative but well grounded in gastronomic sensibility. His culinary imagination can be inferred from dishes like foie gras de canard served with celery rémoulade; potato tart with truffle oil; roast lobster with cardamom and crab polenta; sweetbreads with a sweet and sour sauce that relies on carrots for their sugar; warm brioche with sugar and vanilla ice cream. It is witty, seductive food but not tricksy. The setting and the structure of a meal is formal – including the bonuses of amuse-gueules beforehand, petits fours with coffee – but the staff are young and totally lacking in pomposity. We held our *Evening Standard* Gourmet Competition here last year and felt that every semi-finalist who came to the dinner was a winner.

THERE IS MUCH that is lordly and stellar on this list, but keen intelligence informs the selection (super-seconds have the upper hand on first growths of Bordeaux, for example, and the list is a good guide to those growers in Burgundy – Jayer, Dujac, Pousse d'Or, de Montille – whose efforts often outpace their co-appellationists). Good wines from the Rhône (try the wines of Cuilleron, Juge and Delas) and a selection from the Côte Chalonnaise provide choice at under £30, as does the nascent New World selection which departing sommelier Yves Sauboua would have liked to expand. Sauboua is to be replaced by Claude Douard.

OPEN: Mon-Fri. **HOURS:** 12.00-2.30pm and 7.00-10.30pm. **CLOSED:** 2 weeks at Christmas and 2 weeks in August. **CREDIT CARDS ACCEPTED:** AmEx, Diner's Club, Mastercard, Visa. **NUMBER OF SEATS:** 60. **SET PRICE LUNCH:** £21. **SET PRICE DINNER:** £32. Private room seats 10. **NEAREST TUBE STATION:** Green Park/Hyde Park Corner.

MAP REF: 1,A/1

The Savoy Grill & River Restaurant

Strand, WC2

225

071-836 4343

£50

'A legendary hotel'

The lunchtime clientele at the Savoy Grill are a self-selected sample of the great and the good or, to put it more accurately, the rich and powerful. There is a core of regulars and one supposes that the high prices are a matter of indifference to them. They might not even have clocked that if they choose a plat du jour vegetables are included in the price. Otherwise selecting, say, pommes nouvelles au cumin and épinards palace to accompany a main dish such as les filets de sole poêlée à la ciboulette et aux girolles will add another £7.25 to the £18.75 it costs (excluding service). In the evenings when it is easier for ordinary mortals to book a table the feeling is as if venturing into the first-class dining room on an ocean-going liner. Service is in line with this sensation; very formal and tending towards the patronizing. Chef David Sharland makes an effort with the right-hand side of the menu to include light and modern dishes, e.g. a Caesar salad; sea bass with shiitake mushrooms and artichokes; roasted rabbit and lobster with artichoke and garlic cake and a lime-leaf sauce, and there is a vegetarian main dish. With les scaloppines de veau flambés ' Savoy Grill', you get the theatre of guéridon service. It seems to me that if you choose to fork out to dine in these grandiose circumstances, then a dinner-jacketed waiter at your elbow whooshing flames around the food should be par for the course.

A visitor to the **River Restaurant** has remarked on the dowdiness of the crowd dining there on a Saturday evening – 'surely the clientele of a New York or Paris grand hotel would not look like this?' – and was surprised by the well-worn look of the French-inspired furnishings. These aspects may act as reassurance to some but certainly the lighting in this dining room could be improved, dispensing with messy candles and enlivening the front part which is not near the windows that overlook the embankment; the area where everyone would like to sit. However, Anton Edelmann's menu in grand hotel style has the excitement the surroundings may lack. It is presented as a carte plus various set price menus which offer not only relative good value, but a bill you can predict. An interesting approach is via the seasonal menu worked out between

Edelmann and Werner Wissman, the restaurant's sommelier. Impressive items in this deal were rosettes of lamb wrapped in rösti potatoes served with perfect tiny summer vegetables and a glass of Brunello di Montalcino 1988 and the dessert of gooseberry tart with a yogurt-based orange-flavoured ice cream served with a glass of Château Coutet 1986. Many people go to the River Restaurant in the evening because there is dancing but another time to use it is Sunday lunchtime when the family menu of three courses and coffee is £21.75 (£10 for children under twelve) and seasonal market produce such as caviar, langoustine, lobster and venison is featured in the appropriate months.

NEAT AND TIDY rather than unwieldy, competent rather than exciting, the Savoy's wine list (duplicated by Claridge's qv) most nearly achieves excellence amid the urbanities of Bordeaux (including seven '82s) and the conventional luxuries of grande marque champagne (a berth for most big names). Good Mosels, hocks and sherries (including three finos and a manzanilla – though only by the glass rather than the half-bottle) put worthwhile conservation into conservatism.

OPEN: GRILL ROOM: LUNCH: Mon-Fri. DINNER: Mon-Sat. RIVER RESTAURANT: Mon-Sun. **HOURS:** GRILL ROOM: 12.30-2.30pm and 6.00-11.15pm; RESTAURANT: 12.30-2.30pm and 6.00-11.30pm. **CLOSED:** Bank Holidays (Grill Room). **CREDIT CARDS ACCEPTED:** All major cards. **NUMBER OF SEATS:** GRILL ROOM: 85; RIVER RESTAURANT: 140. **SERVICE:** GRILL ROOM: Optional; RIVER RESTAURANT: 15%. **SET PRICE LUNCH:** £26.50 (River Restaurant). **SET PRICE DINNER:** £32 (River Restaurant).Wheelchair access to Grill Room (but not lavatory). Eight private rooms seating 6-80. **NEAREST TUBE STATION:** Charing Cross/Covent Garden.

MAP REF: 1,F/1

Selfridge Hotel – Fletchers

Orchard Street, W1   226

071-408 2080   LUNCH: £21; DINNER: £26

'This could be your discovery'

It is hoped that this guide will lead you to discoveries. If, when you read this, chef Mark Page is still cooking at Fletchers – my fear is that lack of custom might drive him away – this unheralded hotel restaurant should be one of them. The reason for lack of recognition might well be architectural. The Selfridge is situated between the eponymous department store and a driveway to a petrol station and car park. With the restaurant tucked away on the first floor it is obscurity within obscurity. However, once found, its anodyne, traditional chintzy decor is undemanding and unexhausting (and well lit) and there is the bonus of much of the seating being within comfortable banquetted booths affording privacy, indeed, intimacy. Page's dishes are presented as set price menus for lunch and dinner, an à la carte and sometimes a food festival, for example A Taste of New Zealand. His cooking could be compared to that of Richard Neat at Pied-à-Terre (q.v.) in the ability to think on with ingredients in the attention to intricate detail, for example filling a chicken wing with a basil stuffing to accompany the garlic-roasted breast and the love of crisply fried accoutrements. A recent test meal revealed a classy terrine of freshly cured salmon and halibut served with a dressing that had a kick like the one wasabi can deliver; canelloni filled with calves' sweetbreads poached in a highly flavoured stock served with a chive-strewn beurre blanc; a terrific conceit of Gressingham duck where the breast and thigh is rolled together and made into tournedos placed on a fan of potato slices in a rich dark sauce served with a tartlet of apple and juniper berries; chargrilled pork with the bright accompaniment of pumpkin and chilli fritters. The à la carte menu has a wine-match scheme referring dishes to particular sections of the list with which effort has been made. Service is committed to the idea of customers' enjoyment. The restaurant is named after one Geoffrey Scowcroft Fletcher whose worthy drawings of London townscapes adorn all the walls.

OPEN: LUNCH: Mon-Fri. DINNER: Mon-Sat. **HOURS:** 12.30-2.30pm and 6.00-10.30pm. **CLOSED:** Bank Holidays, 2 weeks in August. **CREDIT CARDS ACCEPTED:** All major cards. **NUMBER OF SEATS:** 65. **SERVICE:** Optional. **SET PRICE LUNCH:** £16.50. **SET PRICE DINNER:** £19.50. No-smoking area. Private room seats 16. **NEAREST TUBE STATIONS:** Bond Street/Marble Arch/Baker Street.

MAP REF: 1,B/3

Seoul

89a Aldgate High Street, EC3

071-480 5770   £13

'Nourishing liquidity at the City's edge'

Few restaurants approach Seoul for absolute decorative simplicity. One is almost grateful that the white wallpaper has been imperfectly hung, since the occasional peeling strip gives the eye something to tussle with. Korean food is, essentially, cold-climate fare, hence the tendency to turn everything into soup – a succession of thick, main-course soups for two, for example, or the nourishing invalid fare of brown seaweed soup with soya oil and spring onion; even rice and noodles come in soup form if you wish, garnished with slices of boiled beef. Savoury fillet pancake with kimchee approaches northern Europe's potato pancakes in texture, though the pickled cabbage provides livelier flavours, and sizzling bulgogi dishes provide further body-heating. The pickles, like crunchy white radish dressed in a red-pepper and garlic sauce, are superb, and counteract the slight over-sweetness of many of the dishes. Drinks are as minimal as the decor, and include the anodyne Korean OB lager as well as hauntingly rooty bittersweet ginseng tea. Pretty Korean girls who smell of soap serve with sweet economy, and play awful unKorean CDs.

OPEN: Mon-Fri. **HOURS:** 12.00-3.00pm and 6.00-10.00pm. **CLOSED:** Bank Holidays, Easter, Christmas. **CREDIT CARDS ACCEPTED:** All major cards. **NUMBER OF SEATS:** 50. **SERVICE:** 10%. Wheelchair access. Private room seats 30. **NEAREST TUBE STATIONS:** Aldgate, Tower Hill.

Shaw's

119 Old Brompton Road, SW7

071-373 4472 **£40**

'Cautious cooking in South Ken'

This quite posh restaurant backed by a consortium of City folk is trading in premises that since the mid-Fifties was The Chanterelle, opened by the late Walter Baxter, friend of Elizabeth David and one of the people who in the post-war years transformed eating out in London. Now the husband-and-wife team of manager Bill and chef Frances Atkins offer mainly fixed-price menus with cooking that is careful but can tilt towards the prissy. A symbol on the menus points towards 'lighter food' and, in fact, the majority of dishes come into this category. A risotto (asparagus, parsley and saffron) has been a success, a jellied terrine – called a flan – considerably less of one. Frances Atkins' skills are better displayed in the main courses where fish has tasted clearly and freshly of itself, duck been richly sauced and grilled chicken with a forest of salad leaves marinated to tenderness. As with much English cooking there is reward to be found in the dessert course, especially in that aptly named Queen of Puddings. Something of a rival to Hilaire, Shaw's seems to have attracted a clientele who live close by in the mansions of the Little Boltons. You can imagine Mark Thatcher liking it.

OPEN: **LUNCH:** Sun-Fri. **DINNER:** Mon-Sat. **HOURS:** 12.00-2.00pm and 7.00-10.00pm (7.00-10.00pm Sat; 12.00-4.00pm Sun). **CLOSED:** Bank Holidays, last 2 weeks of August. **CREDIT CARDS ACCEPTED:** All major cards. **NUMBER OF SEATS:** 44. **SERVICE:** 10%. **SET PRICE LUNCH:** £18. **SET PRICE DINNER:** £30. Wheelchair access (but not lavatory). Tables outside seat 10. **NEAREST TUBE STATION:** Gloucester Road.

Singapore Garden Restaurant

83 Fairfax Road, NW6

071-328 5314 **£23**

'Where Mrs Lim offers her specials'

There are almost as many dishes as seats (about 100) in this plain-looking restaurant in a Swiss Cottage shopping parade which, with its comprehensive South-East Asian menu and friendly approach, attracts a fascinatingly various clientele. Unusually for an Oriental menu there is attached to it a hand-written list of specials, some attributed to the chef Mrs Lim – as in Mrs Lim's mussels with black bean sauce, Singapore chilli or ginger and spring onions – who with her family owns both this restaurant and its branch at Regent's Park Hotel, 156 Gloucester Place NW1 (071-723 8233), not yet tested for the guide. When faced with the long menu with much of it familiar from Chinese restaurants, be sure to turn over to the last page which features Singaporean and Malaysian specialities. Two dishes hugely enjoyed from this list are squid blachan – sizzlingly hot squid served with snow peas and chilli – and Singapore laksa – a big bowlful of spiced coconut cream full of prawns, fish, beansprouts and delicate vermicelli; at £4.30 a perfect one-dish meal. Try also the beef rendang and blachan okra and from the main menu, crispy Teochew meat balls, crunchy from within from water chestnut and from without from deep-fried beancurd skin, and the wonderfully soothing Hainanese chicken rice. There are some dull set menus – only for dull people – and an extraordinarily expensive Chinese steamboat at £31.50 per person. House wine is mediocre and headache-inducing. Go one or two better or stick to beer, tea or grass jelly.

OPEN: Mon-Sun. **HOURS:** 12.00-2.45pm and 6.00-10.45pm (6.00-11.15 Fri-Sat). **CLOSED:** 5 days at Christmas. **CREDIT CARDS ACCEPTED:** AmEx, Diner's Club, Mastercard, Visa. **NUMBER OF SEATS:** 100. **SERVICE:** Optional. **SET PRICE LUNCH AND DINNER:** £16. Private room seats 60. **NEAREST TUBE STATION:** Swiss Cottage.

MAP REF: 6,C/2

Smokey Joe's Diner

131 Wandsworth High Street, SW18

081-871 1785 £9 (Bring your own wine)

'No frills, plenty of trills'

Charlie Phillips, the eponymous Smokey Joe, orchestrates the activity in his cramped caff and takeway from the kitchen/barbecue at the back of the room. This sandwich bar conversion to Caribbean and American soul food is that rare thing – a genuinely original place. If eating in at the plastic-topped tables, you write down your order (at least two courses) on a pad. Peppered prawns comes in a good fish broth with flecks of red chilli. Spare ribs are sticky but deeply savoury. The chargrilled corn, when not overcooked, is excellent. Rib of beef is not the finest quality but good enough and smothered in a doctored-up barbecue sauce. The sauté potatoes are sauté potatoes (not deep-fried) which is unusual in itself. Platters are garnished with rice, coleslaw, lettuce, tomatoes and onions. Specialities change according to the day – Mondays it's callalloo and saltfish, Wednesdays it's red bean stew with rice and salad, Thursday it's braised oxtail; very similar to the Connaught really. It is BYOB – Red Stripe or red wine are favourites – and nearly always party time at Smokey Joe's.

OPEN: Sun-Fri. **HOURS:** 12.00-3.00pm and 6.00-11.00pm (12.00-11pm Sat; 3.00-11.00pm Sun). **CLOSED:** Bank Holidays and Christmas. **CREDIT CARDS ACCEPTED:** None. **NUMBER OF SEATS:** 18. **SERVICE:** Optional; cover charge to eat in. **NEAREST BR STATION:** Wandsworth Town. MAP REF: 3,D/1

Snows on the Green

166 Shepherd's Bush Road, W6

071-603 2142 £25

'Where Shepherd's Bush is lavender'

The denizens of Brook Green and thereabouts have grown accustomed to shafts of Mediterranean flavour piercing the grey of Shepherd's Bush Road. However, we are all less gobsmacked these days by the offer of bruschetta, crostini, foccacia, carpaccio, and other similarly evocative items and here there is sometimes the sense of the same optimistic ingredients being thrown in the air and landing in haphazard pairings and patterns that are not always successful ones. For example there seems little culinary logic in the theory or in the practice of eating foccacia topped with snails and field mushrooms and sprinkled with gremolata (sic); the assembly arrives as little black substances on bread and where you anticipate a snail, you get a mushroom and when you're hoping for another bite of mushroom you find the not altogether welcome piece of chewing gum that is a snail. On another menu the same olive oil bread is topped with the safer combination of sweet peppers, anchovies and basil and the snails etc. come with potato fritters. Snow honed some of his mix and match techniques when chef at Bistrot 190 (q.v.). There too he developed his affection for robust casseroles such as braised knuckle of lamb with white beans and roasted garlic and Chartreuse of Bresse pigeon with zampone and cabbage, a recipe that sounds as if it would miss the point of obtaining Bresse pigeon. Because Snow is now running a much smaller operation, there is a chance that a dish will be immaculately cooked, as was red mullet with roasted potato 'scales' on Puy lentils with bacon and tiny, sweet onions. Desserts are unsurprising. A nice finish to a meal is cheese with figs, the cheese being maybe mascarpone, maybe Roquefort. Service is young and quite keen but hardly professional. You get the feeling that trekking through the snows on the green is, for the Antipodeans, just part of a much longer walkabout. The look of the place; a light, bright front room with a rather dingier part tucked behind the bar, has not changed since its inception. Someone should spend least a mini-break in Provence in order to replace the lavender bunches that are beginning to look dusty.

OPEN: LUNCH: Sun-Fri. DINNER: Mon-Sat. **HOURS:** 12.00-3.00pm and 7.00-11.00pm. **CLOSED:** 24th December to 2 January and Bank Holidays. **CREDIT CARDS ACCEPTED:** Access, Visa. **NUMBER OF SEATS:** 70. **SERVICE:** Optional. **SET PRICE LUNCH:** £11.50 (2 courses) and £13 (3 courses). Private room seats 24. **NEAREST TUBE STATION:** Hammersmith. MAP REF: 7,A/1

Sofra Restaurant

18 Shepherd Street, W1

071-493 3320   **£19**

*'Eat healthily in Shepherd Market and
now Covent Garden'*

Sofra has been voted 'Restaurant of the Year' by that influential, opinion-forming magazine of record (the readership apparently only exceeded by *Pravda*) *Inside Mayfair*. Sofra's owner, Huseyin Ozer, should certainly be voted 'Most Industrious Turkish Restaurateur'. Since last year's guide was published, Ozer has opened a café near his original restaurant in Shepherd Market, another Sofra meze bar and restaurant in Covent Garden in the house where Thomas de Quincey wrote *Confessions of an English Opium Eater*, introduced a £5 'back to basics quick meal' at both establishments and maintained the Healthy Lunch and Healthy Dinner menus comprising ten meze for £8.45 and £9.95 respectively. On the whole the standard of preparation of the long list of dishes is high although a recipient of the 'highly recommended' fried mussels (midye tava) would like to have been forewarned that the mussels are cooked in batter and at the same meal some cod cooked in a foil parcel seemed heated up rather than cooked to order and none too fresh. There is a note on the menu to the effect that anyone not entirely happy with their choice will be given a replacement but at a certain point in a meal you might not want the bother. The healthy meals are a good way of sampling the menu. You could always add on some grilled chicken or lamb or a casserole. One of the soothing creamy, nutty desserts has been described as 'somehow mythological' but the continuous, eventually tiresome music is 'a mixture of Classic FM, Radio 2 and a plane about to take off'. Sofra in Covent Garden is at 36 Tavistock Street WC2 (071-240 3773).

OPEN: Mon-Sun. HOURS: 12.00pm-12.00am. CREDIT CARDS ACCEPTED: Access, AmEx, Diner's, Visa. NUMBER OF SEATS: 66. SERVICE: 12.5%, £1.50 cover charge. SET PRICE LUNCH: £8.45. SET PRICE DINNER: £9.95. Wheelchair access (but not lavatory). 6 seats outside. NEAREST TUBE STATION: Green Park/Hyde Park Corner.   MAP REF: 1,B/1

Soho Soho Restaurant & Rotisserie

11-13 Frith Street, W1

071-494 3491   **RESTAURANT £35; ROTISSERIE £25**

'The whole schmeer from Provence'

Peter Mayle made a mint out of it. The biblical pair Abraham and Isaacson (Neville and Laurence) of Groupe Chez Gerard Ltd see no reason why they too should not capitalize on Provence. The food or anyway some of the ingredients of that evocative, emotive region form the wellspring of inspiration for the menu of the first-floor restaurant. At the time of writing chef Laurent Lebeau is making a good fist of things. Indeed, he sometimes produces that rare phenomenon, dishes that turn out to be better than the description might lead you to believe. Thinking it should be possible to take the temperature of the area via soupe de poissons à la Marseillaise, we were impressed by its intensity, its nice lick of fennel and reined-in kick of cayenne. It is rare to be offered roast calf's liver, as opposed to pan-fried or grilled. Here it is done retaining a heart of pink, and served with pleurottes (oyster mushrooms) that for once were a taste as well as a floppy texture. Brill could have been an inch less cooked but the braised leeks and warm bacon vinaigrette were a gifted accompaniment. Lamb eaten at a private party (there is a salon privé also on this floor) showed that Lebeau has a mastery of this meat. That desserts should appeal to the sweet-toothed is axiomatic but the confections here do seem to throw calories and cholesterol about with gay abandon. The croustillant au chocolate et aux amandes brings with it a small glass of homemade orange wine. A restaurant run by a company – this one recently gone public – cannot escape an air of committee decisions and a slightly mechanical aspect to the niceness of waiters. Good board decisions are the olives, almonds and interesting breads to start, the chocolate coffee beans to finish (all for a cover charge of £1.50) and the provision of free parking in the evening at the NCP in Wardour Street. Bad decision is butter in little foil-wrapped pats.

The **Rotisserie** on the ground floor has a cheaper, more relaxed menu; some quite enterprising hors d'oeuvres such as crespesa, a layered herb omelette filled with tapenade, spinach, onions, tomatoes and mushrooms with a tomato sauce, and tian of sardines; pastas, salads, grills and casseroles and items cooked on the eponymous spit. It is popular from breakfast time onwards and noise can be deafening, augmented by a loud chanteuse in the evenings. Not a place for grown-ups.

THIS IS A WINE list which has set off in the right direction: the 'southern' selection which begins it contains some interesting wines (such as Robert Michel's 1988 Cornas and Armand Maby's 1989 red Lirac). The basic descriptions in this section are welcome, and merit being extended to the 'classic' selection, which includes good Muscadet from Sauvion and white burgundy from Olivier Leflaive.

RESTAURANT: OPEN: Mon-Sat. **HOURS:** 12-3.00pm and 6pm-12.00am. **NUMBER OF SEATS:** 65. Private room seats 60. **ROTISSERIE: OPEN:** Mon-Sat. **HOURS:** 12pm-12.45am. **NUMBER OF SEATS:** 70. **CREDIT CARDS ACCEPTED:** All major cards. **SERVICE:** 12.5%, £1.50 cover charge in Restaurant; 12.5% in Rotisserie. No-smoking area. Wheelchair access. Tables outside seat 30. **NEAREST TUBE STATION:** Tottenham Court Road/Leicester Square. 　　　　　MAP REF: 1,E/2

Sonny's

94 Church Road, Barnes, SW14

081-748 0393 £25

'Barnes storming by Cheltenham chef'

The arrival of chef Redmond Hayward in early '94 seemed to me the moment when Sonny's in Barnes became the restaurant it always thought it was. Hayward, who at Redmond's valiantly tried to persuade the good people of Cheltenham and thereabouts that eating out is something you can do on days other than weekends and anniversaries, has brought an expertise to the execution of a not over-ambitious menu that lifts the establishment above that numbing phrase 'useful in the neighbourhood'. Prices are keen. At time of writing no first course is more than £5, main courses start at £7.95 (with vegetables extra) and there is a fixed price menu at £12.95 for two courses. From this menu chicken terrine with tarragon and chervil dressing was excellent; moist and in possession of two textures, pieces of breast meat surrounding a vigorously herbed chicken mousse, its flavours reinforced by the little sauce. Eating à la carte, successes have been Serrano ham with pear and pousse spinach; roast marinated pigeon breasts (served beautifully tender and daringly rare) with Savoy cabbage mixed with pieces of apple and calves' liver with potato, onion and smoked bacon cake. There is a fish dish of the day plus – taken from the menu already referred to – pot-roasted hake with roast potato, onion, garlic and anchovy, chargrilled tuna with Oriental dressing and seared salmon with creamy Puy lentils, tomato and coriander. The point of this food is not surprise or novelty value but careful attention to more important details like seasoning, timing and temperature. Lunch is the calmer meal. In the evening noise could get you down. There is a deli and café next door and, just in case you should be going that way, a branch in Nottingham.

OPEN: RESTAURANT: LUNCH: Mon-Sun. DINNER: Mon-Sat. **CAFÉ:** Mon-Sat. **HOURS: RESTAURANT:** 12.30-2.30pm and 7.30-11.00pm. **CAFÉ:** 10.00am-6.00pm. **CLOSED:** Bank Holiday lunches. **CREDIT CARDS ACCEPTED:** Access, AmEx, Visa. **NUMBER OF SEATS:** 90. **SERVICE:** Optional. **SET PRICE LUNCH AND DINNER:** £12.95. Tables outside seat 10. Private room seats 20. Wheelchair access (but not lavatory). **NEAREST BR STATION:** Barnes Bridge/Barnes.

The Square

32 King Street, SW1

071-839 8787 £45

'The vindication of the phrase Modern British Cooking'

Philip Howard's food at this now well-established smart restaurant in St James's would be on the list I compiled when required to furnish proof for my contention that food these days in London is as vibrant and seductive as anywhere in the world. I would have to put in parentheses, however, 'when on form' as standards can vary but when Howard is good, he is very very good. A dish in point is a first course of seared tuna served with tartare of vegetables and soy-wilted greens. The slices of fish, purple with a grey rim like a sliced-open semi-precious stone, are rolled in coarse salt and spices. The diced vegetables are minuscule yet beautifully matched. The sweetness of a grilled spring onion and the saltiness of a jaded spinach leaf are the ideal supporting cast. Howard's soups are also worth a special mention. They rarely arrive as just a bowl of liquid; morel, onion and thyme soup is served with potato crisps; chilled asparagus soup – a cream of consummate delicacy – comes with a salad of asparagus, wild asparagus, green beans, tomatoes concassés and shallots. A clever conceit is poached oysters with an iceberg beurre blanc and chives. A concession to the skinny women who hang out at The Square is the first course of green salad, shallots and herbs. Fish and meat are given equal billing in the main course with perhaps fish getting the more carefully considered treatment, viz. fillet of turbot with pea risotto and Parmesan and – a celebration of seasonality this – roast wild salmon with buttered asparagus and Jersey royals. Food at The Square is anything but: this year's wrap – pancetta – is thrown around chicken; the in cut of lamb, rump, is accompanied with aubergines and olive oil. Desserts are expensive enough to persuade the punter who is counting calories not to spend them. For profligates there is a trio of chocolate confections and crème brulée plus more restrained fruit-based assemblies. Note that the lunch menu is shorter (to deal with crowds quickly) and slightly cheaper. Service tends to time the query 'Is everything all right?' to coincide with the point of your anecdote or the punch line of your joke. It is led, at time of writing, by John Davey, proof that restaurant managers never die away, they return in the guise of game show hosts. Some changes have been made to the look of the restaurant but they are structural rather than decorative. It remains defiantly brash at a time when it might seem appropriate to take off the dangling earrings (hanging in the window) and slip into something more comfortable.

OPEN: LUNCH: Mon-Fri. DINNER: Mon-Sun. **HOURS:** 12.00-3.00pm and 6.00-11.45pm (7.00-10.00pm Sun). **CLOSED:** 24th December-4th January (exc New Year's Eve) and Bank Holidays. **CREDIT CARDS ACCEPTED:** Access, AmEx, Diner's Club, Visa. **NUMBER OF SEATS:** 70. **SERVICE:** Optional. Wheelchair access. Private room seats 18-24. **NEAREST TUBE STATION:** Piccadilly Circus/Green Park.

MAP REF: 1,C/1

Sree Krishna

192-194 Tooting High Street, SW17   **236**

081-672 4250/6903   LUNCH: £10; DINNER: £15

'Gentle dishes from the Malabar coast'

Larger than you'd think, with 120 seats in two rooms, this South Indian restaurant maintains its popularity in the teeth of fierce local competition, and despite its rather drab late seventies brown-and-pink decor and early-period Texas Homecare design. A page of Kerala specialities (all vegetarian bar one) begins the long menu, including uthapam, a chilli- and tomato-strewn pizza whose rice-and-lentil- flour base bears uncanny resemblance to thin tea crumpet; bright yellow avial, both creamy and sour, containing green banana and drumstick vegetable; and iddly - steamed cakes served with vegetable sambar and juicily fresh coconut chutney. The elegant and dramatic dosai pancakes, too, are justifiably popular. All these are intended as starters, but you could assemble a whole meal from them if you wish. The rest of the menu is lengthy and more generalized; fair renditions of bhunas, madras curries, kurmas, dansaks and vindaloos abound. The staff, in a bizarre collection of job-lot blazers, perambulate benignly and effectively to piped sitar music.

OPEN: Mon-Sun. **HOURS:** 12.00-3.00pm and 6.00-11.00pm (6.00-12.00am Sat; 6.00- 11.00pm Sun). **CLOSED:** Christmas Day and Boxing Day. **CREDIT CARDS ACCEPTED:** Access, AmEx, Diner's Club, Visa. **NUMBER OF SEATS:** 120. **SERVICE:** 10%. Wheelchair access. Private room seats 60. **NEAREST TUBE STATION:** Tooting Broadway.

Sri Siam

14 Old Compton Street, W1

071-434 3544 £20

'Gratification for the inner child'

Located at the Charing Cross Road end of Old Compton Street, handy for the Palace Theatre (and indeed the Prince Edward), Sri Siam is a better-than-average Thai restaurant, dolled up (quite literally) to look feminine and inviting. The long menu does not focus on any particular region of Thailand so there is good variety – larb from the north, several indigenous Bangkok selections but perhaps a less authentically vivid use of chilli than of old. Thai food obviously appeals to the inner child in all of us who likes deep-fried items and sugar as an ingredient, but too much gratification can, as we know, become counter-productive and the child tetchy. Work on the balance of a meal, perhaps starting with kanom jeep, prawn and pork stuffed cushions pin-pricked with diced fried garlic and beung yon, Thai-style pancakes with a prawn, beancurd and coconut filling, going onto a soup or a salad such as papaya pok pok, a curry, red, green, yellow or jungle, some seafood – marinated fish grilled in a banana leaf and served with a tamarind/palm sugar sauce is delicate and interesting – grilled or stir-fried poultry of meat and, without fail, a noodle assembly. The set price menus are good value, particularly the £9.95 lunch, but its component parts are typically unadventurous. Sri Siam is apparently the only Thai restaurant whose menu is approved by the Vegetarian Society. The owners, Thai Restaurants plc, also have a Sri Siam in the City at 85 London Wall EC2 (071-628 5772) with an identical menu, and a Chinese restaurant, Imperial City (q.v.)

OPEN: LUNCH: Mon-Sat. DINNER: Mon-Sun. **HOURS:** 12.00-3.00pm and 6.00-11.15pm (6.00-10.30pm Sun). **CLOSED:** Christmas and New Year. **CREDIT CARDS ACCEPTED:** AmEx, Diner's Club, Master Card, Visa. **NUMBER OF SEATS:** 80. **SERVICE:** Optional. **SET PRICE LUNCH:** £9.50. **SET PRICE DINNER:** £14.95. Wheelchair access (but not lavatory). **NEAREST TUBE STATIONS:** Tottenham Court Road/Leicester Square. **MAP REF:** 1,E/2

Star of India

154 Old Brompton Road, SW5

071-373 2901   **£29**

'There are many stars here, Reza and the chef are just two'

Reza Mahammad, himself a work of art, has described the decor of restaurant Star of India – started by his family in 1958 – as 'the Sistine Chapel directed by Zeffirelli'. But even as I write more refurbishment is taking place. Diverting and unexpected as the frescoed walls and ceilings are, dishes cooked by chef Vineet Bhatia, who previously worked at the Oberoi hotel in Bombay, can match them. Mr Bhatia has lifted the always praiseworthy cooking here into a new league. The word 'tempered' used on the menu means that spices have been cooked in oil in order that they release their flavours. A dish not to miss that capitalizes on this process is dahi masala, yogurt which as been drained to render it rich and thick, heated gently with onions, tomatoes, mustard seeds, curry leaves and turmeric. It is the ideal foil for the zing in the red pepper paste that coats pan-fried fillets of pomfret. 'Stuffed' is a word that often means no more than mixed, as in the excellent first course murg ke shikampuri, minced chicken and lentil kebabs stuffed with onions, egg and mint. The tandoor is used to good effect, particularly in the novel dish of marinated cauliflower and the lamb chops steeped in ginger. Murg kali murch, chicken cooked with freshly roasted crushed black peppercorns, shows how simplicity in spicing can pay off. Kaju posho thoran, cashew nuts and green beans tempered with mustard seeds and coconut is simply one of the best vegetable dishes I know. Music is sometimes live (upstairs) but always a wonderfully camp choice.

OPEN: Mon-Sun. **HOURS:** 12.00-3.00pm and 6.00pm-12.00am (7.00-11.30pm Sun). **CLOSED:** Bank Holidays exc. Good Friday. **CREDIT CARDS ACCEPTED:** All major cards. **NUMBER OF SEATS:** 94. **SERVICE:** Optional, £1 cover charge. Wheelchair access (but not lavatory). Private rooms seat 12 and 14. **NEAREST TUBE STATION:** Gloucester Road.   MAP REF: 2,B/4

Stephen Bull

5-7 Blandford Street, W1

071-486 9696   **£34**

'Decor in need of HRT'

So close to doctor-land, it is perhaps inevitable that every customer here starts to look like a surgeon, the light fittings to invoke intra-uterine devices, the white-tiled alcove to suggest a sluice, the bottles above the bar to represent samples of bodily fluids and the air-conditioning to seem like the chill of the morgue. However, colour and pattern is in plentiful supply on the often rather overloaded plates. A particularly robust style of cooking has evolved, perhaps to some extent in response to customer demand. I saw someone – for sure an anaesthetist – beckon over the manageress to complain about something and describe as a regrettably small portion a plateful that would have lasted me the week. When the approach works – as it seems more likely to do in the main courses and magnificently elaborate desserts – it is highly satisfactory. 'Tagine' of lamb with tabbouleh, apricots and mint was beautifully spiced meat served with the rather un-North African element of lentils, with the cracked wheat, chopped herbs, oil and lemon juice (tabbouleh) in a pot on the side to be stirred into the juices. Smoked quails with Parma ham, figs, potato cake and Marsala sauce although looking like a multi-organ transplant tasted absolutely delicious. Menus change weekly but certain successful items like the twice-cooked goat's cheese soufflé, the 'delicacies from Spain' and 'variations on a theme of chocolate' are almost constants. The wine list is admirable and, like the menu, does not push its luck with the pricing. Staff were not, I think, found through the pages of the *Nursing Times*.

THIS NEAT, TIDY and clearly organized wine list, much of which can be enjoyed for under £20 per bottle, is full of interest – Pelle's Menetou-Salon, white Saint-Aubin from Gérard Thomas, Leeuwin's Chardonnay, Janodet's Morgon, Colombo's Syrah and the Prince Probus Cahors of Château Triguedina are all worth trying.

OPEN: LUNCH: Mon-Fri. DINNER: Mon-Sat. **HOURS:** 12.00-2.15pm and 6.30pm-10.45pm. **CLOSED:** Bank Holidays and 1 week at Christmas. **CREDIT CARDS ACCEPTED:** Access, AmEx, Visa. **NUMBER OF SEATS:** 53. **SERVICE:** Optional. Wheelchair access (but not lavatory). **NEAREST TUBE STATION:** Bond Street.

MAP REF: 1,B/4

Stephen Bull's Bistro

71 St John Street, EC1

071-490 3127 £22

'No longer must we be so thankful for what have become small mercies'

How quickly in the world of restaurants does the innovative turn commonplace. The well-proportioned double-height white space decorated sparely with mainly primary colours, the overhead gantry, the bare tables, the waiters dressed in black and the vivid menu that Stephen Bull (q.v.) provided for his bistro near Smithfield when he opened it about two years ago seemed almost God-given in the area. Not only city workers but visitors to the Barbican felt that at last someone was watching over them. Now what seemed exciting comes across as ordinary. In large part this is due to staff who seem disaffected and cooking that makes the gestures but ignores the fine points. Someone on the pass who was concentrating or cared would not have sent out a burned slice of brioche with the foie gras. A chef who had enough interest to try it out would not have combined the foie gras with raw clumsily diced peppers. An undercooked piece of chicken with the spooky garnish of polenta mixed with cauliflower, a lobster whose memories of the sea must have been dim and distant ones reclining on practically raw green beans; these dishes needed all the seductive charm a waiter could muster to turn the meal into a nice time. Such interest and/or friendliness was signally lacking. But as 'hit and miss' is a phrase that has been bandied about before now in relation to the cooking here, it is conceivable you could get a string of hits. Choosing constants such as Delicacies from Spain (chorizo, Serrano ham, manchego, olives and quince paste) and the generally delectable desserts will tip the odds in your favour.

WITH A DIFFERENT selection to that on offer in Stephen Bull's restaurant, the Bistro's list is price-ordered, shorter, yet no less eclectic; the beers and ciders are a welcome addition. Rarer grape varieties like Sylvaner, Arneis, Charbono, Chenin and Riesling get a well-deserved outing.

Open: Lunch: Mon-Fri. Dinner: Mon-Sat. **Hours:** 12.00-2.15pm and 6.30pm-10.45pm. **Closed:** Bank Holidays and 1 week at Christmas. **Credit cards accepted:** Access, AmEx, Visa. **Number of seats:** 90. **Service:** Optional. Wheelchair access (but not lavatory). **Nearest tube station:** Farringdon.

MAP REF: 8,D/2

Suntory

72-73 St James's Street, SW1   ④241

071-409 0201   Lunch: £25; Dinner: £55

'Explore the land of the rising bill'

Eating in the low-key ground-floor dining room of Suntory – the only gaijin at a Friday lunchtime – we were given as sake a small flask of very hot water. Presumably the water had been poured in to warm the flask and with barely an apology it was replaced with sake, but the incident served to reinforce the feeling that as non-Japanese it is hard to get the best out of Suntory, praised by those in the know for the excellence of its food. Reports of meals at the teppan-yaki room at the back of the premises have, however, been enthusiastic. Teppan-yaki 'courses' come at various set prices which seem expensive but include tax and service and if you drink beer you can eat for a sum that does not seem altogether unreasonable for the services of a skilled and serious personal chef, a little teapot of a complex and delectable broth, the freshest of grilled fish, the reduction of steak into a sort of tangy crisp and wonderful fried rice mixed with egg and prawn. There are private rooms for kaiseki banquets from £85 a head and in the dining room, chef's specialities are offered in addition to various set meals, sashimi, and cooked-at-table dishes such as shabu-shabu, suki-yaki and yose-nabe. One area where I find Suntory lacking is in the beauty of presentation expressed through serving dishes. Some look as though they come from Tokyo's version of Woolworths. Also presenting sashimi on a metal plate on crushed ice chills the raw fish out of all flavour recognition. An enthusiast has pointed out that Suntory is not the forbidding place it seems.

Open: Mon-Sat. **Hours:** 12.00-3.00pm and 6.00-11.00pm. **Closed:** Bank Holidays. **Credit cards accepted:** Access, AmEx, Diner's Club, JCB, Visa. **Number of seats:** 120. **Service:** Optional. **Set price lunch:** From £18. Wheelchair access. Private room seats 4-14. **Nearest tube station:** Green Park.

MAP REF: 1,C/1

Le Suquet

104 Draycott Avenue, SW3

071-581 1785 or 071 225 0838 £30

'The incorrigibly French fish restaurant'

Pierre Martin, owner of Le Suquet and the chap who 20 years ago with the opening of La Croisette (now Chez Max q.v.) introduced holiday spirit and a breath of ozone into London fish restaurants, now spends a good deal of time practising being retired in Provence. Fortunately Le Suquet carries on in just the same way – with Martin making fleeting visits – and it is still managed by Francis who might have been supplied by central casting when asked for a typically French waiter. The menu of oysters, shellfish, salads. feuilletés, les poissons selon arrivage and the few but interesting meat dishes, is as it always has been; the clientele maintains a cosmopolitan chic and the staff an unshakeable Gallicness. Plateau de fruits de mer, a dramatic and generous array of raw shellfish, makes you glad that life can be a beach. Simply grilled is the best way to have the luxury fishes such as bass and gilt-head bream, both sold by the 100 grams, but there are homelier fish dishes such as raie aux capres or cabillaud Provençale. Pictures of Cannes and Provençal prints can still work their magic in transporting you away from South Kensington, but it is not a bargain break. For that try Cave aux Fillettes, Pierre Martin's authentic French bistro at 116 Finborough Road SW10 (071-370 1722).

OPEN: Mon-Sun. **HOURS:** 12.00-3.00pm and 7.00-11.30pm. **CREDIT CARDS ACCEPTED:** All major cards. **NUMBER OF SEATS:** 70. **SERVICE:** 15%, £1 cover charge. 8 seats outside. Private room seats 16. **NEAREST TUBE STATION:** South Kensington. MAP REF: 2,D/3

Sweetings

39 Queen Victoria Street (East), EC4

071-248 3062 £20

'Some things never change'

This piscatorial dealing floor is one of the few city institutions left completely unruffled by the passage of time. Bookings and credit cards are still off the menu, additionally annoying when prices are high; the culinary ideals remain those of Edwardian Brighton; requests for tea and coffee are the risible solecisms they have always been. What you get is a fast fresh fish lunch. Dover sole, halibut, turbot and skate, all shown a fierce grill or pan, hurtle up and down the service lift; real turtle soup, a meaty oceanic consommé, reassures the nostalgic and gastronomically incorrect; the fish pie, in its stainless-steel canteen dish, is softly adroit. Puddings and salad dressings, by contrast, are too bland and too sharp respectively. Fish and cricketers eye changing City humanity, seated in the insignia-carved wooden chairs, from the double-cream walls. The waiters (either Italian or Cockney) are plentiful and love to bully each other for perceived failures, which in truth are rare. The wine list is brief, and the benefits of a fair choice by the glass (large or small) are offset by the fact that opened bottles are inadequately chilled. Guinness and White Shield look and taste right here.

OPEN: Mon-Fri. **HOURS:** 11.00am-3.00pm. **CLOSED:** 25th December to 2nd January and Bank Holidays. **CREDIT CARDS ACCEPTED:** None, **NUMBER OF SEATS:** 60. **SERVICE:** Optional, Wheelchair access (but not lavatory). **NEAREST TUBE STATION:** Mansion House/Bank/Cannon Street.

La Tante Claire
68-69 Royal Hospital Road, SW3

071-352 6045 or 071-351 0227   LUNCH: £25; DINNER:£70

'The one I would save up for'

Three Michelin stars attached to restaurants in France can quite often lead you to disappointingly formulaic meals and an environment as commercial as a gift boutique. La Tante Claire, currently the only Michelin three-star establishment in London, emphatically does the accolade justice. It is, in its entirety, the most satisfactory restaurant in London. The surroundings are pastel-pretty and light, big enough for each table to create its own pool of intimacy but small enough to reassure that one man – Pierre Koffmann – can handle this number of covers. The waiters are almost burlesque in their willingness to be of service. The food is thrilling in that it takes ideas and flavours a few steps further than you might suppose is possible. Eating a main course of rable de lapereau à la moutarde violette oignon confit was like a gastronomic version of the game of pass the parcel. Wrappings of endive and spinach provided their own flavours as did discoveries of tiny wild mushrooms, broad beans and sautéed strips of the rabbit 'skin'. The squid quill was cleverly utilized as the brochette for langoustines made crisp with subtle Eastern spices in the first course where it is hard to deny Koffmann a demonstration of his atavistic Gascon skills with foie gras, as in galette de foie gras aux Sauternes et échalottes rôties or tranche de foie gras et pain grillé. These luxurious ways of beginning a meal lead gracefully into some of the more rugged main courses such as pied de cochon aux morilles. At my most recent meal here I saw Ken Livingstone eating with huge delight the salmis de Bresse aux champignons, which is as it should be. Desserts prove Antonin Carême's point that the main branch of architecture is confectionery, but those customers looking to trim the bill might make do with the excellent petits fours. Trimming the bill is best left to lunchtime when the set price menu famously provides the best bargain in town.

TANTE CLAIRE'S WINE list is the least ambitious of the restaurant's overtures to the customer; it passes muster rather than impresses. The acclaim of recent years has altered it little: the 'specialism' of the wines of France's south west adds only modest regional flavour; best value comes from the Languedoc with serious contributions from the Château de Lastours Cuvée Simone Descamps and the arrestingly uncompromising

Prieuré de St Jean de Bebian. The list is fundamentally classical: Alsace, the Loire, Burgundy and (especially) Bordeaux furnish its core, drawing on the sure-shot vintages of the '70s and '80s, marked up with a flourish. There is a good selection of half bottles, which is just as well, since drinking less is the best way to leash the bill.

OPEN: Mon-Fri. **HOURS:** 12.30-2.00pm and 7.00-11.00pm. **CREDIT CARDS ACCEPTED:** All major cards. **NUMBER OF SEATS:** 48. **SERVICE:** Included. **SET PRICE LUNCH:** £25.00. Wheelchair access (but not lavatory). **NEAREST TUBE STATION:** Sloane Square.   MAP REF: 2,D/1

Tate Gallery Restaurant
Millbank, SW1

071-887 8877   **£25**

---

*'An eyeful then a glassful and maybe an earful,
what could be better?'*

Perhaps it is the new proximity of the security services lodged in Thames House and across the river at Century House that has caused the improvement since last year in the service at the Tate's main restaurant. The whimsicality of Rex Whistler's mural, *The Expedition on Pursuit of Rare Meats*, with its debts to the gardens at Stowe has little to do with the art on show upstairs but provides gentle diversion for the spies, MPs and tourists who seem to make up the bulk (quite literally in some cases) of the clientele. Believing that those are your fellow diners makes immediate sense of the modern English menu. A secret could be smuggled so discreetly in that filo parcel along with the salmon flavoured with ginger, lime and coriander. Who but the member for Jilly Cooper's Rutshire would contemplate eating brie and Calvados pancakes as a main course? What visitor to these shores would not be pleased to find roast leg of English lamb, even it comes with the Provençal garnish of olives, garlic and rosemary? It is a cannier list than the historical delvings of old and a rather better executed one. Test meals revealed no quibbles about caramelized onion and tomato tartlet (a generous interpretation of the diminutive); watercress soup, served chilled on request; escalope of chicken with smoked gammon and asparagus and that innocent-loking filo parcel. The rendition of summer pudding vindicated what some still think an oxymoronic phrase; English cuisine. This, like all the desserts, brings with it a complimentary glass of champagne. Tables too close together prevent the exchange of important confidences and the complete suppression of the awareness that, to some extent, this is institutional food.

WINEMAKING IS more craft than art, but some of the bottles on the Tate's restaurant list are capable of the sort of profound diversion more usually afforded by gallery exhibits. The speciality here is the big name in the lesser vintage (1987 is justly indulged), or the great vintage as accomplished by the little name. Net result: a bottle of Léoville-Barton for under £16 (1987) or a bottle of 1970 claret for under £40 (Haut-

Batailley). Burgundy is listed along the same curiosity-shop lines as claret, with Sauzet, Blain-Gagnard and Mongeard-Mugneret providing some of the best flavours (proceed with caution on the '83s, though). Apart from that, it's only wayward bottles – like the 1975 Californian Alicante Bouschet, probably the strangest £11.55's worth on the London restaurant scene in 1994. Spirits are largely venerable, too.

OPEN: Mon-Sat. **HOURS:** 12.00-3.00pm. **CLOSED:** Christmas, New Year's Day, Good Friday and May Day Holiday. **CREDIT CARDS ACCEPTED:** Access, Delta, Mastercard, Switch, Visa. **NUMBER OF SEATS:** 100. **SERVICE:** Optional. No-smoking area. Wheelchair access. **NEAREST TUBE STATION:** Pimlico.

The Thai Garden
249 Globe Road, E2

081-981 5748 £20

'A laudably green restaurant at Bethnal'

It was a taxi driver who put me onto Thai Garden, a vegetarian and fish restaurant in the East End. The garden in the name doubtless refers to the produce that is the basis of the cooking. Mushrooms are the main crop. These appear as frequently in the vegetarian dishes as do prawns in the seafood section but there are several varieties and they are used inventively as a stand in for meat, for example as satay and as the basis for a Northern Thai larb where toasted rice, vivid spicing and basil contribute to the hot and sour salad. Contrasts in texture could be provided by mixed vegetable tempura and tau foo tord, deep-fried yellow bean curds served with hot and sour sauce. There is a choice of three seafood soups featuring prawns, main courses of prawns done this way and that – minus any discernible chilli in gra prou goong, fried prawns with basil leaves and hot chilli – plus several fish dishes, all based on pomfret. The noodle assemblies – vegetarian and with prawns – are notably well done. The Thai Garden, on whose menu is a sweetly ingenuous note pointing you to Vatcharin Bhumichitr's book *Thai Vegetarian Cooking* for the recipes, is run by that not unusual pairing of an English man and his Thai wife. It is odd, in those circumstances, that the wine list is quite so banal. Service is sweet.

OPEN: LUNCH: Mon-Fri. DINNER: Mon-Sat. **HOURS:** 12.00-2.45pm and 6.00-10.45pm. **CLOSED:** Bank Holidays. **CREDIT CARDS ACCEPTED:** Mastercard, Visa. **NUMBER OF SEATS:** 32. **SERVICE:** 10%. **SET PRICE LUNCH:** £6.50. **SET PRICE DINNER:** £14.50-£19. No-smoking area. Wheelchair access (but not lavatory). Private room seats 14. **NEAREST TUBE STATION:** Bethnal Green.

Thailand Restaurant

15 Lewisham Way, SE14

081-691 4040 £20

'The perfumes of South East Asia adrift in South East London'

This Laotian restaurant (puzzlingly named after the neighbouring country which annexed chef Khamkhong Kambungoet's home region five centuries ago) is so small it feels as if you're eating in an oriental doll's house. Booking, thus, is essential. The dishes (provided you opt for the hot-and-sour rather than the sweet-and-sour) are often revelatory, aromatic with lemon grass and bergamot leaves and lively with the flavours of tamarind, fish gravy and galangal. Coconut is used to soften and enrich. The salad of hot and sour green papaya with lime, garlic, chilli and fish gravy may be constrained by supply, yet substitutes of bamboo shoots or cucumber are worth trying. The sticky rice served in woven baskets seems to possess an extra dimension of rice flavour and is thus essential. You tear off lumps with your fingers. It comes into its own again at dessert stage, too, simultaneously sweet, salty and buttery, served with banana or mango. Service can be chaotic but is always friendly, and you are quite likely to be seated next to malt whisky scholars of all races, attracted by Victor Herman's range of cask-strength bottlings of rarer malts. The wine list is tiny but sound; yet the best drinking of all may well be provided by the lemon grass tea headily perfumed with fresh mint 'from my Mum's garden', as the waitress proudly said.

OPEN: Tues-Sat. **HOURS:** 6.00-11.00pm. **CREDIT CARDS ACCEPTED:** Access, AmEx, Visa. **NUMBER OF SEATS:** 25. **SERVICE:** Optional. **SET PRICE DINNER:** £20. **NEAREST TUBE STATION:** New Cross/New Cross Gate.

Tokyo Diner

2 Newport Place, WC2

071-287 8777 £8

'Japanese food in what was Chinatown's launderette'

The menu at Tokyo Diner in the heart of Chinatown reads like a Japanese food manual for beginners, which is wonderful for beginners but possibly slightly patronizing for others. The stated aim of Japan-hand Richard Hills is to show you the *real* Japan through serving ordinary, everyday Japanese food that is 'affordable, satisfying and FUN'. I'm not sure about the last – the nature of the food and the place means you are in and out at the double and usually share a table – but the first two objectives are more or less achieved. There are meals presented in bento boxes from £6.90, the price depending on the ingredient you choose to go into the square at the top right-hand corner of the box; from potato-based croquette to breadcrumb-coated fried salmon. There is the cheaper donburi box, rice with a variety of toppings, plus Japanese curries correctly described as like school food, noodle assemblies, sushi and (sometimes) sashimi. I've had better sushi at Ikkyu, better soup noodles at Wagamama (see entries), considerably more skilfully prepared food in the shape of dim sum from nearby Cantonese restaurants, but Tokyo Diner has its charm and seems a laudable enterprise including adopting the Japanese policies of no tipping and offering complimentary green tea. Note cash only.

OPEN: Mon-Sun. **HOURS:** 12.00pm-12.00am. **CREDIT CARDS ACCEPTED:** None. **NUMBER OF SEATS:** 96. **SET PRICE LUNCH AND DINNER:** £3.45-£11.90. No-smoking area. Wheelchair access (but not lavatory). Private room seats 21 or 43. **NEAREST TUBE STATION:** Leicester Square.   MAP REF: 1,E/1

Turner's

87-89 Walton Street, SW3   (249)

071-584 6711   LUNCH: £25; DINNER: £50

'The ladies who lunch love him'

Brian Turner is a warm host and when he is not in his restaurant – as can happen – one misses him. The almost subliminal taped music played is no substitute for his energy and bluff charm. The à la carte price of two courses for £32 (inclusive of tax and service) tends to concentrate the mind on the quality of the dishes and it is sometimes quite easy to let the thought 'old hat' slip in. From the menu du jour – £23.50 for two courses, no choice – more of the delicious mussel risotto would have set off better the well-grilled salmon. However, rillettes de haddock fumé, salade de concombres à l'aneth was a nice balance between salty and creamy and the salad of confit de canard with a mustard dressing just needed the bush of lollo rosso removed to make it good. At time of writing Brian Turner is back in the kitchen looking for a right-hand man to replace chef Alan Thompson who has moved to Pied à Terre to work with Richard Neat. The menu will maintain its style. The good-value three-course £13.50 deal, plus the £8.50 'Turner's one-course salad bar' – a warm salad of, apparently, great appeal to the ladies – will continue to be offered at lunchtimes.

THIS LIST HAS MADE a tentative sortie out of familiar French territory this year but Turner's remains a white-burgundy-lover's address above all, with a royal flush of William Fèvre's Chablis, as well as good tackle from Clair and Thomas further south. Prices are stiffish.

OPEN: LUNCH: Sun-Fri. DINNER: Mon-Sun. **HOURS:** 12.30-2.30pm (12.30-2.00pm Sun) and 7.30-11.15pm (7.30-10.00pm Sun). **CLOSED:** 25th-30th December and Bank Holidays. **CREDIT CARDS ACCEPTED:** Access, AmEx, Diner's Club, Visa. **NUMBER OF SEATS:** 52. **SERVICE:** 10% included in prices. **SET PRICE LUNCH:** £9.95 (2 courses) and £13.50 (3 courses). **SET PRICE DINNER:** £23.50 (2 courses) and £26.50 (3 courses). Wheelchair access (but not lavatory). **NEAREST TUBE STATION:** South Kensington.   MAP REF: 2,D/3

Two Brothers Fish Restaurant

297-303 Regents Park Road, N3

081-346 0469   **£14**

'Which other chippy has its own vineyard?'

North London provides an enthusiastic clientele for fish and chips and it is well served – literally – at the Manzi brothers' (Leon and Tony) dressy chippy which goes those several steps further that merit the description restaurant. First courses range from cod's roe in batter to Rossmore rock oysters via jellied eels, homemade fish soup, Tony's Arbroath smokies in a cream sauce and avocado with prawns. The main course fish dishes are cooked to order and served with exemplary chips, roll and butter and homemade tartare sauce. For 50p extra, the fish can be fried in fine matzo meal or for another 20p it can be steamed or grilled. The desserts, such as peach melba, banana split and sundaes, hark back to windy days in English coastal resorts. Waitresses are brisk, friendly and never stop. Perhaps the most surprising thing of all is the well-thought-out, fairly priced wine list which includes wines from Côte du Duras from the Manzis' own vines. No bookings.

OPEN: Tue-Sat. **HOURS:** 12.00-2.30pm and 5.30-10.15pm. **CLOSED:** Last 2 weeks in August and all Bank Holidays except Good Friday. **CREDIT CARDS ACCEPTED:** AmEx, Mastercard, Visa. **NUMBER OF SEATS:** 90. **SERVICE:** Optional. No-smoking area. **NEAREST TUBE STATION:** Finchley Central.

The Upper Street Fish Shop

324 Upper Street, N1

071-359 1401   **£11 (Bring your own wine)**

'Past meets present over huss and chips'

Upper Street's upper-class fish-and-chip shop bright and clean, though it can't decide which Islington it really belongs in – that of the wartime National Savings Certificate posters or the trendy artworks which surround them. The clientele is similarly divided, so that on most evenings gents who fold their macs neatly over the chairbacks find themselves sharing tables with the exotically dreadlocked. The fish is fresh, generously portioned and battered with restraint; the chips, though, could be externally crisper. Starters include a fish soup which wants to be a parsley sauce when it grows up, and creamy smoked salmon pâté served with packet toast. Departing from the fish-and-chip format for the main course brings you, essentially, the same good fish served in a lower calorie context. Puddings (with decent Bird's custard or cream) are as comfortingly unexceptional as the white pots of steaming tea with which those who have forgotten to bring their own Montrachet or

Guinness must comfort themselves. 'Welcome to London Town', say the wrapped sugar cubes in the bowl, and there are worse places to begin studying Britain than here.

OPEN: LUNCH: Tues-Sat. DINNER: Mon-Sat. **HOURS:** 12.00-2.00pm (12.00-3.00pm Sat) and 5.30-10.00pm. **CLOSED:** 1 month at Christmas and Bank Holidays. **CREDIT CARDS ACCEPTED:** None. **NUMBER OF SEATS:** 50. **SERVICE:** Optional. Wheelchair access (but not lavatory). **NEAREST TUBE STATION:** Angel.

Vasco & Piero's Pavilion

15 Poland Street, W1

071-437 8774 **£25**

'An unpretentious corner of Italy'

Despite the abundance of Italian restaurants in London, few resemble restaurants you would find in Italy. The Pavilion, for a variety of reasons, does. There is continuity. The restaurant used to be located above late, lamented Academy Cinema in Oxford Street (remember where you first saw *Les Enfants du Paradis?*), and in its transfer to premises in nearby Poland Street re-created an impression of the singular Angus McBean interior that evoked the striped and beribboned tents of a festive field. Ownership has remained constant although a member of staff was made a partner when Piero died three years ago and Vasco's son has joined the team. Dishes have moved with the times, capitalizing on the new easy availability of ingredients such as balsamic vinegar, rucola, buffalo mozzarella and sun-dried tomatoes, but they are still prepared with an old-fashioned sort of care and an agreeable lack of the unnecessary flourish. Menus change regularly. The first course features soup – the zuppa di ceci is a particularly homely sort of minestrone – various salads often with shavings of Parmesan as a garnish, frittata either alone or as part of an antipasto based on grilled vegetables and a homemade pasta or two. Try the spinach and ricotta tortelloni if it is on offer. Typical main courses are grilled cod with a herb crust, grilled sea bass with fennel, rabbit in mustard sauce, roast leg of new season lamb, calves' liver with fresh sage. Vegetables tend to be wholesomely cooked in stock rather than smothered in butter. Desserts are authentically unadventurous although a pancake parcelling fresh fruit and cream makes a change from crème caramel or tiramisù. Some of the scope of Italian wines is apparent from the list and the bottles are not greedily priced. Service is affable yet dignified.

OPEN: Mon-Fri. **HOURS:** 12.00-3.00pm and 6.00-11.00pm. **CLOSED:** Bank Holidays. **CREDIT CARDS ACCEPTED:** All major cards. **NUMBER OF SEATS:** 95. **SERVICE:** Optional, £1.50 cover charge. **SET PRICE LUNCH:** £10.50. **SET PRICE DINNER:** £12.95 and £15.95. Wheelchair access (but not lavatory). Private room seats 30. **NEAREST TUBE STATION:** Oxford Circus. MAP REF: 1,D/2

Vegetarian Cottage

91 Haverstock Hill, NW3

071-586 1257   **£15**

'The gentle route towards longevity'

Although most of the death threats I receive through the post are from vegetarians, the staff at this small, sleekly designed Chinese restaurant fulfil the benign, peace-loving, strokeable image that some of us have about those who eschew meat. More to the point, parts of the menu are so reasonable as to be cheap. At the time of writing, crispy spring roll is £1, deep-fried beancurd with salt and chilli is £1.80, soups are mainly £1.60 and no vegetarian main dish is more than £4.80. Seafood dishes, of which eight are offered, cost more, but even these by conventional standards are a snip – e.g. steamed scallops with garlic and spicy sauce £1.60 each. Among the starters there is rather too much reliance on deep-frying to provide a thrill but try the curious dense sweetness of crispy sliced yam roll and experience the delicacy of deep-fried buns with vegetable stuffing. Wheat gluten provides a different 'staple' to beancurd and in Buddhist zhai dishes is fashioned to imitate meat. Vegetarian 'duckling' would be a huge let-down to anyone fond of the real thing. Better is stir-fried wheat gluten which comes with a chilli and black bean sauce that would make mincemeat of anything. If you allow yourself fish, try the fragrant stir-fried scallops with vegetables, or go mad and have baked lobster with ginger and spring onion. The wine list is relatively enterprising and does not attempt to claw back 'savings' on the food.

OPEN: LUNCH: Sun. DINNER: Mon-Sun. **HOURS:** 12.00-3.30pm and 6.00-11.30pm. **CREDIT CARDS ACCEPTED:** Mastercard, Visa. **NUMBER OF SEATS:** 70. **SERVICE:** Optional. **SET PRICE LUNCH:** £8.00. **SET PRICE DINNER:** £13.50. No-smoking area. **NEAREST TUBE STATION:** Belsize Park/Chalk Farm.

Vic Naylor Bar and Grill

38-40 St John Street, EC1

071-608 2181   **£22**

'Where to go for mussels opened in Newcastle Brown with lemon grass'

Vic Naylor's, perhaps inadvertently, has achieved the look of a rough New York bar and grill. As we know, it is not difficult for a pub to look like Camelot, Bohemia, the Last Chance Saloon, the heyday of the Raj, Les Deux Magots etc. but the genuinely rough New York bar is usually beyond the tasteful British who settle for the smoothed-over Joe Allen version. There seems to have been an especially fortuitous combination of circumstances here; a too-high ceiling that can get really filthy in the corners, coarse brick walls, a very long bar under naked bulbs and the propinquity of Smithfield with its beefy menace to health subliminally conveyed. Some of the names of dishes are quite funny; tomozzalada, roasted tomatoes with mozzarella and salad leaves; indostroggo, beef stroganoff using Indonesian spices; and – a touching tribute to jazz musician Slim Gaillard – spaghetti voutaroonie, pasta with a creamy oyster and flat mushroom and dolcelatte sauce. Love mussels, mussels opened in Newcastle Brown with chillis, lemon grass, lime leaves and garlic, were liked as were rosti crab cakes. The choice of beers and ciders has more street cred than the wines.

OPEN: LUNCH: Mon-Fri. DINNER: Mon-Sat. **HOURS:** 12.00pm-12.00am (7.00pm-1.00am Sat). **CLOSED:** Bank Holidays. **CREDIT CARDS ACCEPTED:** Access, AmEx, Visa. **NUMBER OF SEATS:** 100. **SERVICE:** 10% for parties of 4 or more. **NEAREST TUBE STATION:** Farringdon/Barbican.   MAP REF: 8,D/2

Villandry Dining Room

89 Marylebone High Street, W1

071-224 3799   **£25**

'Shopping for a meal'

The balance between tables for eating and space for shopping in this agreeable grocery store is tipping in favour of the eating. When you ring to book a table for lunch, it is worth asking for one in the back dining room where the chance of a loose olive landing in your cleavage reduced. (Men lunch here too but they tend to be outnumbered by the ladies.) The menu reflects to some extent the produce for sale: an assiette of excellent assorted charcuterie; another of cheeses; smoked salmon with nourishing brown bread; Villandry ice-creams served with shortbread biscuits. Cool, deft hands provide the lightest of pastry for savoury tarts and sweet desserts. There is a soup (usually vegetarian), a salad, an omelette, a pasta dish and something heftier. It might be hachis Parmentier (shepherd's pie) or Toulouse sausages with mash and Dijon mustard sauce. It is enlightened home cooking but that very fact, plus the elbows-in schoolroom atmosphere and the exuberantly priced wines, make the bills come to rather more than seems warranted. Service is charming and knows what's what; a request for a citron pressé (not offered on the menu) brought forth a jug of freshly squeezed lemon juice, a bowl of sugar and a bottle of still water. Dinner is served once a month – usually on the last Thursday – but check with the shop.

OPEN: Mon-Sat. **HOURS:** 8.30-11.30am and 12.30-2.30pm. **CLOSED:** Bank Holidays. **CREDIT CARDS ACCEPTED:** Access, AmEx, Switch, Visa. **NUMBER OF SEATS:** 54. **SERVICE:** Included. No smoking throughout. Wheelchair access (but not lavatory). Private room seats 44, evenings only. **NEAREST TUBE STATION:** Baker Street/Bond Street/Regent's Park.   MAP REF: 1,C/4

Vrisaki

73 Myddleton Road, N22

081-889 8760   **£18**

'Greek for "blow out"'

Essential preparation before a meal in this Greek-Cypriot restaurant hidden behind a take-away front is acquiring the kind of appetite that, sketched into your gaze, makes passing pigeons uneasy. Most feast on the set-price meze. The first thing that happens is that 16 different starter dishes swarm on your table. Three more are delivered a little later, then two between times before four fish dishes. Just when you think it's all over, the meat and salad arrives. Highlights include green olives with cracked coriander seeds, three types of beans, nutty hummus, grilled flat-cap mushrooms and grilled halloumi on smoked port loin; the meats are worth conserving the last of your hunger for. The fish, by contrast, can lack freshness, with the boarding-house trout providing a particularly un-Greek moment, compensated by good battered squid rings. With plenty of this order, no wonder the gravel-voiced waiters carry corporations which strain their shirts. The wine list is Greek and inexpensive: try Cambas' '91 Nemea to see the rapid strides Greek winemaking has managed of late.

OPEN: Mon-Sat. **HOURS:** 12.00-3.00pm and 6.00pm-12.00am. **CLOSED:** Bank Holidays. **CREDIT CARDS ACCEPTED:** None. **NUMBER OF SEATS:** 120. **SERVICE:** 10%. Wheelchair access (but not lavatory). Private room seats 18. **NEAREST TUBE STATION:** Wood Green/Palmers Green.

Wagamama

4 Streatham Street, WC1

071-323 9223   **£7**

'Giving good noodle'

The sub-title of the book of the restaurant, *Wagamama* (published November 1994 at £10), is The Way of the Noodle. Becoming a follower usually involves joining a queue. So popular is this simple, stylish, inexpensive and health-conscious endeavour serving ramen, the noodle-based Japanese version of fast food, that a short wait is almost inevitable. The meal you order from staff carrying radio-based electronic hand-held systems that communicate instantaneously with the kitchen and bar tends to be a main course based on ramen, pan-fried noodles or rice, plus side dishes such as gyoza (dumplings) or crumb-coated deep-fried prawns and perhaps raw juices or salads. The assemblies are precise, as can be inferred from my favourite, chilli beef ramen: chargrilled sirloin steak, green chillis, onion, coriander, mint leaf, fried shallots and spring onions. The soup base includes fish sauce, vinegar and chilli sauce. Once a devotee, you can wear a Wagamama house T-shirt and carry a black

Wagamama bag. Go and fill it up with purchases from Muji. There is no booking and sharing the long blonde tables is part of the way of the noodle, but Wagamama is licensed.

OPEN: Mon-Sat. **HOURS:** 12.00-2.30pm (12.30-3.30pm Sat) and 6.00-11.00pm. **CLOSED:** Bank Holidays. **CREDIT CARDS ACCEPTED:** None. **NUMBER OF SEATS:** 104. **SERVICE:** Optional. **SET PRICE LUNCH AND DINNER:** £6.50. No smoking throughout. **NEAREST TUBE STATION:** Tottenham Court Road. **MAP REF:** 1,F/2

Wakaba

122a Finchley Road, NW3

071-586 7960 or 071-722 3854 £30

'Where reductio can become ad absurdem'

Minimalist design, as triumphs here in John Pawson's euphonious interior, is quick to show wear and tear. It is then but a short hop from thinking about scratches on the white-painted bare tables to wondering if the sashimi is not rather inelegantly cut and meanly served. Test meals this year tended to point up the wisdom of concentrating on sushi stylishly served at the bar at the back of the room. A caveat to this is having to sit with your back to the mesmerizing shadow play and lightshow of people and cars passing the opaque glass frontage visible from tables in the main part of the room. Attempts to trace your investment when the bill is presented are thwarted by there being just two sums; one for food, one for drink. And as you visit the fridge late at night back home to forage for a sustaining snack don't have to kick yourself for having paid a service charge twice over: the totals space on credit card slips are left open despite service having been charged.

OPEN: Mon-Sat. **HOURS:** 6.30-11.00pm. **CLOSED:** 3rd week of August, 4 days at Christmas and Easter. **CREDIT CARDS ACCEPTED:** Access, AmEx, Diner's Club, Visa. **NUMBER OF SEATS:** 55. **SERVICE:** 15%. **SET PRICE DINNER:** £23-£32. Wheelchair access. **NEAREST TUBE STATION:** Finchley Road. **MAP REF:** 6,C/2

Walsh's Seafood & Shellfish Restaurant

5 Charlotte Street, W1

071-637 0222 £30

'Old-fashioned fish restaurant'

Walsh's in Charlotte Street is the venture of Elaine Emmanuel, grand-daughter of Bernard Walsh, the founder of Wheeler's restaurants. Her restaurant is designed to keep alive the spirit of the original Wheeler's. Perhaps it was unfortunate that having been given a table in the front room, the oyster bar, and having been told that oysters had 'run out' and having toyed with the small amount of crab on the heap of frizzy lettuce (crab salad) chosen instead, I should look at my hunting scene place mat to see a picture of hounds moving in to the kill with the caption 'Fairly run down'. The meal was redeemed somewhat by good-quality scallops but under a dense cheese sauce given a dark brown skin by the salamander and the old-fashioned excellence of deep-fried sole Colbert with its crisp crust enclosing juicy fish. Sauté potatoes were not sauté potatoes but discs of potato thrown in the deep-fryer. One of the early Egon Ronay inspectors once told me that properly fried sauté potatoes were a test of a restaurant. The house Meursault is fabulous. Have that, some oysters (if they have not 'run out'), Dover sole in one of the many ways and Welsh rarebit – just as you might have done at the original Wheeler's.

OPEN: LUNCH: Mon-Fri. DINNER: Mon-Sat. **HOURS:** 12.00-2.30pm and 6.00-11.00pm. **CLOSED:** Bank Holidays. **CREDIT CARDS ACCEPTED:** All major cards. **NUMBER OF SEATS:** 70. **SERVICE:** Optional. Wheelchair access (but not lavatory). Private room seats 10-40. **NEAREST TUBE STATION:** Goodge Street, Tottenham Court Road.   **MAP REF:** 1,E/3

 # The White Tower
1 Percy Street, W1

071-636 8141   **£35**

'Greek civilization'

The news that Roy Ackermann (who preserved intact the Gay Hussar q.v.) has bought L'Etoile in Charlotte Street gives some hope for the complete restoration of the restaurants of Fitzrovia. All we need now is for fierce ladies dressed in black bombazine to take over the running of Bertorelli's again and for Schmidts to come back. The White Tower had an unfortunate hiccup a couple of years ago but is safely back on the same track that was laid down in 1938 when the late John Stais opened this most sedate of Greek/Cypriot restaurants. His niece Miss Mary runs the restaurant with help of George Metaxas who joined as sommelier 40 years ago. The garrulous menu which has changed little over the years was originally written by Daniel George when he was working as an editor at the publishing house of Jonathan Cape, then located in nearby Bedford Square. It tells you everything that you need to know about the dishes – and sometimes a bit more – in order to make a choice. When I go to the White Tower, I faithfully reread it and order taramasalata (said to have been introduced to London here), the chicken and duck liver pâté Diana and, if it's available and I have a willing companion with whom to share it, the Aylesbury duckling farci à la Cypriote; stuffed with cracked wheat, nuts and spices and roasted to a dark brown. I am then very pleased to see the waiter approach with a silver dish of green peas, cooked from frozen, the proper accompaniment. If the duck is not available – prudent diners order it in advance – I like the chicken Cherkeza or assiette Kalomyra both based on poached chicken with rice and a creamy sauce, the fish salad made with turbot which is a first course you can have as a main course or something charcoal-grilled. The cover charge of £2 per person delivers radishes, celery, olives and bread to nibble on and feel healthy. Finish the meal with fruit salad or pancakes filled with rose petal jam then coffee and Turkish delight. Relying on George for guidance over wine is the best way to approach a not particularly inspiring list.

OPEN: LUNCH: Mon-Fri. DINNER: Mon-Sat. **HOURS:** 12.30-2.30pm and 6.30-10.30pm. **CLOSED:** Bank Holidays, last 3 weeks in August and 24th December-2nd January. **CREDIT CARDS ACCEPTED:** All major cards. **NUMBER OF SEATS:** 80. **SERVICE:** Optional, £2 cover charge. Wheelchair access. Private room seats 16. **NEAREST TUBE STATION:** Tottenham Court Road/Goodge Street. **MAP REF:** 1,E/3

Wild World

264 King Street, W6

081-748 0333   **£25**

'A new take on King Street's ethnicity'

This simply decorated restaurant that opened in the summer of 1994 is one of the places – Robbie's at no. 278 is another – that is changing the image of King Street, Hammermith from a place for ethnic restaurants only. In fact chef Mark Broadbent's cooking might be called ethnic British in the sense of admitting ingredients and ideas from all over the (wild) world. Spanish influences is evident in Serrano ham served with peaches, shaved Parmesan and pickled guindillas (chillis). The Middle East contributes babaganoug (aubergine purée) and marinated Turkish vegetables. Italy delivers wild mushroom risotto and cappuccino brulée and France dishes such as chargrilled tuna Niçoise and confit of duck with truffle oil mash. Broadbent has worked, albeit briefly, at the Brackenbury (q.v.) where this sort of menu also thrives. He is an accomplished culinary backpacker and cooks with the necessary precision with this atlas of influences. The young staff are friendly and keen. The wine list is equally cosmopolitan and fairly priced.

OPEN: LUNCH: Sun-Fri. DINNER: Mon-Sat. **HOURS:** 12.30-3.00pm and 7.30-11.00pm. **CREDIT CARDS ACCEPTED:** Access, Visa. **NUMBER OF SEATS:** 67. **SERVICE:** 12.5%. **SET PRICE LUNCH:** £11.50-£15.50. **NEAREST TUBE STATION:** Ravenscourt Park.

Wilson's

236 Blythe Road, W14

071-603 7267   **£19**

*'A leading contender for London's least
likely success'*

Hard to credit that a Scottish restaurant could quicken metropolitan pulses attuned to Mediterranean or Asiatic rhythms, yet Wilson's does. It's because the culinary ideas are actually rather good, and their realization skilled and boldly stated. Herring and mascarpone pâté may sound like something from the menu of a suburban dinner party in a Mike Leigh film, yet when paired with an apple and cumin purée the flavours assume a strange harmony. Fresh steamed cockles put a lovely shellfish into the limelight without acetic vandalism – though there's a dish of balsamic vinegar if you must. Hot chocolate and almond mousse meltingly engaged with a good toffee sauce, while lemon posset was full of the simple virtue of its ingredients. Service, despite the tartan waistcoats, is kindly rather than parodic, and the wine list is short and intelligent. Limiting the whisky selection here to United Distillers' six Classic Malts, by contrast, seems unnecessarily restrictive, even though they are models of malt probity.

OPEN: Mon-Sun. **HOURS:** 12.00pm-12.00am. **CREDIT CARDS ACCEPTED:** All major cards except Diner's Club. **NUMBER OF SEATS:** 50. **SERVICE:** 12.5%, optional. **SET PRICE LUNCH:** £7.50. **SET PRICE DINNER:** £12.00. Wheelchair access (but not lavatory). **NEAREST TUBE STATION:** Hammersmith/Shepherd's Bush/Olympia.

MAP REF: 7,B/1

Wiltons Restaurant

55 Jermyn Street, SW1   ㉖㉓

071-629 9955   **£48**

'Redrawing the map of a class-ridden society'

Journalists and commentators who like to take the pulse of the nation should pay more attention to restaurants. Wiltons, a retreat of the upper and moneyed classes, some time back started to open for dinner on Saturdays. For decades Wiltons (established 1742) traded only Monday to Friday knowing that its clientele would be in their country houses Friday to Monday. Now it is also open for lunch and dinner on Sundays, and in August of 1994 Wiltons was offering its clientele 10% off the price of dinner. Never mind the balance of trade figures, this chintzy 10% does not augur well. Also, as another restaurant reviewer pointed out at the time, 90% of a hell of a lot is still a hell of a lot. For your money you do get prime ingredients by which I mean the freshest of fish and judiciously hung game. Start with oysters, lobster cocktail or potted shrimps and seize the opportunity to have a savoury afterwards such as Welsh rarebit or angels on horseback (oysters wrapped in bacon and grilled). Captains of industry, royalty and other titled folk get better tables (some in booths) and better treatment from the butlers and nannies who wait but even common folk can enjoy the Edwardiana of the interior.

OPEN: Mon-Sun. **HOURS:** 12.30-2.30pm and 6.30-10.30pm. **CLOSED:** Bank Holidays. **CREDIT CARDS ACCEPTED:** Access, AmEx, Diner's Club, Visa. **NUMBER OF SEATS:** 90. **SERVICE:** Optional. Wheelchair access (but not lavatory). Private room seats 18. **NEAREST TUBE STATION:** Green Park.   MAP REF: 1,C/1

Wódka

12 St Albans Grove, W8

071-937 6513   £20-£25

'Solidarity guaranteed after enough shots'

'The decor and general feeling with the tiled walls chipped by bullets, the iron seats with small bright cushions and the wooden floor all make one feel one is *in* Poland, not long after the Solidarity revolution,' said a satisfied customer. The Eastern European cooking is, on the whole, satisfactory. Barscz, thin, 'like peppery blood' is served with a small roll (pasztecik) seemingly filled with minced bacon. Blinis come with caviar and salmon eggs (keta) but also herring, smoked salmon and aubergine purée, Smoked eel with boczek, new potatoes and capers looks 'exciting and medieval, a clever, cunning peasant dish, made very rich from the eel. We wished we'd been working all day in the shipyards of Gdansk or in the smelting works of Womskz'. Fishcakes come sandcastle shaped but not textured with a dill-flavoured hollandaise. There are authentic side dishes such as kasza (buckwheat); carrots with honey and sesame; sauerkraut and caraway seeds; puréed beetroot and apple mizeria (cucumber salad). Crème brulée for dessert conceals in its creamy depths morello cherries. Wódka is popular and consequently noisy. Crowds of customers can occasion long waits for food, giving scope for testing the range of the eponymous spirit .

IF YOU MUST DRINK wine, there are 40 eclectic and largely well-selected bottles on offer, listed in price order (most under £20). The culturally authentic and alcoholically fearless option, however, is the range of 16 Polish vodkas, the majority of them flavoured, extended by Wódka's own versions. Zubrowka (vodka flavoured by a single stem of bison grass) is hard to beat, but all are horizon-extending.

OPEN: LUNCH: Mon-Fri. DINNER: Mon-Sun. **HOURS:** 12.30-2.30pm and 7.00-11.00pm. **CLOSED:** Bank Holidays. **CREDIT CARDS ACCEPTED:** All major cards. **NUMBER OF SEATS:** 60. **SERVICE:** Optional. No-smoking area. Wheelchair access (but not lavatory). Private room seats 37. **NEAREST TUBE STATION:** High Street Kensington.

Zen Central Restaurant

20 Queen Street, W1

071-629 8089   £35

'Chinese chic'

The Mayfair location of this exercise (by architect Rick Mather) in the sleek, sinuous use of glass and steel attracts a cosmopolitan (on the whole meaning rich) clientele. The menu suits them well; it is not too long, it is divided in a way that is a help towards ordering a well-balanced Chinese meal and although it does not explore the esoteric parts of animals it is by no means inauthentic. For those who appreciate the subtleties inherent in shark's fin and abalone there are reassuringly expensive dishes featuring these textures. Peking duck, crispy aromatic lamb, steamed sea bass or the slightly cheaper Dover sole could also be centrepiece items. Around them try the Imperial hors d'oeuvre (for two) which features spicy jelly fish, abalone, prawns and scallops, pan-fried Peking dumplings, veal cutlets in black pepper sauce and hand-cut pork with dried shredded scallops. There are some good Chinese desserts: red bean pancakes; honey melon tapioca pudding; almond tofu delight. Service is polished, the wine list expensive. On form, Zen Central cracks the problem of combining the buzz of a glamorous restaurant with reckonable Chinese food. At the time of writing, a new menu, more rooted in Hong-Kong style, is planned for Zen Chelsea Cloisters, 85 Sloane Avenue, SW3 (071-589 1781).

OPEN: Mon-Sun. **HOURS:** 12.15-3.30pm and 6.30pm-12.30am (6.30-11.30pm Sun). **CLOSED:** Christmas Eve, Christmas Day and Boxing Day. **CREDIT CARDS ACCEPTED:** All major cards. **NUMBER OF SEATS:** 100. **SERVICE:** 10%, optional. **SET PRICE LUNCH:** £28 and £35. **SET PRICE DINNER:** £35, £42 and £50. Wheelchair access (but not lavatory). **NEAREST TUBE STATION:** Green Park.

MAP REF: 1,B/1

ZENW3

83 Hampstead High Street, NW3

071-794 7863 £25

'The best place to pose in Hampstead'

The loyal North London clientele – 'more Italian designer spectacles than at an evening at La Scala' – need not have noticed a thing when a part of the Zen group went into receivership in 1994 and emerged from that quadrille with a new partner in the shape of the Empress Garden group. Kitchen and service remained and remains the same and the stylishness of Rick Mather's architecture and design continues to float serenely above it all. The recognition that diners might want to choose by form rather than content is sound: wrapped items, pancake specialities, sizzling plate dishes, soups, sataye and salads are listed separately. Ingredients such as wild salmon and veal, not altogether customary in Gerrard Street, are given a dose of imaginative orientalism. Sometimes dishes are more exciting in description than in execution: prawn with tao peng sauce and chicken in five spices both prove anodyne, although quite pleasantly so. Desserts are founded on tropical fruit and toffee combinations with ice cream thrown in for the girls. The staff are efficient, the wine list adequate to the task and the Japanese sake is served (stylish to the last) in outsize vodka glasses.

OPEN: Mon-Sun. **HOURS:** 12.00-11.30pm (12.00-11.00pm Sun). **CLOSED:** Christmas. **CREDIT CARDS ACCEPTED:** Access, AmEx, Diner's Club, Visa. **NUMBER OF SEATS:** 140. **SERVICE:** 12.5%. **SET PRICE LUNCH:** £10.50. **SET PRICE DINNER:** £26.50. Wheelchair access. Private room seats 24. **NEAREST TUBE STATION:** Hampstead.

MAP REF: 6,A/1

Zoë

St Christopher's Place, W1

071-224 1122

£25

'Frenzy and Zoë'

Frenzy could be another name for this Antony Worrall-Thompson enterprise. A characteristic pot-pourri menu, Mediterranean colours splashed on walls and tablecloths, high noise levels and service rushed off its feet, particularly on sunny summer days, all contribute. However, popularity is a necessary ingredient in this frenzy and the imaginative café menu with its oriental incursions and the sandwiches offered on the ground floor and the more expensive menus offered downstairs – divided into one meaninglessly entitled Country & City and another more revealingly headed with the word Seafood – obviously please. Occasionally there seems too much interference with the natural course of culinary events – Do you need mash *and* borlotti bean casserole with pan-fried guinea fowl breast? In hand-rolling mozzarella to put with chargrilled vegetable panino does the cheese act as a sort of Swarfega? – but on the whole combinations that might sound slightly bizarre in print, work well on the plate and palate. A laudable number of wines from the fairly priced list are offered by the glass.

OPEN: Mon-Sat. **HOURS:** 11.00am-11.30pm. **CLOSED:** Bank Holidays. **CREDIT CARDS ACCEPTED:** Access, AmEx, Diner's Club, Switch, Visa. **NUMBER OF SEATS:** 200. **SERVICE:** Optional. **SET PRICE LUNCH AND DINNER:** £10. No-smoking area. Wheelchair access (but not lavatory). Tables outside seat 50. **NEAREST TUBE STATION:** Bond Street. **MAP REF:** 1,B/3

EROS AWARDS*

Aubergine

Bibendum

Bistrot Bruno
(& L'Odeon)

The Brackenbury

Café Royal Grill Room

Le Caprice

Chez Max

Chez Moi

Chutney Mary

The French House
Dining Room

Fung Shing

Le Gavroche

Hyde Park Hotel, The
Restaurant

The Ivy

Quaglino's

Riva

River Café

Les Saveurs

La Tante Claire

The White Tower

TOP TEN WINE LISTS

Bibendum

Downstairs at One-
Ninety

Fifth Floor

Le Gavroche

Gilbert's

Mijanou

Le Pont de la Tour

River Café

RSJ

Les Saveurs

Newcomers

Alfred
The Atlantic
Arcadia
Aubergine *
Avenue West Eleven

Bengal Clipper
Big Night Out

Caviar House, La Brasserie
Café dell'Ugo
Chapel Lafayette
Chester's
Chez Max *

The Fire Station
Fulham Road

El Gaucho
Gaucho Grill
Il Goloso

Green Street

Harveys
The Hospitality Suite
The Hothouse
Hyde Park Hotel, The
    Restaurant *

Jimmy Beez

Kartouche

McClement's Petit Bistro

The Peasant

Rhapsody

Shaw's

Wild World

Restaurants serving Sunday brunch

Al Basha
Al Bustan
Al Hamra
Ali's Indian Cuisine
L'Altro

Babur Brasserie
Bedlington Café
The Belvedere in Holland
    Park
Big Night Out
Billboard Café
Bistrot 190
Blue Elephant
Blue Print Café
Bombay Brasserie
Brasserie du Marché
    aux Puces

Café Delancey
Café des Arts
Le Café du Jardin
Camden Brasserie
The Canteen
Le Caprice *
Chada
Chapel Lafayette
Chester's

Christopher's American
    Grill
Chutney Mary *
Chutneys
Cibo
The Criterion

Daphne's
Del Buongustaio

First Floor
The French House Dining
    Room *

Green's
The Greenhouse

Halcyon Hotel

Ikkyu
Inter-Continental Hotel

Jimmy Beez

Kenny's
Kleftiko

Launceston Place
Lemonia

Ma Goa

Malabar
Mamta
McClement's Bistro

Odette's
192
Osteria Antica Bologna

Pearl
Le P'tit Normand
Pizza on the Park

Le Pont de la Tour

Quality Chop House

Ransome's Dock
The Red Fort

The Savoy, River
   Restaurant
Snows on the Green

Vegetarian Cottage

Restaurants by cuisine

AFGHAN

Caravan Serai

AFRICAN

Calabash

AFRO-CARIBBEAN

Smokey Joe's Diner

THE AMERICAS

Chapel Lafayette
Christopher's American
   Grill

El Gaucho

Gaucho Grill

Jimmy Beez

Kenny's

Rhapsody

BELGIAN

Belgo

BRITISH

Alfred

The Connaught Hotel

The Dorchester, Grill
   Room

The French House
   Dining Room *

Gilbert's
The Greenhouse
Green's Restaurant

The Quality Chop House

The Ritz
Rules

The Savoy Grill

Wiltons

CHINESE

China Court

The Dorchester, Oriental

Feng Shang
Four Seasons, Queensway
Fung Shing *

Harbour City

Imperial City

Mandarin Kitchen
Ming
Mr Kong

Pearl
Poons

Royal China

Zen Central
ZeNW3

CHINESE VEGETARIAN

Vegetarian Cottage

EAST EUROPEAN

The Gay Hussar

Ognisko Polskie

Wódka

ECLECTIC

Alastair Little
Andrew Edmunds
The Angel
Arcadia
The Argyll
Atlantic
Avenue West Eleven

The Belvedere in
    Holland Park
Bibendum Restaurant *
Big Night Out
Bistrot 190
Blue Print Café
Boyd's
The Brackenbury *
Brasserie du Marché
    aux Puces

Café Delancey
Café dell'Ugo
Café des Arts
Le Café du Jardin
Camden Brasserie
Capital Hotel
Le Caprice *
Chester's
Chinon
Clarke's
Cork & Bottle
The Criterion

dell'Ugo

Fifth Floor
The Fire Station
First Floor
Fulham Road

Green Street

Halcyon Hotel
Harveys
Hilaire
The Hothouse

The Ivy *

Kensington Place

Launceston Place
Leith's
The Lexington

McClement's Bistro
McClement's Petit Bistro
Le Metro
Milestone Hotel,
    Cheneston's
Museum Street Café

Nosh Brothers

Odette's
O'Keefe's
192

Pied-à-Terre
Le Pont de la Tour

Quaglino's *
Quincy's

Ransome's Dock
RSJ

Selfridge Hotel, Fletchers
Shaw's
Snows on the Green
Sonny's
The Square
Stephen Bull
Stephen Bull's Bistro

Tate Gallery Restaurant

Vic Naylor's Bar & Grill
Villandry Dining Room

Wild World

Zoë

FISH

L'Altro

Bibendum Oyster Bar *

Café Fish
Caviar House, La Brasserie

Downstairs at One-Ninety

La Gaulette
Grahame's Seafare
Green's Oyster Bar

The Lobster Pot
Lou Pescadou

Manzi's

Poissonnerie de l'Avenue

Le Suquet
Sweetings

Walsh's

FISH AND CHIPS

Brady's

Geales

Two Brothers

Upper Street Fish Shop

FRENCH

Alexandra
Les Associés
Aubergine *

Bistrot Bruno *
Bleeding Heart

Le Cadre
Le Café du Marché
Café Royal Grill Room *
The Canteen
Chez Gerard
Chez Max *
Chez Moi *
The Connaught Hotel

L'Escargot
L'Estaminet

Four Seasons Hotel

Le Gavroche *

Hospitality Suite
Hyde Park Hotel,
    The Restaurant *

Inter-Continental Hotel

Le Meridien, Oak Room

Mijanou
Mon Petit Plaisir

Mon Plaisir
Monkeys
Le Muscadet
Mustard's Smithfield
    Brasserie

Le Palais du Jardin
Le Petit Max
Le P'tit Normand

St Quentin
St James's Court Hotel,
    Auberge de Provence
Les Saveurs *
The Savoy, River
    Restaurant
Soho Soho

La Tante Claire *
Turner's

GREEK

Beoty's

Daphne

Kalamaras
Kleftiko

Lemonia

Vrisaki

The White Tower *

INDIAN

Ali's Indian Cuisine

Babur Brasserie
Bengal Clipper
Bodali
Bombay Brasserie

Chutney Mary *

Diwana Bhel-Poori House

Gopal's of Soho

Jashan

Lahore Kebab House

Ma Goa
Malabar

Namaste
Old Delhi

Ragam
The Red Fort

Salloos
Star of India

INDIAN VEGETARIAN

Chutneys

Kastoori

Mamta
Mandeer

Rani

Sabras
Sree Krishna

ITALIAN

L'Accento
Al San Vincenzo
Arts Theatre Café

Bertorelli's
Billboard Café

La Capannina
Cibo

Daphne's
Del Buongustaio

The Eagle
Enoteca

Florians
La Fontana

Il Goloso
Granita

The Halkin

L'Incontro

The Lansdowne Public
    House

Neal Street Restaurant

Olivo
Orsino
Orso
Osteria Antica Bologna
Osteria Basilico

The Peasant

Riva *
The River Café *

San Lorenzo Fuoriporta
Santini

Vasco & Piero's Pavilion

JAPANESE

Ajimura

Gonbei
Ikkyu

Inaho
Suntory

Tokyo Diner

Wagamama
Wakaba

KOREAN

Jin

Seoul

LEBANESE

Al Basha
Al Bustan
Al Hamra

Beiteddine

Maroush

MALAYSIAN & INDONESIAN

Nusa Dua

Singapore Garden

NEPALESE

Great Nepalese

PIZZAS

Pizza on the Park

PORTUGUESE

Oporto

213

SCANDINAVIAN

Anna's Place

Claridge's, The Causerie

SCOTTISH

Wilson's

SPANISH

Albero & Grana

Rebato's

THAI

Bahn Thai
Bedlington Café
Blue Elephant

Chada

Esarn Kheaw

Mantanah

Sabai Sabai
Sri Siam

Thai Garden
Thailand

NORTH AFRICAN

Adam's Café

Laurent

TURKISH

Efes Kebab House

Istanbul Iskembecisi

London Istanbul Orient Express

Sofra

VIETNAMESE

Saigon

Restaurants with last orders after 11.30pm

Al Basha (12.00am)
Ali's Indian Cuisine (11.45pm)
Atlantic (2.30am Mon-Sat)

Beiteddine (12.00am)
Big Night Out (12.00am Mon-Sat)
Billboard Café (12.00am; 12.30am
    Fri-Sat)
Bistrot 190 (12.30am Mon-Sat)
Bombay Brasserie (12.00am)

Café Delancey (12.00am)
Le Café du Jardin (12.00am)
The Canteen (11.45pm)
Le Caprice (12.00am) *
Chapel Lafayette (12.30am)
Christopher's American Grill
    (11.45pm)
Cork & Bottle (11.45pm Mon-Sat)

dell'Ugo (12.30am restaurant)
The Dorchester Bar (11.45pm
    Mon-Sat)
Downstairs at One-Ninety
    (12.00am)

First Floor (11.45pm)

Gaucho Grill (11.55pm Mon-Sat)

Istanbul Iskembecisi (4.30am)
The Ivy (12.00am) *

Kalamaras (12.00am)
Kensington Place (11.45pm Mon-
    Sat)

Lahore Kebab House (12.00am)
London Istanbul Orient Express
    (12.00am)
Lou Pescadou (12.00am)

Manzi's (11.40pm)
Maroush (1.30am)
Ming (11.45pm)
Mr Kong (1.45am)

Orso (11.45pm)
Le Palais du Jardin (12.00am)
Pizza on the Park (12.00am)
Poissonerie de l'Avenue (11.45pm)
Le Pont de la Tour (12.00am
    Mon-Sat)

Quaglino's (12.00am Mon-Thurs;
1.00am Sat) *

Sofra (12.00am)
Soho Soho Rotisserie (12.45am)
Soho Soho Restaurant (11.45pm)

The Square (11.45pm Mon-Sat)

Tokyo Diner (12.00am)

Restaurants with live music

This is often occasional. Please
telephone restaurants for details

Al Basha
Bengal Clipper
Big Night Out
Billboard Café
Bodali
Bombay Brasserie

Le Café du Jardin
Le Café du Marché
Café Fish
Le Caprice *
Chapel Lafayette
Chester's
Claridge's
The Criterion

The Dorchester Bar
Downstairs at One-Ninety

Efes Kebab House

First Floor
Four Seasons Hotel

Halcyon Hotel
The Halkin
The Hothouse

Imperial City
L'Incontro
Inter-Continental Hotel

Jimmy Beez

Kenny's
Kleftiko

The Lansdowne Public House
The Lexington
London Istanbul Orient Express

Maroush
McClement's Bistro
McClement's Petit Bistro
Le Meridien
Ognisko Polskie
Oporto

Le Palais du Jardin
Pizza on the Park
Le Pont de la Tour

Quaglino's *

Rebato's
The Ritz

St James's Court Hotel
The Savoy, River Restaurant
Selfridge Hotel
Soho Soho
Star of India

Vic Naylor's Bar and Grill
Villandry Dining Room

Wilson's

Restaurants with no smoking areas

Check restaurant entries for details

Ajimura
Anna's Place
Arcadia
Atlantic

Bahn Thai
Beoty's

Bertorelli's
Big Night Out
Blue Print Café
Bombay Brasserie
Café Delancey
Café des Arts
Café Fish
The Canteen

La Capannina
Caravan Serai
Chez Gerard
Chutney Mary
Clarke's

Del Buongustaio

L'Escargot
L'Estaminet

Florians

Gopal's of Soho

Halcyon Hotel

Inter-Continental Hotel

Kleftiko

Launceston Place
London Istanbul Orient Express

Mamta
Mandeer
Maroush
McClement's Bistro
McClement's Petit Bistro
Mijanou
Ming
Museum Street Café

192
Orso

Le Petit Max
Pizza on the Park

Rani
Ransome's Dock
The Red Fort

Sabras
St James's Court Hotel
Les Saveurs *
Selfridge Hotel
Soho Soho

Tate Gallery Restaurant
Thai Garden
Tokyo Diner
Two Brothers

Vegetarian Cottage
Villandry Dining Room

Wagamama
Wild World
Wòdka

Zoë

Restaurants with tables outside

Check restaurant entries for details

L'Accento
Ajimura
Al Basha
Al Bustan
Alexandra
Alfred
Al Hamra
Ali's Indian Cuisine
L'Altro
Andrew Edmunds
Arcadia

Bahn Thai
Bedlington Café
The Belvedere in Holland Park
Big Night Out
Bleeding Heart
Blue Print Café
Bombay Brasserie

The Brackenbury *
Brasserie du Marché aux Puces

Le Cadre
Café Delancey
Café dell'Ugo
Le Café du Jardin
Café Fish
The Canteen
Chapel Lafayette
Chez Gerard
Chez Max *
Chinon
Cork & Bottle

Daphne
Daphne's
dell'Ugo

The Eagle
Efes Kebab House

Florians

El Gaucho
Geales
Il Goloso
Gonbei

Halcyon Hotel

Jimmy Beez

Kalamaras
Kleftiko

Lahore Kebab House
The Lansdowne Public House
Lou Pescadou

Le Metro
Mijanou
Ming
Mon Petit Plaisir

Namaste

Odette's

Ognisko Polskie
O'Keefe's
Old Delhi
192
Osteria Antica Bologna

Le Palais du Jardin
Pizza on the Park
Poissonerie de l'Avenue
Le Pont de la Tour

Ransome's Dock
Rhapsody
The Ritz
Riva *

San Lorenzo Fuoriporta
Shaw's
Sofra
Soho Soho
Sonny's
Le Suquet

Zoë

Restaurants under £25.00 per person

L'Accento
Adam's Café
Al Basha
Alexandra
Alfred
Al Hamra
Ali's Indian Cuisine
Andrew Edmunds
Anna's Place
Arts Theatre Café
Avenue West Eleven

Babur Brasserie
Bahn Thai
Bedlington Café
Belgo
Big Night Out
Billboard Café
Bistro 190
Bleeding Heart
Bodali
The Brackenbury *
Brady's
Brasserie du Marché aux Puces

Café dell'Ugo
Le Cadre

Café Delancey
Calabash
Camden Brasserie
Caravan Serai
Chada
Chapel Lafayette
China Court
Chutneys
Cork & Bottle
The Criterion

Daphne
dell'Ugo
Diwana Bhel-Poori House

The Eagle
Efes Kebab House
Enoteca
Esarn Kheaw

The Fire Station
Florians
Four Seasons, Queensway
The French House Dining Room *
Fung Shing *

El Gaucho
Gaucho Grill

Geales
Il Goloso
Gonbei
Gopal's of Soho
Grahame's Seafare
Great Nepalese
Harbour City

Ikkyu
Istanbul Iskembecisi

Jashan
Jimmy Beez

Kalamaras
Kartouche
Kastoori
Kenny's
Kleftiko

Lahore Kebab House
The Lansdowne Public House
Laurent
Lemonia
The Lexington
London Istanbul Orient Express
Lou Pescadou

Ma Goa
Malabar
Mamta
Mandarin Kitchen
Mandeer
Mantanah
McClement's Bistro
McClement's Petit Bistro
Le Metro
Ming
Mr Kong

Namaste
Nusa Dua

O'Keefe's

Ognisko Polskie
Old Delhi
Oporto
Osteria Antica Bologna
Osteria Basilico

Le Palais du Jardin
The Peasant
Pizza on the Park
Poons

Quality Chop House

Ragam
Rani
Rebato's

Sabai Sabai
Sabras
Saigon
Seoul
Singapore Garden
Smokey Joe's Diner
Sofra
Sree Krishna
Sri Siam
Stephen Bull's Bistro

Thai Garden
Thailand
Tokyo Diner
Two Brothers

Upper Street Fish Shop

Vegetarian Cottage
Vic Naylor's Bar and Grill
Villandry Dining Room
Vrisaki

Wagamama
Wilson's
Wódka

Restaurants under £25 and £45 per person

Ajimura
Al Bustan
Albero & Grana
Al San Vincenzo
L'Altro
The Angel
Arcadia
The Argyll
Les Associés

Atlantic
Aubergine *

Beiteddine
The Belvedere in Holland Park
Bengal Clipper
Beoty's
Bertorelli's
Bistrot Bruno *

Blue Elephant
Blue Print Café
Bombay Brasserie
Boyd's

Café des Arts
Le Café du Jardin
Le Café du Marché
Café Fish
Café Royal *
The Canteen
La Capannina
The Capital
Le Caprice *
Caviar House, La Brasserie
Chester's
Chez Gerard
Chez Max *
Chez Moi *
Chinon
Christopher's American Grill
Chutney Mary *
Cibo
Claridge's
Connaught Hotel

Daphne's
Del Buongustaio
The Dorchester
Downstairs at One-Ninety

L'Escargot
L'Estaminet

Feng Shang
Fifth Floor
First Floor
La Fontana
Fulham Road

La Gaulette
The Gay Hussar
Gilbert's
Granita
Green Street
The Greenhouse

Halcyon Hotel
The Halkin
Harveys
Hilaire
Hospitality Suite
The Hothouse

Imperial City
Inaho

The Ivy *

Jin

Kensington Place

Launceston Place
The Lobster Pot

Manzi's
Maroush
Mijanou
Milestone Hotel
Mon Petit Plaisir
Mon Plaisir
Monkeys
Le Muscadet
Museum Street Café
Mustards Smithfield Brasserie

Nosh Brothers

Odette's
Olivo
192
Orsino
Orso

Pearl
Le Petit Max
Le P'tit Normand
Poissonerie de l'Avenue

Quaglino's *
Quincy's

Ransome's Dock
The Red Fort
Rhapsody
Riva *
River Café *
Royal China
RSJ
Rules

St James's Court Hotel
St Quentin
Salloos
San Lorenzo Fuoriporta
Les Saveurs *
Selfridge Hotel
Snows on the Green
Soho Soho
Sonny's
The Square
Star of India
Stephen Bull

Le Suquet
Sweetings

Tate Gallery Restaurant

Vasco & Piero's Pavilion

Wakaba
Walsh's

The White Tower *
Wild World

Zen Central
ZenW3
Zoë

Restaurants over £45 per person

Alastair Little

Bibendum *

Clarke's

Four Seasons Hotel

Le Gavroche *
Green's

Hyde Park Hotel

L'Incontro
Inter-Continental Hotel

Leith's
Le Meridien

Neal Street Restaurant

Pied-à-Terre
Le Pont de la Tour

The Ritz

Santini
The Savoy
Suntory

La Tante Claire *
Turners

Wiltons

Restaurants with private areas

Check restaurant entries for details

L'Accento
Adam's Café
Ajimura
Al Basha
Albero & Grana
Al Bustan
Alexandra
Ali's Indian Cuisine
Arcadia

Bahn Thai
Beoty's
Big Night Out
Bistrot 190
Bleeding Heart
Brasserie du Marché aux Puces

Café Delancey
Café des Arts
Le Café du Jardin
Le Café du Marché

Café Royal *
The Canteen
La Capannina
The Capital
Caravan Serai
Caviar House, La Brasserie
Chez Max *
China Court
Chinon
Christopher's American Grill
Chutneys
Cibo
Claridge's
Connaught Hotel

Daphne
dell'Ugo
The Dorchester, Oriental
Downstairs at One-Ninety

Efes Kebab House
Enoteca
L'Escargot

L'Estaminet

Fifth Floor
The Fire Station
First Floor
Florians
Four Seasons Hotel
Fulham Road
Fung Shing *

La Gaulette
Le Gavroche *
The Gay Hussar
Geales
Gonbei
Gopal's of Soho
Green's

The Halkin
Harbour City
Hilaire
The Hothouse

Ikkyu
Imperial City
L'Incontro
The Ivy *

Jimmy Beez
Jin

Kalamaras
Kleftiko

Launceston Place
Leith's
Lemonia
The Lexington
The Lobster Pot
London Istanbul Orient Express
Lou Pescadou

Malabar
Mandeer
Manzi's
McClement's Bistro
McClement's Petit Bistro
Mijanou
Milestone Hotel
Ming
Mon Plaisir
Monkeys
Mr Kong

Namaste
Neal Street Restaurant
Nosh Brothers
Nusa Dua

Odette's
Ognisko Polskie
Oporto
Orsino

Le Palais du Jardin
Pearl
Le P'tit Normand
Pied-à-Terre
Pizza on the Park
Poissonerie de l'Avenue
Le Pont de la Tour
Poons

Quaglino's *
Quincy's

Ragam
Rani
The Red Fort
The Ritz
Royal China
RSJ
Rules

Saigon
St James's Court Hotel
St Quentin
San Lorenzo Fuoriporta
Les Saveurs *
The Savoy, River Restaurant
Selfridge Hotel
Seoul
Singapore Garden
Snows on the Green
Soho Soho
Sonny's
The Square
Sree Krishna
Star of India
Suntory
Le Suquet

Thai Garden
Tokyo Diner

Vasco & Piero's Pavilion
Vrisaki

Walsh's
The White Tower *
Wiltons
Wódka

ZenW3

Restaurants with wheelchair access

Check restaurant entries for details

L'Accento
Adam's Café
Al Basha
Al Bustan
Alfred
Al Hamra
Ali's Indian Cuisine
Al San Vincenzo
L'Altro
Anna's Place
Arcadia
The Argyll
Les Associés
Avenue West Eleven

Babur Brasserie
Bahn Thai
Bedlington Café
Beiteddine
Belgo
The Belvedere in Holland Park
Bengal Clipper
Beoty's
Bibendum *
Big Night Out
Billboard Café
Bleeding Heart
Blue Elephant
Blueprint Café
Bodali
Bombay Brasserie
The Brackenbury *
Brasserie du Marché aux Puces

Le Cadre
Café Delancey
Café dell'Ugo
Café des Arts
Le Café du Jardin

Le Café du Marché
Café Fish
Café Royal *
The Canteen
La Capannina
The Capital
Le Caprice *
Caviar House, La Brasserie
Chada
Chez Gerard
Chez Moi *
China Court
Chinon
Chutney Mary *
Chutneys
Cibo
Claridge's
Clarke's
Connaught Hotel
The Criterion

Daphne
Daphne's
Del Buongustaio
dell'Ugo
Diwana Bhel Poori House
The Dorchester

The Eagle
Efes Kebab House
Esarn Kheaw
L'Escargot
L'Estaminet

Feng Shang
Fifth Floor
The Fire Station
Florians
La Fontana
Four Seasons Hotel
Fulham Road

El Gaucho
La Gaulette
The Gay Hussar
Geales
Il Goloso
Gonbei
Gopal's of Soho
Grahame's Seafare
Granita
Great Nepalese
Green's
The Greenhouse

The Halkin
Harbour City
Harveys
Hilaire
Hyde Park Hotel *

Imperial City
L'ncontro
Inter-Continental
Istanbul Iskembecisi
The Ivy *

Jashan
Jin

Kalamaras
Kartouche
Kastoori
Kensington Place
Kleftiko

The Lansdowne Public House
Launceston Place
Laurent
Leith's
Lemonia
The Lexington
The Lobster Pot
London Istanbul Orient Express
Lou Pescadou

Ma Goa
Mamta
Mandarin Kitchen
Mantanah
Manzi's
Maroush
McClement's Bistro
McClement's Petit Bistro
Le Meridien
Mijanou
Mon Plaisir

Le Muscadet
Museum Street Café
Mustards Smithfield Brasserie

Neal Street Restaurant

Ognisko Polskie
O'Keefe's
Old Delhi
Olivo
192
Osteria Antica Bologna
Osteria Basilico

Le Palais du Jardin
The Peasant
Le Petit Max
Le P'tit Normand
Pied-à-Terre
Pizza on the Park
Poissonerie de l'Avenue
Le Pont de la Tour

Quaglino's *
Quality Chop House

Ragam
Rani
Ransome's Dock
The Red Fort
Rhapsody
Riva *
River Café *
Royal China
RSJ
Rules

Sabai Sabai
Sabras
St Quentin
St James's Court Hotel
San Lorenzo Fuoriporta
Santini
Les Saveurs *
The Savoy
Seoul
Shaw's
Snows on the Green
Sofra
Soho Soho
Sonny's
The Square
Sree Krishna
Sri Siam
Star of India

Stephen Bull
Stephen Bull's Bistro
Suntory
Sweetings

La Tante Claire *
Tate Gallery Restaurant
Thai Garden
Tokyo Diner
Turners

Upper Street Fish Shop

Vasco & Piero's Pavilion
Vegetarian Cottage
Villandry Dining Room
Vrisaki

Wakaba
Walsh's
The White Tower *
Wilson's
Wiltons
Wódka

Zen Central
ZeNW3
Zoë